The Best of the
SHEFFIELD CLARION RAMBLERS' HANDBOOKS

'Ward's Piece'

Edited by David Sissons

HALSGROVE

First published in 2002 by Halsgrove
Introduction Text © 2002 David Sissons

British Library Cataloguing-in-Publication Data
A CIP record for this title is available from the British Library

ISBN 1 84114 222 0

HALSGROVE
Halsgrove House
Lower Moor Way
Tiverton, Devon EX16 6SS
T: 01884 243242
F: 01884 243325
email: sales@halsgrove.com
www.halsgrove.com

Printed and bound in Great Britain by
MPG Books Limited, Bodmin

Contents

DEDICATION

In general to all lovers of the Peak District.

In particular to the Sheffield Clarion Ramblers.

ACKNOWLEDGEMENTS

Professor David Hey introduced me to G.H.B. Ward.
Roly Smith instigated this book. Leah Fleetwood checked
and corrected the proofs. The editor is responsible for any errors.

Ward's Piece

The Best of the Sheffield Clarion Ramblers' Handbooks 1902–1964

CLARION CALL

On Sunday 2 September 1900, a group of 11 men and three women caught a train at about 8.30am at Sheffield Midland station. They travelled about 14 miles west into the High Peak of Derbyshire, alighting at Edale station, below and immediately southeast of the brooding, peat-capped plateau of Kinder Scout (at its highest point 2088 feet or 636 metres above sea level). They then set off on an almost circular ramble of about 20 miles, round, but not over, Kinder Scout, calling at the small town of Hayfield on the west of the plateau, and the Snake Inn on the north. Finally, they headed southeast to Hope station, next station down the line from Edale towards Sheffield. There they caught the train at around 8pm and travelled the 11 miles or so back to their starting point of twelve hours earlier.

With perhaps a shorter mileage, a slightly later start and a much earlier finish, this could describe a typical Sunday ramble from the annual prospectus of any of the present-day Sheffield rambling clubs – Ramblers' Association, Holiday Fellowship, Good Companions, Halcyon Ramblers and more. In fact it marks the foundation of Sheffield's oldest Sunday rambling club, the Clarion Ramblers.

The leader of the ramble, G.H.B. Ward, who had previously walked and checked the route, wrote, fifty years later:

> Fourteen Sheffielders responded to an advertisement I inserted in the *Clarion* and, on the first Sunday in September 1900, walked the usual round of Kinderscout, from Edale station. And this, to my knowledge, the first workers' Sunday Rambling Club in the North of England (or South?) was formed. Those present were T.W. Handley, his son and daughter Joseph and Fanny, Sam and Herbert Hodgson, Frank Johnson, John Jordan, Mr King (a manager at Christopher Johnson's works, Portobello St), and his daughters, Isa and Carrie (now Wilford), John Murray, Herbert Stansfield, Fred Watson, and G.H.B.W.[1]

Eight years on from this, just after G.H.B. Ward's death late in 1957, John – or Jack – Jordan, the last survivor who had been on that ramble in 1900, wrote down his memories of the day:

Many may wonder how the name 'Clarion' became that of our rambling club. The fact is that in 1900 there was a weekly paper called the *Clarion* edited by Robert Blatchford, and G.H.B. Ward put an advertisement in it calling for kindred spirits to join him in a walk round Kinder. So it follows that the 13 who joined him were readers of the *Clarion* and when the club was formed it was naturally called 'The Sheffield Clarion Rambling Club'.[2]

Robert Blatchford had edited the *Clarion* since 1891, and his particular brand of socialism, which emphasised culture as much as economics, had spawned Clarion groups all over the country – Clarion Cyclists, Clarion Cinderella Clubs and Clarion Glee Clubs, to list a few. Indeed most of the people on the first Clarion ramble in 1900 knew each other from the vocal union, the Sheffield Clarion Glee Club, whose secretary at the time was Frank Johnson, one of the 14 on that ramble in 1900. In Blatchford's *Clarion* newspaper of Saturday 2 June 1900, Frank Johnson, under the pseudonym of Jay Haitch, wrote, with an opener that has perhaps enough of a hint of irony to remind us that overdue British summers are nothing new:

As we may confidently expect the summer to arrive almost any day, we have commenced this season's Saturday afternoon rambles into the country. These social strolls are very enjoyable: we have taken them during the finer months of several successive years, and can heartily recommend them to other societies. We have a great desire, I may remark, to see more of our local friends on these occasions, and I should be delighted to forward to any who would address a postcard to me at 2 Sarah Street, the printed list of rambles for the present season. It is quite true that these often include an informal open-air rehearsal, but this is not always so painful as some might be led to suppose.

The advertisement inserted by G.H.B. Ward, according to his own testimony and that of Jack Jordan, in the *Clarion* immediately before Sunday 2 September 1900, is a bit of a mystery. I have scanned all the editions of the *Clarion* for the year 1900, which are kept at the British Library in Colindale, North London, but though I carried out a detailed search of the ones for about three months up to the edition of Saturday 1 September, I could find no trace of any advertisement for a proposed ramble round Kinder Scout. What is included in the edition for Saturday 1 September, under the regular heading, 'Notes to Clarionettes', is the editorial comment, 'Received with thanks', acknowledging receipt of a communication but making no reference to its contents. This is followed by the names of the senders: G.H.B. Ward, Frank Johnson, S. King and E. Stansfield. The wife of Mr William King, one of the 14 ramblers on 2 September 1900, was called Sarah, and the 'E' before Stansfield might have been a misreading of 'H'. Bearing this in mind, it seems very coincidental that the surnames of four people either on or connected by family to the first Clarion ramble should be mentioned as having sent a communication to the *Clarion* which was gratefully received but not printed. It is of course possible that when G.H.B. Ward referred to inserting an advertisement in the *Clarion*, he meant that he had inserted a separate leaflet into the Sheffield distribution of the newspaper, in which case this leaflet has yet to surface. However, as Frank Johnson's entry in the *Clarion* of Saturday 2 June 1900 demonstrates, it was not unusual to insert information of purely local interest into what was a national newspaper, and therefore a separate leaflet would hardly be necessary. Whatever the truth is, it seems probable that most people on the first Clarion ramble either knew each other from the Sheffield Clarion Glee Club, or were friends or family, and the supposed advertisement in the *Clarion* had little if any effect on the number that turned up.

What G.H.B. Ward, fifty years later, called 'the usual round of Kinderscout' was not at all usual in 1900. The train journey from Sheffield Midland to Edale had become available to passengers only since 1894, and a section of the ramble's route – from Hayfield to the Snake Inn – had been open to the public only since 1897, after a campaign of agitation lasting twenty-one years.

The fullest account of that first ramble was Jack Jordan's, and it is worth quoting more of it as it reveals a lot of what was in the hearts and minds of the 14 ramblers, though allowances have to be made for the passing of more than half a century:

Sheffield Clarion Ramblers c.1950. G.H.B. Ward (standing, centre) and Jack Jordan (standing, left), two of the original club members. Ramblers' Association

It was a lovely autumn morning. We went by Barber Booth and Upper Booth to Jacob's Ladder; the 'Ladder' was then almost untrodden, not the broken ruin it is today! From the top of it we looked across to Edale Rocks, Pym's Chair, and Crowden Towers, and all of us knew that a new life was opening for us – and we hoped, for those to come after us. The grandeur of it brought a verse to my mind –

> 'For I dipped into the future
> Far as human eye could see,
> And saw the glory of the world
> And the wonder that might be.'[3.]

True, it was not the world, but it was a new world to us, traversed for the first time – even now after fifty-seven years I still remember the thrill and the joy it gave me.

We went from Jacob's Ladder to Edale Cross, Stony Ford and by Coldwell Clough to Hayfield. On entering Hayfield we called at the first local and ate the lunch we had brought with us. After lunch we had a good sing-song, and as we were nearly all members of the 'Clarion Vocal Union' you might imagine singing was one of our strong points.

We turned off past Kinder Bank and Old Pits Plantation and the old shooting cabin, to William Clough, and on to the head of Ashop Clough. We paused by Mill Hill for a breather, and there the glory of Kinder was fully revealed. If possible the lovely views from the top of Jacob's Ladder were surpassed. There was bright sun alternating with cloud, making the Kinder ridges seem most impressive.

Now the descent of Ashop Clough was before us, and after persuading the ladies to go on ahead several of the men indulged in a bathe in one of the deeper pools. There are too many making this journey for that to be possible now!

It should perhaps be emphasised that from Upper Booth to Hayfield, and from Hayfield to the Snake Inn, not a soul was seen, apart from our own party!

So again I stress that the 'Clarion' was the ice-breaker and the pathfinder!

We reached the Snake Inn early and they got a shock when we asked for tea for 14 – such a number in those far-off days was unheard of. In 1900 there were not only no cars, no buses, no coach-parties – there were no other ramblers.

They hadn't enough bread for us all, and to their everlasting credit they SET TO AND BAKED SOME BREAD CAKES!

The memory of that tea is still with me. How much was it, do you say? New cakes, boiled ham, etc., etc., – 1/3d. each.

While we were waiting outside there was an amusing incident. A tale was told of five Irishmen who asked how far it was to a certain place, and on being informed that it was five miles, one of them said: 'Bedad! there's five of us – that's only a mile apiece!'

Standing by was an Irishman, probably one of the waterworks navvies. He had heard the story and at once confronted us with 'An' what's the matter wi' the Oirish?' I thought he would set about the lot of us, but an outburst of laughter calmed him down, and muttering he went away.

In many of our ramble books G.H.B. Ward has quoted from Walt Whitman, and walking round he kept saying, 'Pioneers, oh pioneers!' and I know he felt we were pioneers that day.

After tea it was down the road to Alport Bridge and up to Hope Cross. There we sat around, discussing the day's events, and deciding that we MUST go on, with G.H.B. for leader – and many hundreds of ramblers have since had cause to bless that decision.

We went on to Hope station, and if our feet were on the heather our hearts and hopes were with the stars.

3 SEPTEMBER 1900

On a far-off autumn evening
  In the rays of the setting sun
We sat and talked of Kinder
  And planned for the days to come.
Bert was a man with a vision
  His thoughts on the hills afar
As we pledged ourselves to the Clarion
  And hitched our faith to a star.
There were those who called us dreamers
  But dreams can all come true
If you have faith and work for them
  And ignore the scorn of the few.
Today you roam o'er Kinder
  On paths that are yours by right

But don't forget in your roaming
  For those paths WE had to fight.
Yes, Kinder and many another
  That today you regard as your own
Were keepered and labelled 'Private'
  Till the Clarion came to roam!
So as you plan for the future
  And the way seems bright and clear
Remember the flag-unfurlers
  And all that we held most dear!

Jack Jordan [4.]

Jack Jordan got the date wrong – it was Sunday 2 September – and his location at Hope Cross of the group's decision to do it again differs from G.H.B. Ward's, who had written nearly thirty years earlier:

> Outside The Snake it was decided to have further rambles during 1901, and it may truly be stated that, from this accidental enthusiasm and now historic walk, the Sheffield Clarion Rambling Club was formed.[5.]

For 1901, five summer rambles were organised to places easily accessible from Sheffield, and within about 15 miles – Langsett and Cutgate, Lose Hill, Mam Tor and Castleton, Combs Dale and Monsal Vale, and Kiveton Park to Roche Abbey and Conisborough.[6.] They show a close familiarity with the variety of

G.H.B. Ward pointing out landmarks to the early Clarion Ramblers. The bald gentleman (towards the bottom left) looks like Mr J.G. Graves, the Sheffield businessman and benefactor mentioned in the article on Blackamoor and Strawberry Lee Grange.

local geology and scenery at hand, Langsett being on gritstone, Mam Tor being on the Edale shales bordering between gritstone and limestone, Monsal Vale being on carboniferous limestone and Roche Abbey being on magnesian limestone, all the various rocks and their soils having their own distinctive reliefs, flora and fauna, and history of human interaction.

1902 saw the publication of the first *Sheffield Clarion Ramblers' Prospectus*, edited by G.H.B. Ward, and the nine summer rambles for the year were accompanied by two brief extracts from the poetry of William Wordsworth. Who was this lover of Whitman and Wordsworth?

THE BELOVED VAGABOND[7]

A biography of George Herbert Bridges Ward that does justice to the man and his achievements has yet to be written. The following brief notes, inadequate as they may be, are based on the man's testimony of himself as given in the *Sheffield Clarion Ramblers' Handbooks*, backed up by information from such sources as census returns and memories from a few people who came into contact with him.

G.H.B. Ward was born on 12 June 1876 in Sheffield. His first home was at Derwent Street, off Cricket Inn Road, a short hillside walk from the centre of the growing indus-trial town, but in 1877 his family moved a little further out to Glen Cottage, Park Farm. Here there were fields all around, though Nunnery Colliery and smoky Sheffield were close enough to ensure that the freshness of the air was only relative. Today the site is occupied by Sheffield Work's Department's Manor Lane Depot, and any vestiges of a rural retreat have been obliterated by urban and indus-trial sprawl.

G.H.B. Ward as a young man.

Ward's paternal grandfather, William Ward, had been born in 1814 at Ridgeway, in the parish of Eckington, Derbyshire, to the southeast of Sheffield, and his grandson referred to him as 'the son of a Ridgeway sickle maker'.[8] From about 1600 to 1900, the gently-undulating farmland around Ridgeway, with its fast-flowing and easily-dammed streams, rang to the sounds of the manufacture of sickles, hooks and scythes, tools needed for unmechanized agriculture. Both the area and the dual economy so characteristic of Sheffield's surrounding villages are evocatively described in a near-contemporary account by John Thomas, who, in the fol-lowing extract, is particularly describing the period of August and September, a slack period for the sickle trade, when many sickle-makers took their products into the fields to shear corn.

> The conspicuous and pleasing community of Ridgeway is a pictur-
> esque series of houses and smithies, standing, as its name indicates, on
> a ridge or narrow hill. At this period, which closes what the masters
> and workmen understand by the term year, the anvil and the wheel are
> comparatively noiseless. The black sons of Vulcan enter the service of
> the fair-haired Ceres, and with well-wrought instruments of their craft,
> enter upon the husbandman's task, with all his zeal, and almost all his
> skill. The appearance of the begrimed apron men, thus gathering their
> own or their master's crops, is singular enough, and cannot fail to
> attract the notice of those who have loved to look on the field work of
> purely agricultural districts.[9]

William Ward's father, like a lot of people from the surrounding agricultural
districts, must have found the pull of expanding Sheffield too tempting, as he
is described by some of his descendants, not as a Ridgeway sickle maker, but
as 'a moulder who worked for the once illustrious firm of H.E. Hoole'.[10]
Henry Elliott Hoole was an iron founder who, among other things, made
fenders at his Green Lane works in Sheffield. This may have influenced
William Ward, who started his working life in 1823 as an apprentice fender-
maker with the firm of Stuart and Barton. He elected to go it alone as a fen-
dermaker in 1835, joining the ranks of Sheffield's 'little mesters' or small busi-
nessmen in the light metal trades. So was founded the firm later called
William Ward and Sons, now called William Ward and Son (Wardson). Today
it is an engineering company, based since 1935 at its Centenary Works on
Archer Road, Woodseats, passed by trains travelling from Sheffield Midland
to Chesterfield or the Hope valley.

G.H.B. Ward's father, George Bridges Ward, was born in 1842 at Dobbs Row,
off Wellgate, Rotherham, when William Ward's business may have briefly
operated from there. G.B. Ward grew up within the family business, which
soon moved back to Sheffield, being located, according to local trade directo-
ries and census returns, on Kelham Island in 1845 and at Broad Street Lane in
1861. But the son of 'William Ward and Son' refers to a brother James. G.B.
Ward seems to have left his father's business and gone his own way,
becoming at various times a skilled craftsman or supervisor in the metal
trades. He also became a Sunday School teacher at St John's, Park, a writer of
verse, and a keen rambler, obviously a major influence on his son, though
politically he was Conservative. He married Emily B. Bland in 1875. When
he left his father's house at Broad Street Lane, he moved first to Derwent
Street and then to Glen Cottage, Park Farm. There he lived with his wife and
two children, George and Florence. Emily died in 1885, ten years after their
marriage, as is recorded in a poem G.B. Ward wrote around 1894.[11] He
himself died in 1900.

The 1901 census records G.H.B. Ward (twenty-four), at Park Farm on Cricket Inn Road, head of household, single, living with his sister Florence (twenty-one), single, and Emma Blackwell (thirty-six), boarder, single. G.H.B.W. is described as a fitter and turner in an iron works, while his sister is a school teacher and Emma Blackwell is a housekeeper. In the spring of 1901, G.H.B. Ward was not only about to embark on the first of the five summer rambles which he had been asked to organise by his 13 fellow-ramblers on Sunday 2 September 1900, but he was about to be married to Fanny Bertha Platts, daughter of Joseph Platts, who was from a family of masons based in Dronfield, just over the county boundary in North Derbyshire.

Ward, born after the 1870 Education Act, had left St John's National School in School Street, Park, at the age of thirteen. He had won a scholarship to the Central High School, but he did not take this up, perhaps due to family circumstances, his mother having died when he was about nine. Instead 1889 sees him starting work, not, perhaps significantly, at his grandfather's workshop, but as an errand lad at John Batt and Sons, silversmiths, Broad Street. In 1891 he got a more settled job at James Jackson's, a stay busk manufacturer on Mary Street near Bramall Lane. The company was doing good business, profiting from the crinoline boom of the 1890s, and here Ward served his apprenticeship, qualifying in 1897 as an engineer fitter. The years 1896/97 must have been a decisive period in Ward's early life, for in addition to finishing his apprenticeship he broke his connection with St John's, Park, the church of his childhood and youth. Previously he had followed in his father's footsteps and become a Sunday School teacher, but in 1896 he was attracted to the growing socialist movement and began to move away from the church, mentally at first, then rather more physically in 1897 when the vicar of St John's, Canon H.F. Greenwood, literally drove him out of church! At about the same time, Ward became an active trade unionist, joining the Sheffield No. 1 Branch of the Amalgamated Society of Engineers, which probably qualified him as an 'aristocrat of labour'. On the basis of union activity, he became in January 1903 the first secretary of the Sheffield branch of the Labour Representation Committee (L.R.C.), the precursor of the Labour Party, whose national secretary at the time was J. Ramsey MacDonald.

Ward's political work with the L.R.C. resulted in two publications. The first, in 1905, was the pamphlet, *Infantile Mortality and Municipal Milk Supplies,* which was an augur of Welfare State policies forty years later. The second, in 1911, was the book, *The Truth about Spain.* Ward was to have a lifelong love affair with Spain. Probably from the deaths of his father and maternal grandfather in 1900 he had inherited a bit of money, and this inspired him to leave his job at James Jackson's and follow a roving fancy to the Canary Islands, not a typical holiday destination for a Sheffield fitter at the time. After that, he made himself fluent in Spanish and, through his L.R.C. work, befriended two key figures in Spanish politics, the non-violent, moral force anarchists,

Francisco Ferrer Guardia (1859–1909) and Fernando Tarrida del Marmol (1861–1915). *The Truth about Spain* was written in the aftermath of the execution of Ferrer Guardia on trumped-up charges, and it locates the cause of Spain's problems – its poverty, backwardness and oppression – in three anti-democratic tendencies in its political life, namely Carlism, Caçiquism and Catholicism. Without going into details, it should be noted that the book shook the Spanish government of the time – the Chancellor of the Exchequer, Senor D'Angel Urzaiz, mentioned it in a speech to the Spanish Congress on 13 March 1911:

> Believe me it is one thing to laugh when one is among Spaniards, but I very much doubt, however atrophied is patriotic feeling in many Spaniards, that when they read this book, written by a foreigner, they will be able to say that there is an envy of Spain, but rather a sentiment of commiseration and sympathy. Really, when one reads the volume he feels ashamed, and, at least at the moment, he is filled with a vehement desire to liberate himself from this situation.[12]

The book also concluded with what can be construed as a remarkable prediction of the Spanish Civil War, though it was probably a far from uncommon admonition at the time:

> If Rome, on her part, fails to read the signs of the times, then within a decade – a little less or a little more – a social conflagration will break out in Spain that will light the world.[13]

Ward's L.R.C. days lasted from 1903–11. The period 1910–14 saw an upsurge of labour unrest in Britain, registered to some extent by a doubling of trade union membership. The year 1911, in particular, saw a wave of riots and national strikes during the summer, including in August the first ever national railway strike. The government's short-term response was swift deployment of the police and the army, but a more long-term strategy was to extend its own corridors of power and draw labour leaders into the civil service. This latter process accelerated during the First World War – in 1914 there were 57,706 civil servants, but by 1918 there were 116,241. Perhaps G.H.B. Ward's resignation from the L.R.C. on the heels of the summer of discontent in 1911, and his recruitment to Sheffield and Brightside Labour Exchange can be seen as part of this process.

After the outbreak of war, Ward was posted to the Ministry of Munitions in Whitehall, where he was to stay from March 1915 to July 1919. By this time he had a growing family and had moved his home from Park Farm in Sheffield to the house near Owler Bar in Derbyshire – about five or six miles from Sheffield Town Hall and even to this day surrounded by fields – where he was to live until his death in 1957. His civil service career as a conciliation

The earliest known photo of the Sheffield Clarion Ramblers, taken in Cronberry Clough, 1901.

Sheffield Clarion Ramblers on Lose Hill, 1 September 1946 (G.H.B. Ward is standing third from the left).

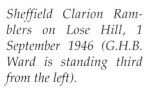

G.H.B. Ward (centre) at the 'Barrell Inn' at Bretton, 7 January, 1941.

The unveiling ceremony of Mr Harry Bragg's viewfinder on Lose Hill, 29 August 1948. (G.H.B. Ward is at the left of the viewfinder, looking over the shoulders of two ladies who may be his wife and a daughter.

officer involved softening the blows and cooling the heat of class struggle, and perhaps as the relatively privileged grandson of a little mester and as someone who had worked his own way up from the shop floor, he was well qualified to see and weigh up both sides in a dispute. He retired, at the age of sixty-five, in 1941 and was offered an O.B.E., which, as a socialist true to his principles, he refused, though he wasn't averse to seeing the same honour bestowed on some of his acquaintances.

If he refused an O.B.E. in 1941, he was happy to accept the offer of two later honours. In 1945 the Sheffield rambling community collected enough money to purchase the summit of Lose Hill, overlooking the vales of Hope and Edale, and this was presented to Ward in gratitude for his services to rambling. Ward promptly gave this panoramic patch of land, under the new name of Ward's Piece, to the National Trust, in whose ownership it remains. A similar recognition of his services and influence came from the University of Sheffield in 1957, with the award of an Honorary M.A. Degree, presented to him on his deathbed in Nether Edge hospital, Sheffield.

A RAMBLER MADE

It is indeed as a rambler that G.H.B. Ward is chiefly remembered, and even during his earlier, more political days, his love of rambling was always bursting to express itself. For instance, he was a regular contributor to the *Sheffield Guardian*, a local socialist newspaper, and there is much about his L.R.C. work in its pages. But even after the outbreak of the First World War, articles by Ward graced the front pages of the newspaper under such 'highly political' headings as 'A Sail to the Irish Sea' and 'Tramping over the Wicklow Hills'. Apart from spells of absence caused by illness and accident, there were two periods in Ward's adult life when rambling seriously got pushed into second place. Early in his L.R.C. period, in 1903, he harboured doubts about continuing with the Sheffield Clarion Ramblers, reflecting nearly twenty years later:

> I began to think that the object had failed, viz, that of inducing men like myself to go during the weekends and enjoy the beautiful scenery sur-rounding Sheffield, and, in this way, get rid of many of the ills and rheums which accumulate largely because men do not know how to throw them off in the abandon with nature.[14.]

During this period of doubt and the pressure of other commitments, it was Father John Murray, a Catholic priest of Irish extraction and a member of the Clarion Ramblers' Committee since 1901 who, despite the Irish joke and its implications in Jack Jordan's memoir of the first Clarion ramble, helped to keep the club going. Something similar happened during the period of Ward's exile to Whitehall during the First World War – club member Harry Inman took over editorship of the booklets, while Ward grumbled in its pages about the relative tameness of the Surrey Downs and the pretentiousness and shallowness of some of the people he encountered.

After his return from down south in 1919, Ward was able to devote all his energies, outside work, not only to the club, but to related organisations which he had either founded, been a founding member of, or had instigated – like the Hallamshire Footpath Preservation Society (1912), the Hunter Archaeological Society (1912), the Sheffield Society for the Protection of Scenery (1924), the Sheffield Federation of Rambling Clubs (1926) and the National Council of Ramblers' Federations (1931). The Hallamshire Footpath Preservation Society was wound up in 1957 just after Ward's death, and its files and correspondence were passed on to the Peak District and Northern Counties' Footpaths Society (now the 'Peak and Northern'), the society responsible for the re-opening of the Hayfield to Snake Inn path in 1897. The Hunter Archaeological Society continues to flourish, with its lectures, field trips and publications. The Sheffield Society for the Protection of Scenery became the Sheffield and Peak District Branch of the Council for the Protection of Rural England (C.P.R.E.) in 1928, while the National Council of Ramblers' Federations became the Ramblers' Association in 1935.

Rambling, for Ward, was not just another leisure pursuit. He often referred to it as 'the trinity of legs, eyes and mind', an activity in which looking and thinking are as important as walking in the fresh air and countryside, and it had a key role to play in the realisation of his particular kind of socialism. Influenced more by the ideas of John Ruskin, Robert Blatchford and Edward Carpenter than by those of Karl Marx, Ward's socialism was based on character-building. And there was no better way of building character than by taking to the hills and battling with the elements. 'A Rambler Made is a Man Improved' was part of Ward's slogan printed on the front of most of the *Sheffield Clarion Ramblers' Handbooks*. But rambling also involved looking, exploring, breaking new ground, for, as the other part of the front cover slogan said, 'The Man who never was Lost never went very Far' (and presumably the same could be said of the Woman, though Ward developed a chronic gender-bias that would combat any suffragette, despite the presence of women in the Clarion Ramblers from day one).

G.H.B. Ward at the Winnats Pass Access Rally, 1933. Ramblers' Association

One consequence of the Parliamentary Enclosures of the late-eighteenth and early-nineteenth centuries was the loss of what had been at least de facto public access to the hills, and many moors in the north of England, in particular the ones adjacent to Sheffield, became private grouse preserves. For example, the first Clarion ramble was *round*, not over, Kinder Scout, which had become heavily-keepered after the re-opening of the public right of way from Hayfield to the Snake Inn. If Jack Jordan, in his memoir of that pioneering ramble, says that not a soul was seen for most of the 20 miles, it is nevertheless unlikely that the 14 ramblers did not come under the discreet surveillance of keepers on and around Kinder Scout so soon after the Glorious Twelfth. Given the paramount importance of hills for Ward's socialist agenda, it is obvious why he became such a passionate campaigner for Access to Mountains and the creation of National Parks. It also explains why so much of his archival research and moorland trespassing was aimed at furnishing evidence to support claims of what he regarded as illegal loss of public access.

The *Sheffield Clarion Ramblers' Prospectus* of 1902 consisted of only four pages but expanded over the ensuing decade. By 1905 it was a mini-booklet, incorporating a couple of Derbyshire photos – Bretton Clough and Win Hill – plus a poem by Ward's father, the late G.B. Ward; a poem by Ward himself about Back Tor (east of the Upper Derwent), and a quotation from the Northamptonshire poet John Clare. The 1906 edition saw the first appearance of the slogan, 'A Rambler Made is a Man Improved', and the first of Ward's essays – a loving description of the view from Win Hill, with a reference to Ashopton's doom, Ashopton being a village to the north of Win Hill, threatened by plans to sink it under a reservoir. Perhaps with some early concessionary significance after the 1905 suffragette rising, 1906 also saw equality of membership for 'gentlemen and ladies' – prior to 1906 ladies had been honorary members. 1907 saw the first Rakes' Ramble, which was to take place on 6 July 1907 on the forbidden heights of Bleaklow. This was effectively the first recorded Clarion Ramblers' organised trespass, an overnight ramble using cover of darkness to gain access to this large private grouse preserve to the north of Kinder Scout.

In ten years the club membership had multiplied by ten. The 1902 four-page *Prospectus* had, by the 1912/13 edition, become the pocket-sized booklet whose basic format of about 100 pages was to be retained until 1963/64, six years after Ward's death. The 1912/13 edition also saw the first appearance of the slogan, 'The Man who never was Lost never went very Far'. The booklet contained the annual prospectus of rambles, a few photos, a relevant map, some rambler-related advertisements (mostly outdoor equipment, boots, clothing, ingredients for packed lunches, pubs and cafés) and many literary quotations, with an occasional list of recommended books thrown in. The literary content of the booklets is quite encyclopaedic – Wordsworth and Whitman had gained the company of Henry Thoreau, Ralph Waldo Emerson, Richard Jefferies, George Borrow, John Ruskin, Edward Carpenter, William Morris and many lesser-known authors, all of whom had something to say about the sheer spiritual joys of walking, looking, breathing fresh air and living life to the full. Because of Ward's Spanish interests, he included translations of Spanish and Latin-American writers who had similar concerns and interests, and he was always glad to include other people's translations of writers in languages like Chinese, with which he had no familiarity. While Ward regarded ramblers as the true patriots because of their love of and intimacy with the hidden depths of the countryside, he was always an internationalist, never narrowly chauvinistic. A book is waiting to be written that will put together in one volume a selection of the literary extracts and quotations that so enrich the pages of the *Sheffield Clarion Ramblers' Handbooks*, and must have enriched many a ramble.

Of equal importance though were Ward's original articles and essays, all of relevance to the 'rambler made'. When more than half-a-century's worth of Ward's articles are listed from the booklets, the result is quite staggering – it is a wonder how a man in full-time, non-academic employment, ever found time to write them, given the amount of foot slogging and archival burrowing each article represents. There are articles about tramping in Wales, Scotland, Ireland, the more northern Pennines, and such places as Madeira and Spain's Galicia, but the majority of Ward's articles are about the moorlands and valleys fairly close to his home. As he himself often said, 'These

G.H.B. Ward.   Ramblers' Association

booklets contain much unrecorded information upon place names, associations and history of the moorland and valley recesses of the Peak and South Yorkshire, and many chapters of local lore, anecdote and wit'. It was his wish to publish his articles in book form, and towards the end of the Second World War this looked likely to happen. In the Foreword to the 1944/45 edition, he wrote, 'By arrangement with a member, I forwarded six items of £25 to the Sheffield and Peak District C.P.R.E., Ramblers' Association, Sheffield and District Ramblers' Federation, Hallamshire F.P.S., Peak District and Northern Counties' F.P.S., and to the Trust Fund for the publication, in permanent book form, of the topographical and other researches dealing with the valleys and moorlands of the High Peak and South Yorkshire area printed in these S.C.R. booklets. The Annual Meeting of the S.C.R., 2/1/44, opened this latter Fund with £50.' Sadly, the book never materialised, and in the 1957/58 edition, the last to be edited by Ward, he wrote, 'The greatest regret is that, due to the latest troubles, and costs, in the printing trade, the hope that a book of our researches on these Peakland hills and moorsides, cloughs and peaty tops (often obtained from farmer friends, many of whose ancient homes are now reservoir-drowned); and a volume of original moorside wit and humour, will not be printed in my day'.

The book never was printed in his day, for he died within twelve months, but nor has anything remotely resembling it been printed during the more than half a century since. Ward seems to have suffered the fate predicted by one of the best of the Sheffield Clarion Rambler poets, Joseph W. Batty, who wrote a

G.H.B. Ward, 1953.

poem on 4 April 1949, which was included in the *Sheffield Clarion Ramblers' Handbook* Jubilee Edition of 1950/51. The following is an extract:

> Fifty years more, and time will still stride on,
> To bring more changes in the hearts of men:
> The once-important may become despised,
> The once-despised a sudden fame achieve,
> And all the present whirligig of time
> Fade out as shadow in a shadow-dream.
> Who is remembered when his work is done?
> Or who remembered for his guiding hand?...
> Who minds it so? – if grandeur yet unknown
> Lies undiscovered for our sons to boast,
> While we their forbears, from our fretted day,
> Move to the cypress trees, a silent host...
> Will Ward gain thanks in all the years to be
> For all he did to help the poor roam free
> On moor and hill? It may be that he will,
> But more than likely that his name will pass
> Along the mem'ries of his printed page.

WARD'S PIECE

Time will stride on and maybe Ward *will* gain thanks in all the years to be, after a long period of neglect. In celebration of the Labour Government's Countryside and Rights of Way (C.R.O.W.) Act, which became law at the end of the year 2000, the group, Sheffield Campaign for Access to Moorland, set up in 1982 after the fiftieth anniversary of the Kinder mass trespass of 1932, commissioned the making of three bronze plaques, dedicated to all ramblers who had worked to make the C.R.O.W. Act possible. The plaques bear the image of G.H.B. Ward making a passionate speech at a ramblers' rally in the Winnats Pass, the design, by local Ramblers' Association member, Doug Hewitt, being based on photographs taken during the 1920s and 1930s. One plaque was located, at the end of December 2000, in the Winnats Pass near Castleton, site of many ramblers' rallies at which people like G.H.B. Ward called for the creation of National Parks. A second was donated to the Sheffield Clarion Ramblers, who celebrated their centenary in September 2000 – they later located it in the Peak National Park Information Centre at Fieldhead, Edale, near where the first Clarion ramble began. A third was fixed in the entrance of Sheffield Old Town Hall during the year 2001. Soon afterwards, in the autumn of 2001, the National Trust put the place name, 'Ward's Piece', on their signs at Lose Hill Pike.

Ward's articles in the *Sheffield Clarion Ramblers' Handbooks* have continued over the years to be a major influence on local historians, ramblers, archaeologists and others with a specialist interest in the Peak District. A typical example in the 1990s was a major archaeological dig on Gardom's Edge near Baslow, which was triggered off by articles Ward published in the *Handbooks* in the 1940s. The articles have also provided a fairly easy and rich quarry for the plagiarist – Ward himself noted his own original research being lifted from the *Handbooks* and appearing without acknowledgement of sources in lucrative magazine articles, and this process has certainly continued since his death. This book represents an attempt to bring some of the best of Ward's researches on his beloved Peakland hills and moorsides, cloughs and peaty tops, to the attention of a wider public. The writings and associated maps provide a tremendous and inspirational resource for anyone interested in the Peak District, as relevant to today's concerns as to yesterday's, and they are testimony to a truly remarkable lifetime's achievement.

SELECTION AND EDITING

The selection comprises 11 of Ward's articles which were published between 1924 and 1950 in the *Sheffield Clarion Ramblers' Handbooks*. As the articles were written for an annual pocket book for ramblers, Ward did sometimes repeat himself, and most of such repetitions have been cut. Ward's style of writing was idiosyncratic – he often piled on asides and parentheses to such an extent that his sentences grew to an unwieldy length, and the main point was lost. Where possible these long sentences have been broken up. Nevertheless, footnotes have been incorporated into the main body of the text, and this has occasionally led to long, bracketed chunks which interrupt the main flow.

Essentially the articles consist of very detailed guided walks and anecdotes, backed up by archival research. A lot of the guided walks were trespass walks in Ward's time, though he did sometimes ask the landowners for permission to wander at will. More than half a century after the creation in 1951 of the Peak District National Park, some of these walks are still trespass walks, and whether this situation will change after the Countryside and Rights of Way Act of 2000 remains to be seen. For the anecdotes, which Ward picked up mainly from locals, he did not use a tape recorder – they were jotted down from memory and often reconstructed in dialectal form. Sometimes, when he quoted a bit of dialectal speech, he inserted his own comments, and there are occasions when it is not quite clear to the reader whose voice is speaking.

Ward did not claim to have the last word on anything – he was always prepared, in writing at least, to admit his own errors, and he always encouraged people to check his research and observations. It is hoped that this selection from his articles will inspire people to do just that.

REFERENCES

1. *Sheffield Clarion Ramblers' Handbook (S.C.R.)*, 1950/51, p. 40.
2. *S.C.R.*, 1958/59, p. 5.
3. The quotation is from Alfred Lord Tennyson's poem, 'Locksley Hall'.
4. *S.C.R.*, 1958/59, pp. 5–7.
5. *S.C.R.*, 1927/28, p. 162.
6. *S.C.R.*, 1950/51, p. 40.
7. William J. Locke's popular contemporary novel, *The Beloved Vagabond*, often appeared on Ward's booklists in the *S.C.R. Handbooks*, and the title was applied to him on a photograph in the *Handbooks*.
8. *S.C.R.*, 1948/49, p. 33.
9. John Thomas, *Walks in the Neighbourhood of Sheffield*, 2nd Series, 1844, p. 112.
10. The information comes from a periodical, *Inside Industry*, a copy of which is in the Local Studies Section of Sheffield Central Library.
11. *Sheffield Guardian*, 3 January 1908.
12. Press clipping from an unknown newspaper, 22 March 1911, found in a copy of *The Truth about Spain* in the Local Studies Section of the Sheffield Central Library.
13. *The Truth about Spain*, Ch. 6, p. 40.
14. *S.C.R.*, 1921/22, p. 100.

'The Duke of Norfolk's Road'

The Loneliest, Wildest Walk in West Yorkshire

From S.C.R. Handbook, 1924/25. This article on 'The Duke of Norfolk's Road' influenced the mass trespass which took place on it in September 1932, in the immediate aftermath of the more famous Kinder Scout mass trespass of April 1932. The reference to Handsome Cross is picked up in the later article on 'New Facts about Broomhead and Bradfield Moors'. Derwent village is mostly demolished and its remnants now submerged by the northern part of Ladybower Reservoir, though the Derwent packhorse bridge was reconstructed north of Howden Reservoir at Slippery Stones, and dedicated to John Derry, author of Across the Derbyshire Moors *(1904). Abbey Grange Cottage is long demolished, though its site is still discernible.*

The Duke of Norfolk's Road' provides the wildest Yorkshire moorland walk south of Wharfedale. It crosses the Don–Derwent watershed and leads down Abbey Clough, one of the finest of Peakland's upland stream courses. The route – six miles – is entirely within the Yorkshire boundary. The 'Road' begins at the S.S.W. end of Bardike – eight miles (as the crow flies) from Sheffield Town Hall – where you have backward views of the Walkley Bank, Malin Bridge, Hillsborough and Owlerton suburbs of the beloved city of smoke. It is a 'public' road legalised for ever (save the word!) by the Ecclesfield Tithes (or Enclosure) Act of 1811 which, then including the chapelry of Bradfield, closed the commons to the freehold farmers and labourers of the wide Ecclesfield parish. The commons then enclosed hereabout stretched from Foulstone Delf and Bradfield Gate Head (to each side of the Agden watershed), along the Derbyshire county boundary to Abbey Grange, and up the Derwent (here properly called the Wronksley or Ronksley) to Swains Greave and the little known boundary turf heap at Swains Head, as one crosses from Swains Greave, over the moor, to Black Clough and Woodhead.

THE ENCLOSURE ACTS

18,128 acres of ancient moor, common pasturage and surface rights, chiefly in Bradfield, were 'taken in' by this Act, while the total acreage of combined Ecclesfield and Bradfield parishes today is 34,244 acres. The then Duke of Norfolk (as Lord of the Manor of Sheffield) scooped nearly 5000 acres in one patch and Earl Fitzwilliam 741 acres on Thornseat Moor, 23 acres in Hall Field, to which, by easy purchases of two awarded allotments, he added 736 acres on the east of Foulstone Delf.

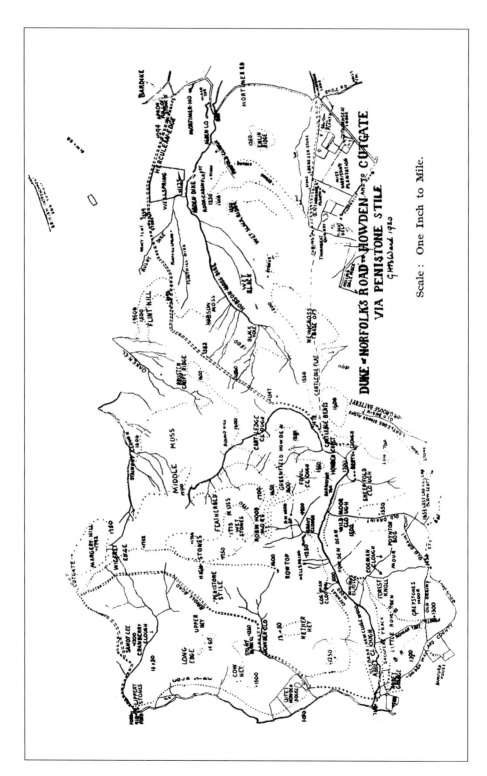

DUKE OF NORFOLKS ROAD HOWDEN AND CUTGATE VIA PENISTONE STILE

G. H. B. Ward 1920

Scale : One Inch to Mile.

THE DUKE OF NORFOLK'S BOUNDARY

The Duke's boundary line of the land awarded by the 1811 Act is from Bradfield Gate Head, on the county boundary trench and wall to Abbey Grange, up the Derwent to Swains Greave and the turf heap at Swains Head, and then on the watershed line to Margery Hill, Wilfrey Edge, Oaken Clough Head, Lost Lad and Bradfield Gate Head. The extremity of this plot, although in Bradfield parish, is 17 miles from Sheffield Town Hall. Altogether the Duke of Norfolk obtained common lands 'supposed to contain nearly 7000 acres.' This plot of 11 square miles, however, included roughly four square miles of 'Holden Heys, Little Holden and Holden Pasture', which, in 1811 'freehold lands', may have been granted to the Earl of Shrewsbury when the Welbeck Abbey lands were divided after the Dissolution of the Monasteries – post 1535. 'Holden Heys' is the land north of Abbey Brook, to Cranberry Clough; 'Little Holden' the land south of Abbey Brook to the county boundary; and 'Holden Pasture' probably the lower-lying brook and Derwent side pasturage and fields.

The (Rimington) Wilsons of Broomhead Hall, awarded about 300 acres, purchased then and subsequently another 925 acres of awarded common lands. These Enclosure Acts, however, had one good side. They gave the commons and profits to the principal landowners and odd strips to small freeholders, and some of the lower lands, in consequence, were considerably improved. The ancient moorland commons, however, now turned into grouse moors, give smaller returns in food value (sheep and cattle-feeding) than before they were 'taken in', and the Sheffield papers, now the 1914–18 war is over, have forgotten some of their articles and paragraphs about more sheep on the moors, etc.

In addition to the legalised filching of moorland common pastures, these Acts – by ignoring their existence in the Awards – deprived the unorganised public of many old bridleways and paths which, today, would be valuable routes for walkers and 'neart cuts' or alternatives to the moorside main roads which, due to motor traffic, and the absence of side paths, can no longer be traversed in comfort or safety. Today we may point to their existence and my map records of the old tracks are made. Tomorrow's men will, it is hoped, be given, or claim, legal freedom to walk over them in peace.

The enclosures under the Ecclesfield Tithes Act of 1811 were not concluded until 9 March 1826, when the Award and its map was sworn and issued at the 'Tontine Inn', Sheffield. Two of the ancient ways leading from the Bradfield to the Derwent valley were preserved by it. One, the Holden Road, 60 feet wide, leads up Foulstone Delf to Bradfield Gate Head stone guide stoop and down to Abbey Grange – with a certain physically marked branch down John Field Howden and Mill Clough to Derwent village which, during recent years has been disputed by the gamekeeper and his employer. The other is legalised in the following terms:

One other Public Carriage Road and Highway of the width of 30 feet from Mortimer's Road on Broomhead Moor, and leading westward and southwards to or near to a place called Cartledge Delph which Road I call the Duke of Norfolk's Road and which I set out and appoint as one of the two Roads which I in and by the said mentioned Act was directed to set out across the said Commons, Moors and Wastes, to the tract of Land directed to be allotted to the Duke of Norfolk.

EXPLANATIONS

The 'Road' was never finished and remains practically as in 1811 in part a stone crackers' rough cart way, and, at the Abbey Grange end, a foot track and occasionally, a bridle, and sledge-deepened, trench way. The only reasonable apology is that the 30 feet width of this road and the 60 feet width of the 'Holden Road' (Foulstone Delf–Bradfield Gate Head to Abbey Grange and Howden) was a plan and wild cat scheme of the infant years of the 1800s to make a new Sheffield–Manchester turnpike from Moscar and along the tops from Derwent Edge to Margery Hill and Dean Head Stones, Fiddler's Green and Woodhead, and that the 30 and 60 feet widths were to give 'connecting by-roads from Sheffield, Stannington, Oughtibridge and Bradfield: villages, etc.' with feeder routes from Derwent and Abbey Grange. Certainly these were ancient ways in 1811 and before the Glossop Road (1821) was substituted for this more elevated route. The whole proposal, however, may have been a sop to make the Act less hateful to the inhabitants.

The 1811 Act 'directed and ordered Joseph Bishop (the Commissioner) or his successor, to set out at least two good and sufficient carriage roads across the rest of the commons moors and wastes to the said Tract of Land directed to be allotted to the Duke of Norfolk and one of such roads shall be of the breadeth of 60 feet at the least and shall be set out from a place called Moscar Cross to a place called Lost Lad, being the most eligible direction for a road between Sheffield and Glossop Dale, such roads to be set out and made by and out of the moneys to be raised for defraying the expenses of this Act and afterwards kept in repair by the Inhabitants of such District, Hamlet or Division as the road shall pass through'.

The Commissioner cautiously avoided the setting out of a direct road beside the county boundary from Moscar Cross to Lost Lad, and used the existing Mortimer Road to Strines Brook and the old track up Foulstone Delf for the 60 feet road that was never made, obliterated the useful Emlin Dike Road and preserved the ancient way which he called 'The Duke of Norfolk's Road'. The abandonment of this Glossop road was possibly reasonable, but the landowners saved their money.

'Mortimer's Road', made about 1770, goes from Strines Lane End to Strines Inn, Agden and Ewden Bridges, Midhope and Penistone. Mortimer was the contractor. 'Broomhead Moor' is today's name of these moors owned by the Wilsons of Broomhead Hall. 'Cartledge Delph' is the upper end of Abbey Clough. The name, 'Duke of Norfolk's Road', perpetuates the handing over of this huge patch of moorland to the Duke of Norfolk and his successors.

THE COMMENCEMENT – BARDIKE
The walk really begins exactly opposite the S.S.W. end of the Bardike trench and, if you come from Broomhead Hall or Wightwizzle hamlet on the Agden to Strines Mortimer's Road, you will pass – on the summit and watershed between Ewden and Agden Brooks – a recently made, railed-in, Ordnance datum stone. Coming from Bradfield, by the Penistone Road, or Rocher Head path or, from Oughtibridge, through Coumes Wood, and the sandy road by Edge Mount Farm and Handsome Cross, you can turn left and follow along the length of Bardike (S.S.W.) from the right roadside wall above which (N.N.E.) the trench ends on the near edge of the Kanyard Hills – a sign that the kanyard landslip was before the dawn of history. (Handsome Cross is now a 1753 road guide stone, possibly near the site of the old cross. The markings are: 'Penistone 5m., Sheafield 6m., Bradfield 1m., 1753', and the other side, indistinct, like 'I P' and '17'.)

Bardike is only a few yards S.S.E. of the watershed and stretches between the Agden–Strines and Bradfield–Worrall and Oughtibridge Roads. The complete length from the edge to Mortimer's Road is 370 yards. The S.S.W. end of the trench is about nine feet deep, the centre is shallow, and part seems to have been removed rather than washed away, while the N.N.E. end deepens above the wall and approaching the kanyard edge. There is little doubt that Bardike was an ancient British defence work placed there where an enemy would cross at the most obvious point – avoiding the wide peaty and boggy moorland between here and the Derwent valley.

HERCULEAN EDGE AND APRON-FULL-OF-STONES
The 'Duke of Norfolk's Road' begins exactly at the S.S.W. end of Bardike, across the road, and for the first ¾ mile the direction is N.W. half W. Incidentally, Mortimer House, south of the commencement of 'The Duke of Norfolk's Road', is named after the road maker, Hans Winthrop Mortimer, but according to Mr Wm Bramall, it was built after the enclosure by a Mr Uttley, of Thurgoland, who cleared at least some of the land. He used to pen the farmer's moorland sheep and "hang t'grouse by snickling 'em". But at last he was caught on the Howden side and "his game was up". Mortimer House, however altered, was built about ninety years ago. To return to 'The Duke of Norfolk's Road', after the first ¾ mile, ten yards away there is a small quarry hole. Keep this on your left and then follow gently up and close beside the Herculean Edge, by, at first, a faint track through benty grass and then heather, and presently becoming more defined. The Rev. A.B. Browne, of Marton-cum-Grafton and late vicar of Bradfield, tells me that he has asked

the Ordnance Survey to re-name Herculean Edge 'Ercklin: or Hercklin' Edge', a local word for crouching. My copy of Jamieson's *Scottish Dictionary* (1846), in the words *Hurker, Hurkle* and *Hurkle-Backit*, gives a similar explanation. The edge seen at a distance resembles a crouching or recumbent beast and before the stone-getters cracked and almost stripped the edge top there were dozens of the flattish grey weather blocks on the moor similar in character to the stones which, near Whinstone Lee Tor on Derwent Edge or at the Holmesfield boundary on Big Moor, are today called Hurkling Stones or Stone. Mr Wm Bramall of Watch House, Bradfield, who was born at Smallfield eighty-three years ago, also tells me that he well remembers the local use of a sentence such as "'urklin' under t'wall", used to describe a man crouching along the side of a wall, and proves that the late vicar's contention is correct.

En route and 330 yards from the commencement – part of it once covering the present track – is the site of the Apron-Full-of-Stones – apparently a former cairn 60 feet in diameter and probably 20 to 25 feet high, an ancient burial place of the pre-historic Britons of which I have failed to trace a written descriptive record. It may have been removed about 1770, for the making of Mortimer Road or later, to build the lower field walls or dwellings. Mr Wm Bramall never heard of any person in the parish who could give a description of it. The cairn would be similar to that on Nether Moor, Edale, and the present, although disturbed, great cairn by the Circle, on Eyam Moor. The Apron-Full-of-Stones was once a great local landmark. Near by, if you can find it, is the Ordnance bench mark (left) 1235 feet, and, just beyond, is a cluster of shapely grey-weather gritstones – the few survivors after the moorland stone cutters and wall builders of a hundred years ago or so had done their work. A few yards hence note a small cairn (right) and a wall (left) alongside our once cart-trodden way. It is the north boundary wall of the Wellspring Field, enclosed after the Bradfield Award 1826.

NIXON HOUSE
Is on the slope south of Herculean Edge. The ruins and a small croft beside a spring can be seen today. Possibly built after the enclosure, it was erected and inhabited by a Nixon, who gained a livelihood by making besoms. But the house fired one day and Nixon found another home.

Following close beside the wall we turn at the bend and, for half a mile, the direction is west. Beyond the wall end, 200 yards ahead, is a small land boundary stone (marked 'C'). Make for it.

The track, now in the heather, is broad and unmistakable and with a sandy path beside it. To the right of the boundary stone and track is a ruined hut, once called 'Nancy Tent'.

IN LONELY LAND

You are now leaving the rearward beauties and views of Agden (Agden may mean the woody hollow of the oak tree) and Bradfield valleys – on the north side of the upper Agden Brook – and, although not ten miles from Sheffield Town Hall, passing into the land of solitude and its smooth slopes of bracken, heather, cotton grass, bilberry and cranberry briar, and treeless to the skyline. The opposite long gentle slope is Rook Cabin Flat merging higher up into Wet Slack Ridge (Slack, old Norse, means a hollow, boggy place, and is found on the north Yorkshire moors. It also means a hollow – as apart from boggy). The only feature, nearly due S.W., is the rock top of Back Tor, and, due S.W., the smooth heather top of Howshaw Tor. For the next quarter of a mile we go slightly S. of W. and approach and cross the little hollow and peaty streamlet called Rushy Dike – the rushes are higher up – and a little lower and S.E. of our way is the 'Wellspring', more S., and clearer bubblings of Flint Hill Spring, near Agden.

The moor, roughly from Rushy Dike to Flint Hill Dike and Hobson Moss Dike, *vide* Mr Wm Bramall, was called 'Hollin's Ground', from an enclosure given to the Hollins, who, for many years, kept the 'Sportman's Arms', at Wightwizzle. This licence lapsed about 1907.

So far you will have noted that 'The Duke of Norfolk's Road' has been used by carts to convey the stone split from the surface rock, and presently, that the stone-cutters and carters went Bradfield way homewards.

Until forty years ago, the Bradfield farmers used to drive their young stirks this way to the 'summerings' on Howden Heys. Beyond Rushy Dike, our way, gently rising, is still W. half S.W., between the slight banks of peat, and with no landmark to guide us. Soon, at a slight curve, it narrows and deepens, and for another quarter of a mile we proceed almost S.W. The eye fastens upon the sandy track, and the practised man thinks of an ancient bridleway.

THE DIVIDE OF AGDEN AND EWDEN

At the next bend (1436 feet) we are in the open and look, rearwardly, into Agden valley and S.W. to Back Tor. Onwards we go for another half a mile, due W. On the near left is the shallow depression of Flint Hill Dike and the highest bracken growth. Beyond it is Hobson Moss Dike – the chief source of Agden Brook. Near Back Tor we now observe the isolated gritstones, called Cakes of Bread and Wheel Stones.

The track is again renewed and plain – like a cut-out roadway through the peat – and Flint Hill's flat top (about 1580 feet) is on our near right. Prehistoric man lived or worked hereabouts, as my friend Leslie Armstrong, F.S.A., has found flint flakes, which, obviously enough, were imported from other districts.

Nearing the summit ahead we keep a good eye on the track direction due W. Two little tummocks of heather and peat on the skyline are a good guide. I placed a wee cairn there, and hope it will be allowed to stay there and increase. At the tummocks (a left bend to follow) we are 1551 feet above sea level and at the divide of Agden and Ewden drainage areas. The depression to N.W. is the Oaken Clough tributary of Ewden Brook – Margery Hill is ahead, and Pike Low and its unseen tumulus on the extreme north of the near view. The famous 'Candlerush Springs' are one-and-a-half miles to the N.W. (a rough walk), but it is no longer necessary to gather them for the glimmer of winter's night in upland farmhouses – they were formerly gathered on the Moors and, dipped in tallow, used for candle-lights.

THE VIEWS

The view westward is just that dreary moor and loneliness which only has a call for the active vagabond and restless wanderer who is still called 'trespasser'. The ordinary man would curse it and walk home again. But let everyone beware and bring compass and map, for, on a misty day, here is one of the most bewildering moorlands in the Peak District.

The altitude is 1551 feet and we bend sharply left (acutely S.S.W.) for about 200 yards, and see and pass six broken gritstones (possibly the remains of an old guide), and then, at the stones, for about one mile further, go due S.S.W. along the smooth flat divide between the two stream sources.

The highest point of our walk, 500 yards beyond the six stones, is 1582 feet, and there is a good view of smooth Low Tor (hardly acceptable as such), then comes Howshaw Tor showing a face crag, and, to the right, the plainer Back Tor (1765 feet) and the pimple of Lost Lad – falling from the flat of Lost Lad Hill End into the Abbey Clough. The isolated Wheelstones of Derwent Edge are to the left of Back Tor and Stanage Edge still further to the left and more distant. Strangely enough, one can look behind and see the slope of Walkley Bank, Malin Bridge and Hillsborough side of Sheffield. From the last bend, the direction, for about half a mile, is first direct for Lost Lad Hill End, and then hardly a compass point to right of Lost Lad pimple summit.

IN PEAT STREET

The broad way hereabouts reminds one of the better known Cut Gate track, almost appearing to be cut out of six or seven feet of brown peat – a sort of Devil's highway, or of man's intention and attempt, and then an abandonment of the idea. It might be suggested that this was an ancient boundary or a road begun by the Duke of Norfolk's men or others in anticipation of the new road to Glossop and Manchester, which, in the earliest years of the nineteenth century, was intended to go from about Moscar top and straight across the summit of the moors to Glossop. I have doubts about the road or the rough paving of it, and a few sections cut through with pick and shovel would soon settle the point. It may be assumed that as the Glossop ('Snake') Road Act was passed in 1818, finished in 1821, and prepared for in 1816, they did not waste money on this road. Besides, the Award was not issued until 1828. At the most it might have been rough paved by the early grouse shooters, who (pre 1860 and shooting butts) came over the moor on horse-back.

The little peat soaking we cross is the brown trickling and head feeder of Agden Brook (at 1560 feet above sea level), and, by following its trench windings E.E. by S. a short distance (to the next bend E.E. by N.), we arrive at the peaty bog hollow, which, named Black Hole, is the beginning of Hobson Moss Dike.

In a few hundred yards we descend gradually towards the Cartledge Clough beginnings of Abbey Clough and Brook, and, still in this curious way which I call Peat Street, pass (left) two boundary stones marked 'RRW' – evidently the boundary of Rimington Wilson's Broomhead Hall estate. The wide street of peat, curiously enough, ceases a little short of the stream side – at the commencement of the deepenings of Cartledge Clough, an altitude of 1547 feet. If we kept to the same course we should reach the little stream at an altitude of 1500 feet.

CARTLEDGE, CROOK(ED) AND BENTS CLOUGHS
The track, from the termination of Peat Street, and for the next half-mile, was always more or less go as you please, and, in the sense of exactness, not easy to follow. The best plan is to proceed a little W. of S., along Cartledge Bents, just above the east-side bank of the deepening Cartledge Clough, until, opposite a prominent precipice of gritstone, the clough, now bending S.W., falls into the well-named Howden Chest and opposite the remarkable twist-ings of Crook (probably meant for Crooked) Clough – its first important trib-utary. The green flat just beyond, above, and W. of Crook Clough is called Greenfield Howden and, if pasturing was renewed, it would be greener. The long Cartledge Stones Ridge and Flat (about 1650 feet) is the higher ground to the east.

We now pursue the summit of the edge and the gritstone cliffs – with the peat deposits two or three yards on our left – and, in ¾ mile S.S.W. of the end of Peat Street, a plainer track turns southwards towards the head of Bents Clough and a clearer-marked track which, already, we have seen descending, westwardly, down the side of Cartledge Clough, and towards the keepers' hut (another is seen later) in Sheepfold Clough. The one-and-a-half miles from Peat Street to Sheepfold Clough is one of the finest clough-side walks in the Sheffield walkers' district and vies with Kinder, Grindsbrook and the three Black Cloughs near Woodhead.

The stream-side walk is rough going, but excellent reward. There is a small fall in Howden Chest and good rock views on the way.

THE ABBEY CLOUGH AND ITS FEEDERS

We cross the stream by the shooters' huts, avoid the upward and follow the downward track, passing (right) the low ridge and ancient stream course, and the two rock 'Gates of Abbey Clough' – so I have ventured to baptise this interesting place, which is similar to the 'Gates of Kinder', above the Downfall. Berrister's Tor is the north 'Gate' and Foul Clough is beside it. We pursue along the high south side of the now named Abbey Clough and cross steep, narrow, and often dry, Wild Moor Clough. Howden Edge is the opposite steep slope. Half a mile from Sheepfold Clough we pass Gravy Clough's clear stream – and bracken slopes – draining from Robin Hood Moss and Robin Hood's Spring, and, in another half-mile the shorter Cogman Clough, which drains Nether Hey. Opposite Cogman Clough and Catholes Wood, the track turns S.W., away from Abbey Clough, across the shoulder and down to a wider, more shapely clough, which is also named Cogman Clough. (The coincidence of two names in the same valley is curious, and one may be a modern misnomer. In any case, there are ancient tracks across either side of the valley, and cogman is an old word for a pedlar.)

Before crossing the latter we have noticed a trench way going in the same direction (S.W.), straight ahead to the near skyline, beyond Cogman Clough. We cross the stream, below the ruined shepherd's stone hut, go up the slope and, 200 yards beyond the stream, the shorter shooters' used track goes to the right (and west) on the low side. We go uphill (under the treeless Forest Knoll) and ahead (S.W.), and the trench way, quickly seen and followed, ends at the top of the slope. The track, now intermittent, goes along the 1250 feet level (S.W.) straight to the beginnings of the next un-named clough, just above the highest of three rowan trees, which, if no other name is discovered, I shall call Rowan Tree Clough.

We cross Rowan Clough and avoid two trench ways, one going west and then southwest – to Bamford House. Our way, now going N.W., and indistinct, is along the top of the clough side (1250 feet level), and a good guide is to steer a course 10 to 30 yards to the left (S.E.) of the highest patches of bracken. In a quarter of a mile from Rowan Clough we arrive at the beginnings of another bridle and sledge trench way (going almost west) and, a little lower down – in the same direction – a second trench way leads down to the gate, the Derwent Valley Water Board's boundary wall, and the exit of the track – beside the outhouse of Abbey Grange cottage.

THE REVERSE ROUTE

The late vicar of Bradfield, Rev. A. Browne, M.A., now vicar of Marton-cum-

Grafton, told me that the farm wife of Abbey Grange used to ride regularly on horseback to Sunday service at Bradfield church, and Mr Wm Bramall tells me that Mrs Eyre (the wife of a descendant of the yeoman eighteenth-century Eyre, of Crook Hill, who worked Ronksley and Howden Farms), who lived at Howden Farm probably ninety years ago, and whose husband held Ronksley and Crook Hill also, often rode across the moors to Bradfield and its church. Mr Wilson, the Duke of Norfolk's steward at Howden, forty years ago was also a regular moor rider to Bradfield.

We approach via Slippery Stones or Derwent village and the reverse route – for Bradfield, Sheffield, Wightwizzle, Bolsterstone or Penistone – begins at the north side of the outhouse of the good-natured Kennedy's – late game-keeper's – cottage. The present cottage, although map-called Abbey Grange, was built in 1829, and the outhouse was once inhabited. The site of the original Abbey Farm or Grange – once a farm worked, or afterwards leased, by the Canons of Welbeck Abbey in the twelfth to sixteenth centuries (1535) – is 200 yards S.S.E. and covered by the Derwent Reservoir. Hence, the origins of Abbey Brook and Clough.

We pass by the outhouse wall and the plain track (going east) goes up the green slope to a wired field gate and the water board's boundary wall. Beyond the gate are two routes. The modern used, shorter and lower track, goes tolerably on the level – slightly N. of E. – and, in two miles reaches the two shooters' huts in Sheepfold Clough. The older and longer right of way, giving the best views, goes ahead, up slope – slightly S. of E. In 500 yards this deep trench track ends, and for another 200 yards the way is fainter, but, bending and mounting (S.E.), the trench resumes, but again becomes more intermittent. The direction is still S.E., and, keeping the highest patches of bracken perhaps 20 yards to our left, we make for the mountain ash tree at the head of the unnamed clough which I call Rowan Tree Clough.

The Derbyshire–Yorkshire boundary line follows the wall on the (S.E.) skyline in front, and, on Sanderson's 1836 map, is called Howden Wall.

After crossing Rowan Tree Clough the way is fainter, but the direction is due N., then N.N.E., on the 1200 feet above sea level, and a direction point is the summit of Howden Edge–High Stones, 1750 feet. In a quarter of a mile we follow down a deepening trench way, under treeless Forest Knoll, and, now joining the lower shooters' track, arrive a little west of (below) an old stone shepherd's hut and the confluence of the two streamlets which make the wide foldings of the Cogman Clough on the south side of Abbey Brook. The more southeastern streamlet rises in a drain from Poynton Bog, and both rise near Lost Lad Hill End. But before descending Forest Knoll we sit and take the view of our moorland temple.

THE VIEW FROM ABBEY CLOUGH

Hey Bank is on the north side of Abbey Brook – nearing the reservoir. The firs were cut down a few years ago, and the thin plantation is doomed. Further east, and beyond the short Hey Clough, we have New Close Wood, and a good mile from Abbey Grange Cottage, Catholes Wood (wild cat?). Next we have the second Cogman Clough, on the north side of Abbey Clough. The long flat summit behind (north of) Cogman Clough number two is Howden Edge leading along the 1750 feet level, to High Stones, Wilfrey Nield, Margery Hill, and Cutgate. The easterly summit is Robin Hood Moss – merging into the higher Featherbed Moss – another problematical haunt of Robin Hood who, apparently, was an original Clarion rambler. (Robin Hood's Spring is one-third mile N.E. of the foot of Gravy Clough.)

Looking away N.N.W., we see, five miles away, beyond Steanery Clough, the nosey slope of Horse Stone Naze (Horse Stones is 1726 feet), and the infant Derwent (Ronksley Clough) is to the left of it. More to the west is flat-topped Barrow Stones (1939 feet), the sharp edge of Grinah Stones, and the hollow of the Westend stream. Bleaklow Stones (2050 feet) is to the right of it, and Shelf Stones (2039 feet) at the left end of this long plateau of peat groughs. The views of Kinder, hereabouts, are spoiled by the intervening Alport Moor and Rowlee tops.

The six-inch-to-mile map, although incomplete, is full of odd place names which prove what the eye can see – that on either side of Abbey Clough the land below the skyline was a great heathland pasturage which, within the last forty years, summer-pastured from three to four hundred horses and young beasts each year – in addition to sheep. Some day the production of beef and mutton will, in law, be more important than grouse, and these modern-made waste lands be restored to their original, and more valuable, usage.

THE WAY RESUMED

We cross Cogman Clough below the old and ruined shepherd's hut and fold, go up the bank, have a sod bank on our left and soon cross a ruined wall fence and enclosure called on my 1836 Ordnance Map, 'Howden Close'.

Our now level way for half a mile is along Howden Dean, with the sources of Gravy Clough and high Robin Hood Moss beyond. The track approaches the steep side of Abbey Brook, we pass Gravy Clough and cross steep, and often dry, Wild Moor Clough. We have already observed, and now approach, two dark projecting outcrops of gritstone which I call the Gates of Abbey Clough. The north-side 'Gate' is, however, map-called Berrister's Tor, and, near it, is a good view of the fine foldings of the upper Abbey Brook, now called Cartledge Clough. (An old document calls Cutgate 'Cartgate', and one would like to see old estate plans and the origin of Cartledge.)

CARTLEDGE CLOUGH

Beside the 'Gates' is steep, shaly and slimy Foul Clough, and, on our side of the stream, we see that the sharp ridge and hollow – a few yards to our left – ending in the south 'Gate', was the ancient stream course of Sheepfold Clough, which has cut through the strata a little to the east. We cross the two, now rotting, bridge poles and pass the two shooters' huts – the one on the west bank being within the walls of the old sheepfold. (At the head of Sheepfold Clough is Howshaw Tor, 1650 feet.) But before arriving here we observed a fainter, but evident, track which, going beyond the second hut, almost due east, and rising slowly and then more steeply, up the southwest side of the main Cartledge Clough, presently crosses the head of the next feeder – Bents Clough.

Between Sheepfold and Bents Clough is one of the finest clough pictures in the Peak, of foldings and twistings – chiefly of Crook (crooked?) Clough, the feeder of Cartledge Clough, which, seen under proper atmospheric conditions, leaves a lasting impression. The rearward view of Abbey Clough and moor flats beyond should also be noted. This deep steep-sided clough near Crook Clough confluence, and well named Howden Chest, is best seen from Lost Lad Hill end.

Crossing Bents Clough we turn left (N.E.) along Cartledge Bents and the top of the clough side, and, above the gritstone outcrops. The path almost dies away – but we keep two or three yards left of the peat. The open moor is now ahead, along Cartledge Stones and Ridge (1650 feet) on our right (the 1836 official Ordnance Map calls it Carter Stones Ridge, and the name may have some reference to Cartledge, and certainly adds to the confusion of origins), Crook Clough and Greenfield Howden on our left (my 1836 Ordnance Map marks 'Grinfield Howden' on either side of 'Sheepfold Clough'), and, looking half a mile ahead, and slightly E. of N., we see and make direct for, the faint wing-folding or depression on the front skyline. Keeping the shallowing clough on our left hand, and taking a rough course, we shortly arrive at the S.W. end of the wide way I have called Peat Street, and the two boundary stones marked 'RRW'.

ALONG AND ACROSS THE WATERSHED

The direction is N.E. and, for a mile, it is difficult to leave Peat Street. We cross the dribbling western sources of Hobson Moss Dike, and, on the west, have Round Hill and then the Brusten Croft Ridge divide of the Ewden watershed. In two-thirds of a mile the highest point, 1582 feet, is reached, and about 400 yards beyond it we pass by half a dozen cracked stones (right and east) which may be a distributed road guide. About 200 yards beyond them we turn due east and avoid crossing the low ridge of Flint Hill (N.), 100 yards ahead, or, turning N.W. into the sources of Oaken Clough. At the turning point, altitude 1551 feet, I have placed a little cairn which might be improved by a party of ramblers. We now descend gradually under the low summit of Flint Hill. The way is indicated by the grey benty grass between the heather, due in part to the fertilisings of the sheep and beasts often driven along the line of the way – in the years gone by.

In a short half-mile, at 1436 feet altitude, we have a bend (direction, for one-third of a mile, E.E. by N.) and pass above the highest brackens and beginning of Flint Hill Dike streamlet. Crossing the low east shoulder of Flint Hill we pass over the shallow cloughlet of Rushy Dike and proceed for the last one-and-a-half miles eastwards, and, latterly, a little S. of E. The first guide is a boundary stone beside the track on the right hand, and a ruined stone hut to the near left, called 'Nancy Tent'. Mr Wm Bramall, who gave me the latter name, says that until shooting butts became fashionable, and the dog and gun and ten brace a day were improved upon, the Sheffield, Wadsley and Ecclesfield crowds came up Foulstone Delf, Emlin Dike and Herculean Edge every 'Glorious Twelfth' of August. Some made a night of it, and you could always buy grouse in Sheffield by 8am on the morning of the 12th. There used to be a tent fixed near 'Nancy Tent' and beer was sold to the thirsty crowd who "made a day of it", and bought other refreshments from the trundlers of handcart or barrow, who followed up the side of these streams.

Then, for a distance, the track pursues the side of a wall and, along Herculean Edge, descends to the S.S.W. end of Bardike and the alternate roads to Bradfield or Oughtibridge, Wigtwizzle, Bolsterstone, etc.

THE INJUNCTION
Take a map and compass with you – and a few choice friends – and give three hours to the full route, three-and-a-half hours for the route between Abbey Grange and Bardike – and a good hour for study and contemplation. The walk down or up Abbey and Cartledge Cloughs and Howden Chest can be taken by a good walker, and the reward is great – but although an attractive, hard walk, by the stream side and the waterfall cannot be a right of way.

This is the first printed description of the 'Duke of Norfolk's Road', so go over and learn until you can throw article and map away, and find your course at midnight.

The Emlin Dike Road

From S.C.R. Handbook, 1924/25. This short article complements the previous article on 'The Duke of Norfolk's Road'. The Ebenezer Stone is still standing, but the keeper's gallows nearby is no longer used. The Biblical reference for the Ebenezer quotation is 1 Samuel 7, verse 12, and, as Ward says, Benjamin Elliott's quotation is wrong. Curiously, Ward makes no reference to the carving of a sword on the base of New Cross, yet a contemporary photo in the Clarion Handbooks *shows that it must have been visible. New Cross used to be a prominent landmark from 'The Duke of Norfolk's Road', until the cross shaft was vandalised in the early 1990s. Ward refers at the end to an article by John Wood, the Penistone postmaster. This was published in the* Barnsley Chronicle, *and titled* A Walk Across the Penistone Moors. *The exact quotation is, 'The path up Abbey Brook Clough and across the moor, is a short cut of about 4 miles to Strines Inn, and some fine moorland scenery is met with on the way'. It is possible, even likely, that John Wood followed the route Ward described – past New Cross and down Holling Dale to Strines Bridge – but Wood's description can hardly be called 'clear'. Ward was optimistic when he wrote that the Emlin Dike Road would probably remain private until the Access to Mountains Bill became law. He was referring to the Bill that became law in 1939 and was superseded by the 1949 National Parks Act. The Countryside and Rights of Way Act 2000 might change things, but in the more than half a century since 1949, the Emlin Dike Road has remained private.*

One of the old inhabitants of Bradfield told me quite twelve years ago that the elderly natives of the district remembered five 'Cut Gates', as they usually called them, which were, or had been, in their days, public rights of way across the moorlands from the western end and sides of the Bradfield valley. They are named as follows, and in order:

(1) 'The Duke of Norfolk's Road'.
(2) Emlin Dike Road.
(3) Holden Road – up Foulstone Delf (Holden is Howden).
(4) Cutthroat Bridge or Derwent Edge Road leading to Grainfoot and Derwent.
(5) 'Derwent Road' – from Moscar Cross over Derwent Edge, by the Wheelstones, to Derwent village.

'The Duke of Norfolk's Road' and the Abbey Grange route of 'Holden Road' are still public ways. Number (4) is only 'free', or undisputed, as a path to Riding House and Grainfoot, and 'Derwent Road' has been reopened (after the article published in the *Sheffield Clarion Ramblers' Handbook* of 1920–21, which revealed the secrets of sale plans). The Emlin Dike Road will probably remain 'private' until the Access to Mountains Bill becomes law, but it crosses a most interesting stretch of moorland and was clearly an old right of way which was legally stolen by the Ecclesfield Tithes Act of 1811 and enclosures covering Bradfield parish. It was the obvious sheep and cattle drovers' route for the one-time commoners, farmers and shepherds coming from Low Bradfield and Dungworth, Thornseat or Ughill, and their direct way for the upper Derwent valley.

A half-mile of old bridleway, still marked 'BR' on the six-inch-to-mile maps, goes N.N.W. out of Bradfield Dale, passes the Holes Farm house, up a wee hollow, and the last field, in Mortimer Road, to a gate now wrongly obstructed by a pole, and to a point a few yards east of the boundary wall of Thornseat Plantation – where the plantation wall follows along the top of the south bank of Emlin Dike stream. Thornseat Lodge, to the S.W. down Mortimer Road, was built by Sydney Jessop during the Crimean War for Mr Jagger, his first gamekeeper and, *vide* Mr Wm Bramall, his more famous brother William afterwards used it for a shooting and weekend lodge. It was built inside the originally called 'Miss Harrison's Plantation'. The first tree in Thornseat Plantation was planted by Jossy Sanderson, the uncle of Mr Wm Bramall's mother, who lived at Fair House. Before the Enclosure Act it was called Thornseat Moor.

This half-mile of bridle road and remnant of Emlin Dike Road is awarded and shown on the Ecclesfield Tithes Act Award Map. The other approach is from Low Bradfield by the modernised Windy Bank Lane beside Agden Reservoir. This metalled lane, once a bridleway, formerly crossed the southwest side of Agden Reservoir and came out at Low Bradfield. The two old ways, Windy Bank Lane and the awarded bridleway, meeting at this point, are eloquent proof of the once continued public route. 'Windy' means 'winding'.

Emlin Dike is the first clough south of Agden Clough. It is crossed by Mortimer's Road, and Windy Bank Lane joins Mortimer's Road by the bridge, over Emlin Dike stream. At the road junction, looking S.W., and up towards Thornseat Plantation wall, we see evidences of the old heather-covered trench way which is observable for half a mile along the side of the plantation wall. The plainer cart track and continuation of the bridle road from Holes Farm, beside the plantation wall, which is used occasionally, is followed and, in half a mile, we have the first of two rough open fields on our left – the part of Thornseat Plantation cut down during the First World War. Opposite (N.) is the smooth brown summit of Emlin Ridge (about 1275 feet). Next we see a stone boundary pillar 4ft 6in high (no markings) and near a small wooden gate – another boundary stone, now leaning over, is noticed 200 yards further to the west. Mr William Bramall, of Watch House,

Bradfield, tells me that this first upright stone is called 'Ebenezer Stone', and was a boundary stone between William Jessop's and Mr Cadman's moors. When the men, after the Enclosure Act, were marking out the boundaries of moorlands some eighty years ago, Mr Benjamin Elliott, of Smallfield Farm, after the stone was fixed, suddenly exclaimed – "Theer's a bit i' t'Boible 'at says, 'Thus far shalt thou go, Ebenezer, and no farther'. They then threw up the bottles they had emptied and shouted hurrah, an' it's bin called Ebenezer Stooan ivver since." The quotation doubtless is wrong, but the incident shall survive. Beside it (and just beyond the next cross wall) is a rough field gate made of rough poles – the gamekeeper usually hangs his enemies upon it – sparrowhawks, magpies, stoats, etc. The path beyond and east of the second gate is modern and leads to (a) a shooters' hut and shed and (b) the twin wooden shooting cabins at the Clough divide where Emlin Dike ends and we observe the source of the Holling Dale Brook which runs to Strines Bridge – below 'Strines Inn'.

Through the second, widest, and pole-made gate, is our old Emlin Dike 'Cut Gate'. The rough road going south soon ends at an old small quarry, but a few yards along it is the right and west branch – our 'Cut Gate', which goes consistently about 40 yards inside the field south of the wall and comes out at the hollow where the two furthest huts are placed and a track goes N. of W. to a line of shooting butts.

We are now one mile from our starting point and the route forward was never plain to follow. Sledge or cart scarcely went up this moor and the usual mode was on horseback or Shanks' mare.

We have already seen a moorland boundary stone (in a socket and marked 'BJY') standing 700 yards slightly N. of W. beyond the corner of the wall we are leaving behind and near the two last huts. Looking S.E. we see the top of the extensive, but now disused, Thornseat Quarries.

Our direction is due west and, almost a mile away, is New Cross, which when again seen, after rising up the dry part of the moor, has the appearance of a thin, tapering cairn. The track, intermittent, becomes plainer as we approach the little mound and wonder if this rudest of new crosses is on the site of an ancient tumulus. It is marked 'New Cross' on my 1836 Ordnance Map and, while I suggest that it may be eighteenth century

New Cross.

and was, obviously, placed to point the way at a confusing point – to prevent an exit to Strines Bottom, or along the obvious route of Wet Slack Ridge into the Agden Clough – it is not known whether there was a medieval cross at this spot. It is, however, a curiosity and, of its class, quite unique upon our local moorlands. The rough measurements are: base of cross 2ft 6in deep, bottom of base about 2ft 6in square, tapering to about 1ft 6in. Shaft of cross above mortice-hole 2ft 6in, mortice-hole in base 12in x 9in x 6in deep. There are no letterings, and it is the coarsest moorland cross I have seen in the district.

Our direction is still west, across the faint near depression which, flowing southwards, is the source of Rushy Flat Dike; and in half a mile from New Cross, we reach the summit level of the north end of Cartledge Stones Ridge – here called Cartledge Flat. We keep a similar course and in another half-mile have, descending easily, reached the side of Cartledge Clough and the track to Abbey Clough.

The late John Wood, Penistone postmaster (died 1888), who was a walking local gazetteer and tramped all the moorlands for miles around, refers in one of his articles, to a path up Abbey Brook Clough and across the moor being a short cut of four miles to 'Strines Inn'. From his description it is clear that he went up Abbey Clough, Howden Chest, Cartledge Stones Ridge and from New Cross, down Holling Dale to Strines Bridge. But his walking was done in the seventies and early eighties of last century.

New Facts about Broomhead and Bradfield Moors, Howden and 'The Duke of Norfolk's Road'

From S.C.R. Handbook, 1926/27. *This article is based on a reading of the Ronksley Manuscripts, now housed in Sheffield Archives, and it refers back to the article on 'The Duke of Norfolk's Road', particularly adding information about Handsome Cross, Hurkling Stones and Apron-Full-of-Stones.*

This article, and the comments therein, is almost entirely due to my perusal of the thousands of extracts from the MS. which Geo. Ronksley copied, now to be found in the Ronksley MS. in Sheffield Public Reference Library, and I am not aware of their publication in any previous book or publication. They are a quarry in which I have dug dozens of hours, and the topographical notes were, I am of opinion, entirely made by the great John Wilson, of Broomhead Hall (1719–83). Joseph Hunter, the historian of Hallamshire, who owed tremendously, and acknowledged his indebtedness, to John Wilson for much of his material for the standard history of Hallamshire, did not use the notes and quote *in extenso*.

Wilson's note on the prehistoric earthwork called Bardike (across and near the summit of the two roads which come from Strines and Agden, and Bradfield, and, joining, proceed to Ewden Bridge and Midhope or Wigtwisle) is as follows:

'At the west end is a large ditch called Bardike about 380 yards in length and 36 yards broad and in some places the same height. It [is] now a boundary betwixt this common and that of Smalfield and the horseway from Broomhead to Sheffield and Nether Bradfield lies through it'. (See Ronksley MS. 1541.)

It will be noted that Wilson, who had made a topographical survey of his district 'in 1741' (Joseph Hunter), and may have written this before 1750, states that the ditch is '36 yards broad' and that, quite apparently, he means 3–6 yards broad. The height today as I examined it is only three yards. The word 'lies' today would be changed to 'goes'.

'Near the west end thereof on a place on the north side is a huge heap of stones called 'THE APRONFUL OF STONES' (see Ronksley MS. 1542), 'being about three yards high, hollow in the middle and about 80 yards in circumference [and] containing several hundred loads. It was once much bigger, as great quantities are sunken in the ground and grown over so that it may be conjectured that there are as many in the ground as are exposed to sight. The occasion of this ditch and heap of stones is uncertain. There is a tradition that two armies came, the one from the north, the other from the south, and that the commander of one of them consulted with a sorceress to know the success of the battle which was about to ensue. She told him he should be victorious unless he met a white bear or boar which, if he happened to do, he should be slain and his army routed, which he, thinking himself not likely to do, marched on with his army, and upon this place the two armies met and fought in which battle the commander before-mentioned was slain and his army routed, the prediction of the woman being verified in the adverse party having on their standards a white bear or boar. After the battle the heap of stones was thrown over him by the soldiers for a memorial. If this be true it most likely occurred during the Saxon Heptarchy and that the southern army were the Mercians. I take this dike to have been their encampment before the battle and that afterwards they would probably bury their king or commander near the encampment'.

Similar Names Elsewhere
Similar names to the Devil's Apronful of Stones, denoting man-made heaps of stones or mounds, are found in other parts of the British Isles and also on the Continent, and they are often beside or near ancient trackways – as in this case. Examples are the Three Men cairns on Gardom's Edge near Baslow and the once great cairn on Nether Moor, Edale, which was called The Druids Altar, etc. Mrs Leather, in *Folk Lore of Herefordshire*, gives a local folk-lore explanation of the White Rocks at Garway:

'The Devil was helping Jack to stop up the weir at Orcop Hill, in order to flood the valley and make a fishpool. But as the Devil was coming over Garway Hill his apron strings broke; and down fell all the stones he was carrying. Then the cock crew and he had to go home, so there are the stones to this day'.

Similarly Colwall Stone in the Malvern Hill district was said to have been carried by the Devil in his apron when the string broke and it fell there – told by a roadman in the Yew Tree Inn at Colwall Green to Mr A. Watkins. (*The Old Straight Track*, Methuen & Co., 1925.)

This is the only description I have read anywhere of the Apronful of Stones before it was removed for wall building or other purposes. It was then diminished, and I still think that it became a common quarry for road metal when Mortimer's Road was made – about 1770 or not long after that date.

The Historic Wigtwisle–Howden Track and Boundary

It may also be noted that the site of this ancient cairn burial mound and once great landmark and direction indicator, in the site fixed on the large-scale Ordnance Maps, is not far from the junction of the old tracks from Bradfield, Low Bradfield, and Agden to Wigtwisle and Midhope – and the exact site may be nearer than shown on the six-inch map, which I have suggested is 330 yards from the S.S.W. end of Bardike. I cannot be sure. We can, however, assert that there is ample evidence from a prominent landowner who used it that the way to Howden was by the Apronful of Stones, and that a line of oak guide-stakes was fixed there before his time. Further it is apparent that, from the new evidence discovered, I must now assume that the whole of this historic right of way from Wigtwisle to Howden as far as Cartledge Brook was the boundary line of Wigtwisle Common from Smalfield (or Agden) and Howden and the broad road-like part of it a trench cut out of the turf and afterwards widened by the washing away of the peat. It may also be something more than coincidence that Cartledge and Cutgate are both trench-cut boundaries of commons, also ancient rights of way, and that Cutgate, in a 1574 document, is 'Cartgate'. The Clough by the Cart or Cut ledge may be guesswork, but it is at least suggestive.

The following (Ronksley MS. 1543) is a description of the long defensive trench work over the S. side of the Ewden and about one mile N.N.W. of Bardike and the Apronful of Stones:

'I take the ditch on the adverse or north side of this Common of Wightwisle, lying by a close belonging to the Duke of Norfolk called the Lea, to have been thrown up as the encampment for the army from the North or the Northumberland army. It is probable also that the common soldiers killed in the said battle were buried on the plain'.

The Hurkling Stones

The following (Ronksley MS. 1544 and 1545) prove my contention that Herculean Edge is another Ordnance surveyor's error and that in Wilson's day there were great quantities of isolated gritstone blocks along this Edge. I still prefer the local explanation of hurkling as crouching or bending, similar to the naming of grey wether, ox stones, etc., which denoted flattish stones which resembled recumbent animals on the moors and edge tops.

'Hurkling Stones is a boundary of the said common. It is open on one side and the other three sides environed with prodigious large stones, some of them above four yards high on the back side thereof, but the wonder is that upon one of these stones though so high lyeth another huge stone which hath holes worn into it like basons but is certain was not laid so by hands. These stones standing so close together and upon a heap as it were occasioned the place to receive the name of Hurkeling Stones'.

MS. 1545 – 'Along this edge are great quantities of stone (though not so big as those already mentioned) which are of a sort of rough sand or grit and used by the inhabitants for various domestic purposes'.

The foregoing probably refers to soft rotten stone used for domestic rubbing-stone on flagged doors, door steps, and window sills.

ROBIN HOOD'S CHAIR

The following (MS. 1546) is a mystery which, some time, may be solved by the production of an old estate map. It is, however, apparently on the line of boundary between Wigtwisle and (thus far) Smallfield Common and the head of Agden Clough at its source called Hobson Moss Dike. John Wilson, however, only says 'there is a pile of stones distant from here', i.e., from Hurkling Edge, and the only suitable stones I know are about two miles W. of the S.S.W. end of Bardike, 200 yards beyond where 'The Duke of Norfolk's Road' turns from a westwardly to southwesterly direction. Those half a dozen broken gritstones may have been a little quarry for making stone boundary posts on these moors after John Wilson had passed away.

'Robin Hood's Chair. There is a pile of stones distant from hence amongst which is a large stone with a semi-circular hollow place in the side thereof as if made for a seat it is commonly called Robin Hood's Chair and a person being placed therein finds at the right height with rests for his arms so that it is easy to sit in. There is, moreover, a stone before which may well serve for a table'.

KITT'S STAKES AND PATH OBSTRUCTIONS

Kitt, as may be known, is 'short' for Christopher. Here again, if evidence were required, is proof that 'The Duke of Norfolk's Road' was a public way to Howden and beyond long before the Ecclesfield (Bradfield was a chapelry) Enclosure – or Tithes – Act of 1811 and its Award of 9/3/1826 was dreamed of. And why, oh why, is 'The Duke of Norfolk's Road' left off the latest (1925) one-inch-to-mile Ordnance Maps and printed in the previous editions? When our club walked over it officially in late 1924 and early 1925 we were met on each occasion and told that it was not a right of way – an honour which was paid to us by the fixing of the gate and wire at the foot of the Westend–Alport track on the week before our ramble of 22 April 1923. These oak stakes, still existing about the middle of the eighteenth century, were, as we may conclude, placed there by one of the Wilson family. ('Christopher Wilson of Houlden, in the chapelry of Bradfield, gentleman. Born 14th August, 1681. Died 2nd June, 1730, and was buried in the church of Bradfield. He married Alice the daughter of Richard Bilham'. See the Wilson pedigree in Hunter's *Hallamshire*.) They were direction posts placed by a Wilson of Wigtwisle to guide himself and others over the most dangerous part of the route! A boundary of 1653 (see later) also gives a High Stake – another indicator placed at the awkward turning place near (Brusten) Croft Ridge or 'hill'.

MS. 1547 – 'Kitts Stakes. There is a row of oak Stakes goes from these stones' (Robin Hood's Chair is meant – G.H.B.W.) 'to a place called Holden and set there by Christopher Wilson of Wigtwisle as a guide for people going thither and called from him Kitt's Stakes many of them are pulled up those which remain are set some about 20 yards and others 10 from each other'.

TREES ON MOOR TOPS
The next paragraph (MS. 1548) is further confirmation that good trees formerly grew on these high moorlands.

'Fir trees are often found buried on this moor generally about half a yard deep in the earth whole and round without the loss of its peculiar smell and changed to a darker colour'.

'THE DUKE OF NORFOLK'S ROAD' AND HOWDEN EDGE
The next MS. 1549 (Holden Edge), takes us along and beyond the wider course of 'The Duke of Norfolk's Road' which I christened 'Peat Street', and I must now suggest that this boundary of Wigtwisle and Smallfield Commons and then, after the head of Agden watershed, the Howden Common, is a boundary ditch widened by some centuries of floodwater washings. The boundary, from the end of 'The Duke of Norfolk's Road' at Cartledge Clough, goes straight west to the 1550-feet nose at the south end of Howden Edge, at the top of the boundary wall and Seward Lode – coming up E.E. by S. from upper Howden Clough. It then follows the Edge by another boundary and water-widened ditch (one mile long) to Margery Hill, where the water flows into Spring Gutter and forms the Ewden. Wilfrey Edge is the northern end of Howden Edge nearer Margery Hill.

MS. 1549 says, 'Holden Edge. At the upper and west end of this Common is an edge called Holden Edge which is the boundary of the Common Wigtwisle and Holden'.

BOUNDARIES OF WIGTWISLE COMMON IN 1635
The following is Ronksley MS. 1653:

'These are the [limits] and Boundaries of Wightwisle free common ridden and viewed and seen the 20 Oct. 1653 by Christopher Wilson, Christopher Morton, John Hill, Wm Garlicke, Henry Hawksworth, John Morton, Richard Gillott and many others.

'First by a common way leading from New Milnes unto the fall of Turnbrooke Water running to the north end of Hartley Rocher and from Hartley Rocher by a ditch to Bardike and thence to the Hurkelin Stones and so along the lower edge to the Black Dike and so to Tom Bowr.

'Thence to the High Stake and then along the Edge to Croft hill from there to Cartledge Dike and so to Holden Edge. From Holden Edge to a ditch near Uden and from thence on the [north?] side the river to the way leading from Bradfield to Midhope.

'Wightwisle Common contains 1960 acres.'

Lonely Cottage near Wightwizzle.

I am not quite clear in regard to the first portion of the boundary, but if we can accept the 'New Mill' which lies at the foot of today's Rocher Lane (going N.E. from White Lee Farm) and Fairhurst Lane, it is possible that today's 'Raynor Clough' was Turnbrooke Water. This apparent natural boundary line would then cross over by Swan Cottage, Swan Height and West Nab (the highest point 1300 feet), and then lead direct to what is now called Rocher Top or the Roches – a line of rocks and edge above the path from Bradfield church, Bailey Wood to Bowsen, Rocher Head Farm and into Smallfield Lane. The reader may study the later reference to 'Hartley Rocher'. I have also an old reference to 'Harcliff'. 'Haranclif' is Anglo-Saxon for boundary cliff, and the probable origin of the word Rocher is from 'roche' – for rock.

I have not looked for the ditch from Hartley Rocher to Bardike, but the boundary line from Hurkling Stones along the lower edge to Black Dike is clearly the course of 'The Duke of Norfolk's Road', and Black Dike is probably today's Rushy Dike. 'Tom Bowr' may be a mis-spelling, and I cannot identify it. The High Stake would stand as a mark and guide at the place where 'The Duke of Norfolk's Road' bends from a west to a south-southwesterly direction, and Croft Hill is clearly the Brusten Croft Ridge between the Oaker Clough feeder of Ewden and Hobson Moss Dike (Agden). The 'Peat Street' boundary goes immediately east of Brusten Croft Ridge and then descends to Cartledge Clough stream, where it first bends to the south. Due east to Howden Edge is apparent, but there is no mention of Margery Hill. The rest of the boundary is not clear, but the course of the Ewden to the Bradfield–Midhope Road at New Milnes may be intended.

HARTLEY ROCHER
The Ronksley MS. 1486 gives the following account of this place name and the 'round holes' may be looked for:

'Hartley Rocher. On the other side of the common lies Hartley Rocher, a huge precipice of rock. There are two round holes in the steepest part thereof which are much frequented by Ravens which hatch their young there'.

WIGTWISLE HAMLET AND COMMON RENTS
Ronksley MS. 1528 explains the extent of the hamlet in 1741:

'Wightwizell or Wigtwisle or Westmonhalgh. From which last it gives its name to the Liberty or Bierlow formerly called Westmonhalgh Bierlow now Westnal Bierlow. It is a very ancient village but now (1741) consisting of only four mess(uages) and a cottage'.

And MS. 1529 explains the origin of its grant of common from Thomas Lord Furnival, the Lord of Hallamshire:

'To this village and its territory or liberty Thomas fil Thomas Lord Furnival granted a free common of pasture on the moors for the inhabitants to depasture their cattle (which moor extends itself near four miles in length and more than two in breadth and contains 1960 acres of land'.

The Thomas Lord Furnivals were three in number, dying respectively in 1332, 1339, and 1366, and the first was a baron recorded in 1292. This may be the second or the third Thomas. MS. 1530 stops when we would learn more.

'He likewise granted divers other privileges to the inhabitants thereof'.

A WIGTWISLE–SMALLFIELD COMMON DISPUTE
Ronksley MS. 1531 also gives confirmation of my contention that Hartley Rocher is the place now called 'Rocher Top' on the six-inch-to-mile map.

'In 1652 there was a suit betwixt the inhabitants of Wigtwistle and Smalfield about the said common in consequence of one Edmund Hobson of Smalfield graving peats on the south side the Bardike being within the Common of Wigtwisle but after a tedious suit the inhabitants of Smalfield were forced to submit by reason they had no writing or precedent to show for so doing'.

Wightwizzle Hall Farm.

Ronksley MS. 1532 gives the name of the spring not far from Hartley Rocher. Is it the one on Agden Side?

'Here is a fine spring of cold water called Dank Spring'.

Bradfield Moorland Rents in 1441

A Stewards Rent Roll of the Manor of Sheffield for the moorland pastures of Bradfield from Michaelmas 1441, to Michaelmas 1442 (Ronksley MS. 1241 and British Museum Add. MS. 24467), informs us that John Page was the forester (for Bradfield forest moors or waste), who had 2d. per day, and that £4. 13s. 4d. was paid for 'rent of pasture in Ewden and Akeden', the same amounts for 'the pasture of Middle Holden, Hordron and Stanning Clough demised [transferred] to Barton Ronksley', and 40/- for the south part of Holden demised to Thomas Hawksworth.

Ewden pasture would include Wigtwisle, and Agden and Smallfield are probably the same. 'Holden' will be understood, but Hordron is not necessarily the Hordron Edge part of Lady Bower, while 'Stanning' may not be the Steanery (stan, stean, or stone) Clough in the Upper Derwent. We know, however, that 'Bartin de Ronksley' 'took the pasture of Mickle Holden and Holden hedes' in 1425, and therefore Stanning Clough could be today's Steanery Clough – in the Ronksley infant course of the Derwent.

A further Ronksley MS. (1488), presumably one of John Wilson's notes, is as follows:

'Smalfield. About a mile from Bradfield and probably having its name in contradistinction to it. The inhabitants pay 3/5? to the Duke of Norfolk for commoning in Agden for their cattle'.

The number of inhabitants or freeholders is not stated, but the payment apparently was a nominal sum, and the period presumably about 1750.

Wigtwisle – I prefer this spelling to the present Wightwisle or Wightwizzle. Twizzling is turning or twisting, and the Anglo-Saxon 'weg' for way is perhaps the nearest guess one can offer and perhaps preferable to the twist or fork of a stream.

ADDENDA

ROWAN TREE CLOUGH

On the 'Duke of Norfolk's Road', Mr E. Dearden, Lord Fitzalan's head gamekeeper, informs me that the name of this first clough on the south side of Abbey Clough is Hey Clough. So please mark it on your maps.

'THE DUKE OF NORFOLK'S ROAD'

I have nothing further to add to what I wrote in my article about this ('The Loneliest, Wildest Walk in South Yorkshire'), save that I gave a description of the commencement of the track from and to Abbey Farm and indicated the highest and most ancient track. The plain track to the right of the Water

Board's wall is the shooters' new track, and the track which before the making of the reservoir was used by the residents is below the shooters' track, and inside below the wall, and as we reach Hey Clough blocked up by the Water Board's wall. True enough the wall has apparently been knocked down or fallen, but the obstruction is there. I am waiting to receive written evidence contesting what I wrote in my article, and the records quoted in this issue give further point to my contention that this is, at least, a medieval right-of-way, perpetuated by the Bradfield Enclosure Act and Award of 51 Geo. 111 and 9/3/1826 respectively.

HANDSOME CROSS

The reader can now erase this blunder from his Ordnance Map. It is Hanson Cross. It dates earlier than today's road guide stone, which reads 'Penniston 5m, Sheafield 6m, Bradfield r lm 1753'. The other side, not distinct, is like '1 – P 17'.

'SCOTCHMAN'S CORNER' is apparently the junction of Smallfield Lane with the Bradfield–Penistone Road – at the S.E. corner of Cowell Plantation. Smallfield Lane going N.N.E. (from this junction) becomes Load Field Lane.

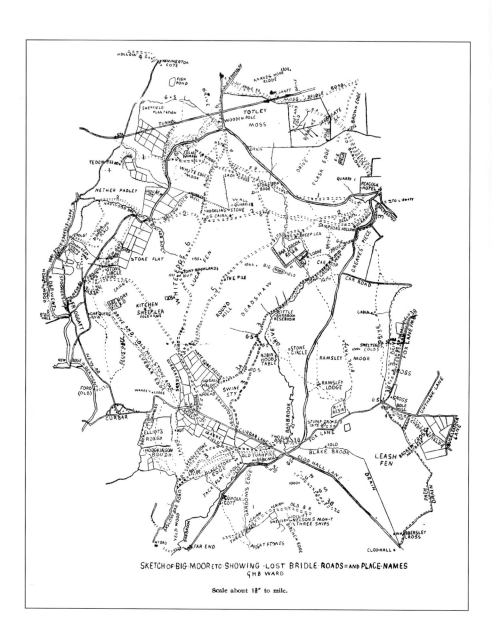

SKETCH OF BIG MOOR ETC SHOWING LOST BRIDLE ROADS = AND PLACE NAMES
G H B WARD

Scale about 1⅜″ to mile.

The Story of Baslow's Big Moor

or Bridleways and Moormen's Ways, in History, Topography and Anecdote.

From S.C.R. Handbook, 1927/28, this is a Ward 'magnum opus', not surprising, perhaps, considering Big Moor is only half-an-hour's walk from the house Ward lived in from 1915 until his death in 1957. While there may be little doubt that Lady Cross was erected by the Premonstratensian Canons of Beauchief Abbey, Ward's suggestion of a similar link between Beauchief and the Fox Lane–Shillito Wood crosses is probably wrong. Professor David Hey, who has been helping to edit the Beauchief Abbey Cartulary, suspects that these crosses belonged to either Lenton Priory or Louth Park Abbey, both of which had possessions in the area. Big Moor is now part of the Peak National Park Authority's Eastern Moors Estate, but today most of it is still without public access, this time on grounds of its designation as a 'wildlife sanctuary'.

THE FOREWORD

It is big and brown, wide and drear, featureless and lonely, flat and boggy as any moor in Peakland, and yet, to those who know it most intimately, full of interest, and, in the treading of it, verily, a big man's moor. Big Moor is a modern name, as, before the Holmesfield and Baslow Enclosure Acts, it was, and indeed still is, known in parts as Curbar, Bubnell and Froggatt 'commons' or moors. But the big has absorbed the small, and the common is a memory only recalled by the native who has a family history going down to the days when every freeholder and farmer had some portion of the common pasturage, and a dozen or more shepherds tended unlimited numbers of sheep and young cattle during the 'summering' days. Then, verily, the moors produced meat and wool.

It was, in those days, a moor crossed by half a dozen ancient and even early British bridleways, and possibly by some of my own ancestors who, on the male side, hail from Ridgeway and, having persisted about Dronfield and even Holmesfield for many generations, may have trod the heather and tufty grasses either as shepherds or during their journeyings with pack-horses. Indeed, it may be suggested that, if Sheffield is in my heart, Derbyshire is also in my bones.

It stretches from the road between Owler Bar and the Wooden Pole and down to the 'Grouse Inn', then along Froggatt Edge to Curbar Gap, down Curbar Lane to the Sheffield–Baslow Road, and so back to Owler Bar. One could almost add the stretch of Eaglestone Flat between Baslow and Blackstone Edges.

Its eastern neighbours, the flat Ramsley Moor and the boggy Leash Fen, are only parted by the Baslow Road, and, similarly, there are dreary flat stretches on the southeast side, above Gardom's Edge and Birchen Edge, towards Clod Hall Farm, and above the 'Robin Hood Inn'.

Big Moor would bear another ten years' investigation, but the facts now gathered are presented in the knowledge that they will make a first record, and be improved upon by another generation. No rights are claimed and no demands presented.

The city creeps moorwards, and everywhere the new standard of about 12 houses to the acre claims much of the best valley land, and will continue to do so. The higher lands thus become more valuable, and many changes are coming – some, it is fervently hoped, not before they are appreciated.

The moors today are private property, and rights are strictly guarded, and yet one may hope that those who desire to investigate and enjoy may be given the opportunity to follow some of these ancient tracks and obtain a picture of the past which, despite today's wonderful motor cars at 60mph and the daily deaths they cause, were the every-day form of travel before 1781, and did not pass out of general usage, as roads, until the opening of the Sheffield–Baslow Road in 1818.

The article is dedicated to those men of the moors who travelled in very truth (and worked as we, fortunately, never shall), and to some of their descendants who, as I know, have family records and stories going to the days of common pasturage. If there are any errors in it or additions to be made, I shall be glad to be corrected and to learn still more. The various old ways are numbered in the articles and also on the map.

The 'sharp' Sheffielder and 'slow' Derbyshire Man
I am reminded of a story told of the late John Silcock, who lived near Bank Green, in Fox Lane, Holmesfield, and worked on the roads.

A couple of sharp Sheffield grinders were 'having a day off', and, walking on the road from Totley towards Owler Bar, met 'John', at work, on the highway. He asked where they were going, and, very promptly (and in rougher adjectival parlance), they said they were going into Derbyshire "ter tak' sumbody dahn a bit".

"And", quoth road-mender John: "Yo' won't go varry far o'er t' brow, or yo'll varry sooin be takken dahn yersens" – meaning, no doubt, that if the Derbyshire 'tup' looked a little slow and did not say quite so much as the townsman, "he worn't asleep all t' time", and, as my friend Taylor, of Totley, would say, "he doesn't allus sleep all t' neet other". Take him all for all, the Derbyshire and moorside man who has his chance can hold his own in the all-round tasks of the day, and motor 'bus and wireless, in due time, will bring him nearer and quite as cutely, to the doings and thoughts that interest the man in the town. And, with my pen, I greet them – big men and hard men of the moors.

(I) A DRONFĪELD–TĪDESWELL BRĪDLEWAY BY LADY CROSS

This route from Holmesfield and Lidgate follows the present highway to Owler Bar. From Owler Bar it proceeds along the main road towards the Wooden Pole, Fox House, or Froggatt Edge, and (left side) to the top of the first and only ploughed field. Here it turns (left) and, crossing Saltersitch, and with the brook 20 to 30 yards on the right, the way proceeds slightly N. of W., along an indefinite track in the heather. (The connection of Saltersitch with the salt-carriers road cannot be ignored, for there are too many Saltergates, Salterways, Salterbrooks, etc., and several in the Peak District.). In 150 yards it crosses the road and the two walls and, turning west (left) uphill, leaves a little quarry hole a few yards on the left hand. At the top of the rise the road is about 100 yards away (left), and there are wide views down Cordwell valley towards Chesterfield and Hardwick Hall, the prominent green height of Stone Edge (S.E.) between Chesterfield and Ashover, and the East Moor and Harland Edge behind Chatsworth Park. The track is now plain, and, parallel to the road, becomes trenchy. It passes a few stones which, before the early-nineteenth century wall makers and chippers began their work, must have been a prominent and, possibly, a named landmark. Turning a little to the left, it passes a few yards right of another small quarry hole, and regains the road at about 350 yards short of the Barbrook Road – culvert bridge – at an altitude of 1150 feet.

A Slab Bridge

Crossing the road there is at once a surviving, wind beaten thorn tree – and also a number of shallow trench ways passing through a long bed of cranberry briars. It continues in the same direction, and, in about 450 yards from the road, reaches the rude stone stoop (five feet high) which, beside the two-slab bridle bridge and known to have existed in the eighteenth century and called 'Stone Bridge', is, in the Baslow boundary of 28/8/1812, called 'an ancient bridge'. This stoop was *the* guide across the moor. The stoop is also a survivor from the days of bridle roads, and is not a rubbing stoop for cattle. It is also apparent that many tracks and 'short cuts' have been made to this bridge and stoop. It is also clearly stated, in other boundary evidence of 1811 and 1812, that 'Froggatt Old Gate' from 'Froggatt to Holmesfield' joined this road and crossed at this point.

The spring immediately across the slab bridge is perhaps the only one which runs into the Barbrook peat-drainings above the reservoir.

A Public Footpath for part of a Bridle Road

Some of the Enclosure Act commissioners, although having power to close any road or path deemed to be unnecessary, adopted a convenient practice of "saying nowt abaht 'em", and thus on landed or entail estates place the public in these days in the position of proving usage through living memory and beyond it, after the date of the Act – usually, in Derbyshire, 1790–1830.

The Holmesfield Act, in its Award of 10/11/1820, gives the following in lieu of part of this bridle road:

One other Public Footway from Holmesfield and Stoney Middleton Turnpike Road, where Barbrook crosses the same in a westwardly direction, over an allotment No. 169, made to the Duke of Rutland, to Hathersage Moor'.

It would be interesting to know when the following instruction, in the Award, was observed:

'The several Public footways shall, from time to time, and for ever hereafter, kept in repair by and at the expense of the owners and occupiers respectively of the Lands over which any such footways are hereby set out and appointed'.

This 'public footway' was awarded to save half a mile between Holmesfield and Grindleford and to link up with the Tedgness track. The Award Map shows the path to begin just across the Barbrook by the gate at the left side of the road and slightly N. of W. and, from near Lady Cross, to follow the course of the bridleway as far as the turnpike road above the 'Grouse Inn'. The path on the Award Map is only shown as far as the Holmesfield boundary at about 400 yards E. of the gap on White Edge. I have not heard of any legal closing of this path and feeble substitute.

Crossing the spring, leaving the hollow slightly to the left, and proceeding N. of W., the track soon passes two small rude guide stones. Beyond are quarried holes (in 400 yards), another deep bridleway (Hope to Chesterfield) and, if it still remains, a dead rowan tree. One cannot dogmatise unduly, but the evidences on this moor on the near left side – going from Owler Bar to Barbrook Bridge – point to the gradual extinction of an old or natural wood of thorn, birches and rowans, except for a few stragglers. Blame the natives for chopping an odd tree, and the landlords, and the rabbits who eat the bark and are allowed to swarm and interbreed on moorlands. (Perhaps no edible quadruped is more subject to sexual disease than the popular rabbit.) In 60 yards, the track arrives at Lady Cross.

Lady Cross – the measurements of Lady Cross are as follows: base 2ft 1in x 2ft 1in x 1ft 6in and mortice hole about 13in x 13in. The shaft, possibly a post-reformation bridle-road indicator, is in two pieces, each roughly 2ft 6in, and, when put together, about 4ft 6in above the base. On the east and Totley side of the base of the cross is the lettering of ' + I R 1618' and, on the side, 'T'. The meaning is James Rex (king) 1618 and Totley – for Totley parish. On the opposite side of the base is '+ + M B' for Manor of Baslow. These were marked when the inhabitants were 'beating the bounds' of Totley and Baslow parish common lands and when Baslow (although a complainant in 1816) had claimed part of the common which, at least since the Enclosure Award, was placed in Holmesfield parish – the present boundary being the wall going N.N.W. from Hurkling Stone and three-quarters of a mile west of Lady Cross. The earliest copy of a boundary riding of Holmesfield in my possession (25/8/1777) records that 'the Shaft is part broke off' and markings on the base of 'I R 1618' '+' , 'M B' and '+'.

Beauchief's Monastic Moorlands
There is little doubt that Lady Cross was erected by the Premonstratensian Canons of Beauchief Abbey as a bridle cross road guide and to mark one of the then boundaries of the waste or common of Hathersage – a grant which was made to them by Matthew of Hathersage, the Lord of the Manor, who died a little before 1263.

The boundaries were as follows: 'Fulwood to the head of Burbache [Burbage brook] down Burbache brook to Hyggehase [High House?], thence descending to Lightokford [is it the old ford by the old Padley saw mill by Grindleford station, or the old Hollowgate ford?] and Paddely [Padley], and ascending to Levidicros [Lady Cross] and by the boundaries of Totinley [Totley] and Dore to the boundaries of Halumshire'.

This, as will be seen, is a goodly tract of more than 2000 acres of moorland and heathland pasturage.

To White Edge Lodge and Tedgness
The last half-mile and the next quarter-mile could be named Cranberry Briar Road. The course is N. of W., the many trenches continue, and it passes (to left) an old stone gate-post and (right) another indicator, and, in about 700 yards from Lady Cross, comes to the deep gapway at White Edge, where the Totley Moss to Bakewell Road crosses the track. White Edge, as a place name, was well known to the natives at the time of the 1816 boundary dispute between Baslow, Holmesfield and Totley. 'The Whites' are an old Tedgness Farm and Grindleford family.

The way is now straight down, leaving the White Edge Lodge a little to the right, and after skirting the edge of the old gritstone slate quarry (right) it comes, in 800 yards W. of the 'gap' on White Edge, to the Froggatt Edge Road, at a point some 600 yards short of the 'Grouse Inn'. A trespass board is probably beside the steps in the wall. Crossing the road, it goes through the narrow plantation, down the wooden step-stile and, diagonally, across White's Moor, over the bridleway stones which, in 1912, decided the legality of the Tedgness footpath. The higher, paved portion, is the continuation of the 'Tedgness' track. It is also possible that a paved way could be exposed on the moor flat W. of Lady Cross. Arriving at the foot of White's Moor, the usual public way is inside and down Oaks Wood to the Tedgness, now ex-farm house and Grindleford, etc. The older way, however, kept to the right of the wood and, between the walls, along the green lane to the left (at the foot of White's Moor), passed through Tedgness Quarry. It is now slightly diverted between the new villas above the Grindleford Road. The route then followed the Sir William Road and, short of its summit, there are traces of an older bridleway to the near right – on Eyam Moor.

(2) A DRONFIELD–TIDESWELL BRIDLEWAY BY HURKLING STONE

This ancient bridle track is also first observed at the top left (S.) corner of the ploughed field on the road to Froggatt Edge, etc. – 160 yards west of the 'Peacock Hotel' at Owler Bar – and formerly appears to have followed the course of the present highway (1781 Act) from Lidgate and Holmesfield, etc.

Across the narrow rough field, the wall and Saltersitch, across the brooklet; and about 40 yards west of the brookside wall corner, there is a bonny rowan tree and, from it, a deep trench way going S.S.W. for perhaps 40 yards until, at the skyline, it turns W. by S.

Bucka – or Bucca – Hill and Bell Pits

Bucka Hill is not 200 yards S.E. from here, overlooking the Owler Bar–Baslow Road, and there, as all over this part of the now almost treeless moor, are deep pudding-holes or bell pits, from which the forefathers in the eighteenth, or even seventeenth, century, extracted thin surface coal and carried it on pack-horses across the moor. (Glover's *History and Gazetteer of Derbyshire* (1829) registers the following coal working – 'Salters-sitch, S.W. of Owler Bar, one-and-three-quarter miles W. of Holmsfield, 2nd coal (formerly) crowstone'. The distance and direction corresponds almost exactly to Bucka Hill, and the coal working as stated is pre 1829.)

A deep trench way starts from the Baslow Road, just south of the newly extended culvert bridge, over Saltersitch, and widened road corner (during 1925). At first going S.S.W., on the bank top, it soon swings to S.W. and, across the swampy Sampson's Hollow, turns W., by some shooting butts, and joins the above track, half a mile ahead near the crossing of the Duke's Drive.

The continued route is easily followed and, shortly, passes one of the bell pits (left). On approaching the Sampson's Hollow, it keeps a few yards to the right of the bracken and, now turning almost west, the short remnant of a line of thorn and rowan trees is a good guide. There was a goodly natural covering of stubby rowan, hardy birch, thorn and sallow willows on this part of the moor, but the majority have given up the ghost, and the eating of the bark from the trees in winter time by rabbits is partly to blame. You may also ask the moorside farmer how the young moorland rabbits nip off the green blades of his young oats – "just as if they'd used a pair of scissors", says he. The grouse can also ruin a field of young oats.

The Wide View
About 100 yards short of the next skyline (ahead) it passes through a patch of bracken nearer the hollow and, crossing the head of it, is joined by the track from Bucka Hill – and the Duke's Drive from Barbrook Reservoir Lodge crosses it – going N.W. The drive, which starts from almost opposite Ramsley Reservoir and follows the Barbrook, formerly pursued the side of the brook throughout to the Owler Bar–Froggatt Road, but was diverted to the E. and N. side of the reservoir. At this point there is a good view over Barbrook Reservoir, the Derwent valley across Chatsworth Park, and the heights of Stanton Moor south of Rowsley – with Harland Edge (East Moor) and Ramsley Lodge on the left hand.

A Freak Cairn and Sheep Lea Wall
A thin, tall cairn is seen near the north side of Barbrook Reservoir, but the explanation is that George Herrington, of Robin Hood, Baslow, and Mr J.W. Stone, a Duke's gamekeeper (one or both) built it, during the making of the reservoir, out of the walls of the old four-sided shelter or 'lea' for sheep. Stone, at this period, lived at Thickwoods Lodge, one-third mile N.E. of and below Owler Bar, and died about a year ago, at Stanton Ford farm, near Baslow. A son is at present a Sheffield police officer, and another, George, an ex-police-man, is gamekeeper at Badger House, on the old Ankirk Road. Badger House is also called Ox Dale Lodge – on today's maps.

This sheep wall may, quite possibly, date from the days of common pasture in Holmesfield, but its name is not known to me.

The Barbrook and a Guide Stone
The direction is still W., and the twin track, deepening, approaches the moss, and, in the long grasses, is almost lost. But, beyond the moss, there is a green strip. The way to it is by a gentle crescent bend (left), and there is proof of a rough paved track. Beyond the green strip is a quick approach to the Barbrook and an alternate trench way proceeds northwestwardly up the heathery moor beyond. The correct way, however, is to turn north of west (right) at the end of the cranberry beds – perhaps 200 yards W. of the last skyline – and, by

another crescent way which soon turns more westwardly and, if discerned, is a paved slab way which, presenting a deepening trench, descends and crosses the Barbrook, perhaps 200 yards N. of the lower crossing. The track which goes within 50 yards of the freak cairn and sheep wall is the Curbar old carriage road.

Any former slab bridge or stone ford has disappeared, and the way up-moor is a deep trench way which, at first, looks like a drain, and, going between the heather (N.W.) makes towards a birch tree, and two dead rowans on the left of it. Just beyond the birch – about 400 yards from Barbrook – is a Chesterfield-Hope alternate track. About 60 yards beyond is the junction with the Hope-Chesterfield track, and on it, about 20 yards to the left, lies the spigoted stone shaft, and an old guide stone, now very faintly marked. The correct reading is given below.

A 1709 Guide Stone

Old guide stone north of Barbrook Reservoir.

The shaft is 3ft 3in x 13in x 10in, the guide stone 2ft 3in x 8in, and the faint marks as follows: AST–R–FELD–ROAD–+DM (five lines), HOOP–E–ROAD, (three lines) DRO–NFE–LD–ROAD (four lines) and TIDSE–WALL–ROAD (three lines). The CH and E in 'Chasterfeld' have worn away. The date is probably 1709, but I can only decipher '17'. Had I rediscovered it a few months before the trial of the Grindleford–Tedgness footpath case (1912), the two owners might have refrained from wasting their money in trying to filch the lower, White's Moor-to-Tedgness part of the bridleway from the public.

There were three hardy birches here, but the dead trunks will soon fall down. The several trench ways on the near right are a sign of the once busy cross-bridleway for Hope and Chesterfield, but the Tideswell way is forward (about N.W.) up the shallow heathery hollow, towards the end of a wall.

The Parish Boundaries

This wall corner denotes the site of the historic Hurkling Stone and the parish boundary wall which, going thence W.W. by N. (over the anciently named Windlow Hill part of White Edge) to Windley Well spring, under White Edge, is, so far the boundary between Baslow and Hathersage – the Baslow U.D.C.

and older manor boundary then following the outer wall of the rough pastures east of the 'Grouse Inn' and down Hay Brook. (The Nether Padley boundary from Windley Well is the northerly side of Sallow Sitch and Haybrook and, from Windley Well, slightly N. of W. it follows the course of the stream down White's Moor and Oaks Wood bottom to Grindleford station, etc.) The

Leash Fen Cross.

Baslow boundary comes from the junction of Blake Brook with Barbrook, just north of the bridge at the foot of Curbar Lane, and following up the stream, and through Barbrook Reservoir to the shuttle of the former small 'still' reservoir – at the north end and exposed in a dry summer – then proceeds direct N.N.W. to the Hurkling Stone. The Holmesfield–Hathersage boundary from the Hurkling Stone goes N.N.W. by the wall, and, then on the edge, passes the side of the northeasterly of the two small plantations. Then it goes almost due N. to the junction of the Owler Bar to Froggatt and Fox House Roads, where the Totley boundary now begins.

Holmesfield and Baslow Awards

The land generally, on the eastern side of this boundary, is in the wide parish of Holmesfield, which, in its Enclosure Act of 1816, lost 2650 acres, out of a total area of 4600 in the parish, or a little over four square miles of common lands. The Duke of Rutland got 1998 acres of it, and added other pieces by exchange or purchase. The Baslow Award of 10/3/1826 enclosed 1501 acres 0–20 in Baslow parish, 1691 acres 1–19 in Bubnell hamlet, 573 acres 1–13 in Curbar, and 149 acres 3–28 in Froggatt, and the total acreage in the four divisions (1879 *Gazetteer*) is 2602, 2403, 1202, and 248 acres respectively – or 3913 out of 6455 acres.

These two Enclosure Acts and Awards account for the whole of the moorland between Fox Lane to Clod Hall Farm and 'Robin Hood Inn', down the road to Baslow, from the Derwent to Hay Brook, up Sallow Sitch on White Edge to the Wooden Pole and the road from the latter, to Owler Bar – including Flask and Brown Edge to the junction of Moorwoods Lane, the first road below Owler Bar.

A little to the right of the track, and about 100 yards S.E. of the Hurkling Stone, in the proper place, are the remnants of a small low cairn and probably an old guide. The expert alone could point to an ancient and rifled barrow.

The Historic Hurkling Stone

The walling of the moor hereabouts would not be required before the Holmesfield, Hathersage and Baslow Enclosure Acts of 1808, 1816 and 1823, and the two hollows, 30 and 60 yards to the N.E. of Hurkling Stone, are small wall quarries. (The Hathersage Award for some reason was not issued until 23/6/1830 and the Holmesfield and Baslow Awards on 10/11/1820 and 10/3/1826 respectively.) The present markings on the low Hurkling Stone – the only survivor hereabouts – appear to be as follows:

I M / H T W 22 (for 1722, the '17' is obliterated) E C 1743 + another H, E H (deeply cut) and R H.

My evidences for these letterings are as follows. My copy of a Baslow and Bubnell boundary taken by Sir George Manners, 'in the sight of my Tennents the 12th of July 1614', records 'the Hurking Stone where it is marked w(i)th the Crosse'. Another boundary of Baslow, 18/7/1721, records 'Herklin Stone marked on the north end + M B' – meaning: a usual cross mark and, 'Manor of Baslow'. The same lettering appears in a Baslow boundary of 10/9/1736 on 'Huckingstone' and, in another boundary record of 4/8/1773, 'Hurkling Stone, marked M.B. with a cross and divers other marks'. A Holmesfield boundary taken by John Mander and John Barker, stewards of John the Duke of Rutland, on 25/8/1777, records 'Hurkelin Stone which seems a native low rock on whose sides are cut divers marks and Ltrs [letters], on the east side H 1722, on the N.E. is a cross X and the letters M.B'. The same marks are also recorded in a Holmesfield boundary of 10/10/1801, and in Wyatt, Bishop and Gould's (Enclosure Act Commissioners) boundary of Holmesfield taken on 15/3/1817, which settled the dispute between Holmesfield and Baslow for the former's claim to Deadshaw – on the W. side of Barbrook – and also tolled the knell of free common. The word 'Hurkling Stone' assumed its present form, meaning a low, recumbent stone, in the sense of hurkling – or crouching or bending. This word is now almost lost and seldom used by today's moorside dweller – i.e., 'hurklin' up t'side o' t'wall'.

The letters 'I M' could be for John or James Mander of Bakewell, Solicitors, who were stewards to the Duke of Rutland and rode these boundaries with the freeholders during the latter part of the eighteenth and early-nineteenth centuries. 'H' probably denotes a Holmesfield boundary mark and 'H1722' another Holmesfield boundary taken in that year – although, as stated, only '22' now remains.

The 'EC 1743' may be another boundary marking made by the Holmesfield or Baslow freeholders, but I have no records. 'EH', 'RH' and 'TW', similarly, are not explained, and, to quote Edward Heathcott and Robert Holmes, who attended the Baslow boundaries of 1721 and 1773, or Edmund Hallom and Robert Heyward (Baslow boundary witnesses in 1614), and Thomas Worrall, a Froggatt freeholder who attended the Holmesfield boundary in 1777, is only coincidence and not fact.

Samuel Buxton, a Curbar witness (aged seventy-eight) and farmer of 80 acres, in the 1816 case of Holmesfield claiming pieces of common (Deadshaw) from Baslow and part of Totley Moss from Totley, refers to removing the letter 'H' and inscribing 'MB' for Manor of Baslow on 'Herculan Stone', by order of Mr Barker, the then steward of the Duke of Rutland. He declared that "Baslow and Curbar people went to knock the mark out of Herculan Stone" and that "none of the Holmesfield people were there", and said they "never let Holmesfield people know of knocking out such marks". He added that the date was "about thirty-nine years ago" and the marks were put on and knocked out the same year – thus corresponding with the Holmesfield boundary riding of 25/8/1777 and, probably, the erasure of 'H.17' from 'H.1722'.

Guide stoop on Big Moor with bullet scars from Army training practice.

It will thus be understood that our moorside forefathers have held many a meeting and told many stories at this truly historic stone.

The Buxton homestead, at Curbar, has been pulled down and rebuilt, in the cross lane north of the Kennel Farm – so called because William Hallam, who died about 1893, kept hound puppies for the Duke of Rutland's Belvoir Hunt and put them out 'to walk' among the tenants – and also did 'tenting' or assistant 'keeping' on the moors.

A White Edge Guide Stone
The track onwards goes westwardly and, in places, is raised and, some years ago, I exposed part of the paved slabway which appears to have been broken and taken away, and, in other places, is covered with bilberry briars. In about 300 yards, after passing the Hurkling Stone, there is a rowan tree on the near left, and a birch tree further away.

The track deepens and, some 50 yards short of White Edge, and perhaps three yards to the right of the track, there is a short guide stone (and proof of this way) which, until six years ago, stood erect in the hole which (just beside the stone) is still visible. These old guide stones should be made national monuments and protected by law.

Sallow Sitch to Hay Brook
At the edge is a good view of Longstone Edge, Sir William Hill and the Derwent valley. The track now swings abruptly to the right, aslant the slope,

and the deep trench almost disappears at the foot of the edge. Thenceforward is somewhat go-as-you-please along the harder ground (about W.W. by S.), leaving, on the right, the field walls and the tricklet properly called Sallow Sitch, and making for the road bridge below the 'Grouse Inn', a few yards below the junction of Sallow Sitch with 'Blacker Sick' – both early-nineteenth century and almost lost names of which the late Mr Samuel White, of the 'Grouse Inn', who died in June 1926, was not aware.

Sallow Sitch and Blacker Sick are authenticated, and almost lost names; Sallow referring to the sallow willow, and Blacker probably to the dark peaty streamlet rising in Lucas Fen. Richard White, a Sheffield shopkeeper born at Grindleford Bridge and then forty-eight years of age, testified in the Baslow–Holmesfield boundary case of 1816 that he began shepherding for his father, who kept two to three hundred sheep. He shepherded for his father nineteen or twenty years, 'and drove the sheep up by Sallow Sitch to Windlow Hill' – clear evidence of the name, and the course, of Sallow Sitch from one of the ancient family of the Whites, of Tedgness Farm.

The Froggatt 'Old Gate' joined the route at this point.

A Stopped-up Horse Gate
Two or three yards above this road bridge, and until three or four years ago (east side of road wall) there was a horse gate which the Duke's men (I am told) blocked up with stone. The track then crossed the road and along the low side of the field – just above the now called Hay Brook – and may be traced down Hay Wood, on the north side of Hay Brook, into the lane below Hay Wood Farm and, opposite the old toll bar cottage to the road short of Grindleford Bridge, where, at one time was the supposed original 'ford' near to which, a few years ago, an ancient stone axe was discovered. Further ahead, the ancient trench way can be seen on Eyam Moor – on the right side of the Sir William Road, in the last half-mile, on approaching the summit of the road.

Another Route towards Eyam
At the Blacker Sick bridge below the 'Grouse Inn', just inside the moor, is a trench way going southerly and soon lost in the (Enclosure Act made) rectangular fields. (The few natives still call this 'Blackter' brook and Bridge; there is trace, in the pronunciation, of 'Blacktor' for this part of White Edge.) One branch is recovered a few hundred yards along the north end of the Froggatt Edge drive going steeply down the bank to the Froggatt Edge Road – below its acute bend. It is now usually obstructed with thorn or other brushwood on reaching the roadside. There is a well-known track going through a gateway and leading towards Grindleford station, along Haywood. Further S.W., towards the 'Chequers Inn', on the same W. side of the road, are two narrow 'Pieces'. The first is 'Stoke Plantation' and the second called 'Parish Piece'. The latter was sold by Froggatt parish people fifteen years ago. A track goes

through Stoke Plantation, passing an old smelting mill in the wood; and another keeps to the nearer (N.) side of the little stream which flows from above the (Froggatt Edge) roadside cottage, once called 'The Masons Arms'.

Another Old Guide Pole
The way is difficult to trace down the wood, but it comes out by the brook, where it is crossed by the well known track from Grindleford Bridge to 'Spooner's Lane', and thence into Froggatt hamlet. A little further south of the brook crossing, below the path, and nearer the river Derwent, is a narrow elliptical field and house ruin (and gate post) of the Froggatt family of Gregory called 'Toad Pole'. I strongly suspect that the true meaning is T'Owd Pole, and the place where a post or pole once stood. The longer, narrow field (a quarter of a mile long), on the river side, is 'Long Field'. Just S.W of 'Toad Pole' field was an old river ford. This track, across the Derwent, turns S.S.W., and is lost in the three flat fields, but recovered in 'Home Wood', beneath Stoke Hall. It came out on the road 300 yards N. of Stoke Hall outbuildings, and went due W. and steeply up the enclosed dark, tree-girt (and slate-quarried) 'Blind Lane', which leads to the main road to Eyam. At the top it crossed the road, went S.W. across the field, and into the old Riley Road, which was the older main road, leading past Riley Quarry and Riley Graves to Eyam. This is a charming road, but – to Blind Lane – a pack road lost probably almost a hundred years ago.

Lost Bridleway to Froggatt Bridge from Holmesfield
Two other lost bridleways towards the culvert bridge below the 'Grouse Inn' came from Froggatt Bridge – once 'Stoke Bridge' – up the 'New Road' which goes N.E. to the Froggatt Edge Road. It then pursued a similar course towards and over Froggatt Edge just north of the 'Stone Circle' beside the second field on Stoke Flat and again is lost in the fields nearer the culvert bridge. This road is called the 'New Bar Road'. The 'Old Bar Road' went out of the New Road and zig-zagged up the edge a little south of the New Bar Road, and then followed a similar course to it on the top. These were also the cattle and sheep driving tracks to the commons used by the Froggatt freeholders before the Baslow Enclosure Award of 10/3/1826. John Rollinson, of Froggatt, aged eighty-eight, in the 1816 boundary dispute, refers to a pack-horse road from Froggatt to Holmesfield.

(3) SHEFFIELD–BAKEWELL BRIDLEWAY BY BARBROOK AND EAGLE STONE
Lidgate to Saltersitch
The possibly pre-historic, deep bridleway gap in the road, at Lydgate – by 'The Robin Hood' inn – 928 feet altitude – is now part of the (1781 Act) highway, but the old course of it can be traced down the hay field on the left, and to the foot of the hill across the damp hollow, to the gorse bushes – a few yards inside the second field – and to the second wall and gate, almost

opposite the end of Moorwoods Lane. (The course from Holmesfield to Sheffield may have been through Bradway and Beauchief Park, and a bridle-way from Dronfield to Holmesfield came by Gosforth (otherwise Gorsey Bank) Lane to Kitchen Wood at Cowley.)

Beyond (west of) Moorwoods Lane, the old track is almost obliterated by the ploughing of the third field (left) but, turning left (and south) and following inside the fourth field, beside the wall, and to the bend, it becomes a hollowed way through the reeds and marsh. The surviving trees are also a good pointer.

The track goes direct to the high, and quite modern, wall of Major Wilson's (Horsleygate Hall) thickly populated rabbit warren. (Cockshutt's Wood, with its also modern rhododendron bushes and good cover for foxes, is immedi-ately below.) Going S.W. it crosses the flatter top corner of the warren between the bracken and along a trench way, quite recently deepened into a drain. A good half-way across the warren, beside the track, and possibly hidden by the bracken, is a low stone stoop which may have been an old guide.

At the next wall, and leaving the rabbit warren, the altitude is 900 feet. The direction is now N.W. along the edge for about 400 yards, but again passing along cleared fields, the traces have been obliterated by the plough. Two fields' length short of Owler Bar Cottage and the 'Peacock Hotel', there are signs of it, going downwards (due W.), across a rough bank and, on crossing the wall, it is again lost in the ploughed field. Crossing Horsleygate Lane – now often called Cordwell Lane – and about 100 yards below the widened culvert bridge (1925) over Saltersitch – there is an ideal bridleway ford, over the flat rock, and above a small, and ferny, waterfall.

Greaves Piece, a Guide Stone and Long Causeway
The track now turns southwards, and, although soon lost in the fields, goes about 100 yards below the Owler Bar to Baslow Road. In 600 yards from the Saltersitch fording place it crosses a green lane, at about 60 yards below the main road, and, turning more westwardly along Greaves Piece now becomes a plain trench way. (Greaves Piece was one of the sweets of the Holmesfield Enclosure Award, granted to George Bustard Greaves, a prominent local landowner.) It crosses the next marshy hollow, and, bending to the south, soon resumes W.W. by S., goes between two thorn trees, and, crossing the Baslow Road, at Sampson's Hollow, follows beside the drive to Barbrook Reservoir Lodge until, in 100 yards, there is an old guide stone. This stone, fallen weary and almost lying on the ground, was, I am pleased to state, re-erected about two years ago. The stone, 6ft 3in high, is marked 'Bakewel Way', and 'Shefield Way', and two rudely carved hands point the direction. There is no date upon it, but the likeliest guess is 1737 or 1709.

The course, now S.S.W. may be traced through the bracken and heather to the head of the hollow (on the left) at two couples of thorn trees – here called Car Top – about 1050 feet altitude. The direction is continued across the flat towards another thorn tree (a second tree is not seen at first) and a low waste heap of the reservoir is passed 20 yards to the right. On the way along Car Top may be seen a stretch of stone slabs or paving, part of which I re-bared perhaps fifteen years ago and which, to the few natives who still know it, gives the name of 'Long Causeway' to this mossy part of the bridleway. The slabs are probably eighteenth-century work, and there is abundant evidence in the 1816 boundary dispute that this and the Curbar–Sheffield Road were repaired by the inhabitants. Charles Rushton, of Holmesfield (aged seventy-six), in the Baslow–Holmesfield boundary dispute of 1816, stated that he had repaired the road from Owler Bar to Deadshaw Sitch, and 'has repaired the same on both sides the Sich over Barbrook for twenty years and upwards and repaired it every year when it wanted repairing until the Turnpike Road was made. Flags were led to mend the road, from Bottoms Mill, near Smeecliff, and taken to both sides Deadshaw Sich'. Perhaps he also repaired Long Causeway? 'When a young man', he went this road three or four days a week with pack-horses for coals.

Half a mile from the guide stone is the ford across Barbrook – at the extreme S.W. bend of the stream below the reservoir. The hollow slope on this side of the ford has disappeared in the frittering-away of the bank, but the signs of a trench way on the far side are plain. The ford today is called Saltersford, and (wrongly, I think) also Sandy Ford. Thomas Parker, aged fifty-seven, a Curbar weaver, in the boundary dispute of 1816 stated that when about eleven years of age he went along this road with a pack-horse to Stubley Pits – at Stubley Hollow, near Dronfield Woodhouse.

On the Bank of Barbrook
Over the ford, the course, for a while, is on the right bank of the stream, about 20–30 yards to the right (W.) of another drive lower down, above the pond – an early Chesterfield R.D.C. water supply – it nears the stream and there is all old stone-ford crossing and a plain stone guide-post on the ground. A few yards further is another length of paved way. Immediately short of the pond is another paved crossing over a second tricklet. There is a low cairn (right and N.) and a drain comes into the pond. The stone crossing below the pond is almost destroyed. (One of these tricklets may be the 'Sallow Sitch' named in the 1816 boundary dispute.) This moor drain comes out of the middle part of 'Deadshaw', the lost natural wood of hardy trees named in records I have seen dating from 1777 to 1816.

The first flat-topped height perhaps half a mile W. of the pond is called 'Round Hill', and there is a ruined sheep wall under it. The trench way can be followed on the right bank (now steepened) and through the bracken and heather. The direction (still S.W.) is to the old guide stone standing just beyond the crossing of the next streamlet which, in the 1816 Holmesfield-Baslow boundary dispute and 1836 Ordnance Map, appears to have been called 'Deadshaw Sick'. A large stone beside the guide stone may have been the original crossing place.

Robin Hood's Table
Following beside the main Barbrook stream from here for about one-third of a mile towards Baslow, on the right (W.) bank, is a now rapidly decaying grouse shooters' foot bridge. Here, on the same west bank of the stream, and beside it, are two slabs of gritstone forming a low platform two feet high and about 3ft 6in x 3ft. It was, I understand, made during the time of the grand-uncle of the present Duke of Rutland (the 'Shooting Duke', whose men made the drives across Longshaw Moors estate), and was used for an al fresco dining table. 'Robin Hood', the supposed Sherwood sportsman, had nothing to do with it.

Between this point and the foot of Curbar Lane there is a pleasing stretch of woodside on the east side – Big Moor Plantation – and also a town of rabbit burrowings and 20 sinuosities in the Barbrook.

Two-Slab Bridle Bridge on another Bridleway
200 yards north of the bridge at the foot of Curbar Lane is the two-slab bridle bridge marked 'H1777'. The marking corresponds with a Holmesfield boundary taken on 25/8/1777. This was the crossing place of another original ancient bridleway from Dronfield and Chesterfield to Curbar and Tideswell, (a) via Holmesfield, and (b) from Cutthorpe and near Spitewinter Farm (?) – and which, between this point and the first Fox Lane stone cross, generally followed slightly on the N. side of the present line of Fox Lane.

The Barbrook Guide Stone
The markings on the sides of the guide stone are as follows:

(1) 'TO–TIDSWA–LL' (three lines).
(2) 'IS–1737' and lower down in ruder, later lettering, '1775–IS' (two lines each).
(3) 'TO–SHEFFEILD' (two lines). 'TO–BAKWAL' (two lines), and, below it, the letter 'H' – 1775-RC (three lines).

The letterings of '1775' – 'IS' – ,'1775' and 'RC', are additions, and '1737' is the probable date of erection – as upon other guide stones placed on some of our Derbyshire moorland bridle roads.

(3a) The Curbar–Tideswell Branch Bridle Road
The Tideswell Road, from this guide stone, goes in a southwestwardly direc-

tion and, in the first few yards, there are evidences of some rude gritstone flag pavement – probably eighteenth-century work. It at once climbs a trench on the left (S.W.) side of the little hollow of 'Deadshaw Sick', and, after passing the flags, goes between a few rough gritstones.

The direction is maintained for about half a mile along the open moor and the route is shown by thin ribbon tracks through the heather which, if bared, might produce evidence of wheel tracks upon a rough paving. In about 600 yards from the guide stone, it crosses a short, greenish flat and then, rising, follows a strip of grass. (There are supposed to be remains of prehistoric British village dwellings on this part of the moor, and also on 'Stoke Flat' – in an easterly direction from the Stone Circle – which in turn is slightly east of the Froggatt Edge drive. These should be examined and decided upon whether for or against.)

300 yards beyond the flat it approaches the skyline and the plainer straighter track, now going more towards the west, crosses the smooth edge of Swine Sty and descends to the last 20 yards N.W. of the corner of the field wall. (This first of the so-called 'White Edge Fields', the small one below it, and the next (N.W.), are called 'Siddall's Fields', from the name of the Curbar family who, I am told, first cleared them, after the Baslow Enclosure Award of 10/3/1826. The lower ten fields are 'Curbar Fields', and the third from the north end is 'Rushy Field'.)

The alternate and easier track maintains a more S.W. course on the level and turns under the edge, among the thick beds of cranberry briars, and, making a dog-leg bend, descends to the source of Sandyford Brook. Across the brook the way proceeds on the outside (S.E.) of the first wall, to the first and then to the second wall corner, and, turning to the west, reaches Curbar Lane, Curbar Bar Head, and its guide stone – at a point about 700 yards from the Sandyford Brook, and one-and-a-quarter miles from the guide stone at Deadshaw Sick.

Another Old Sheep Wall or Fold
About 100 yards S.S.W. from the wall at the today's source of Sandyford Brook, which, in the fields, may be drained, are the ruins of an old and unnamed sheep fold and, beside it, what may be the foundations of another or older one or stone hut? On the S. side of it is a short, upright stone and also, on the low side, another similar stone. It was a Curbar (Buxton's?) sheep fold.

(3) Sheffield–Bakewell Way Continued
From the guide stone the way towards Baslow for about 30 yards turns abruptly S.E. in the direction of the lettering 'TO BAKWAL' – and, reaching the skyline, resumes the former direction (S.S.W.) along the hard, flat ground, and 1000 feet level. The track, in 100 yards, passes an ancient, thin and rude,

stone guide, 6ft 3in high, and marked 'R.BAS' (for 'Baslow Road to') and, about 350 yards further, a second rude guide (6ft 3in) marked 'S' and probably intended to point the way to Sheffield. (The carved guide stone and the two rude stone guides were marked on the 1897 edition of the six-inch-to-mile map, but although not shown in the 1919 revision, are still upright and in situ.) Shortly after there is a slight bend towards the left and, in about 300 yards, a third stone stoop (5ft 6in) which for at least fifteen years has lain on the ground. This moderately traceable track, hitherto along hard ground, now proceeds under the bank, above the coarse long moor grasses, and through the bracken, and then, proceeding across the moor grasses, becomes fainter – and may have been paved and overgrown (?). The course for quite half a mile has been almost straight towards the westerly end of Blackstone Edge and the Wellington Monument.

On reaching the smooth slope of Swine Sty it descends, bends more west-wardly, quickly crosses the head of the shallow, marshy hollow, and goes through some bracken. Then, for about 400 yards, it pursues a faint course (S.S.E.) some yards on the east side of the reed-skirted tricklet called Sandyford Brook – as far as Curbar Lane. It may possibly be an overgrown, paved way, or have been filled-in. Crossing Curbar Lane, a similar course (due south) is now taken across two fields, but the track has been obliterated by the plough or other means. (These moor-side fields, set out in the usual straight lines, were probably reclaimed and walled-off after the Baslow Enclosure Award of 10/3/1826.)

At the far wall corner, called Sandyford, it becomes apparent that the course across this heathery part of the moor called Eaglestone Flat has been a busy medieval bridleway.

The Junction of the Dronfield–Tideswell–Chesterfield Way
A continuing trench way going eastwardly on the moor, outside the field wall, coming from Curbar Gap and bifurcating, crosses Curbar Lane and through workings (?) descends to the Barbrook and over it by the previously men-tioned two-slab stone bridge marked 'H1777'. This lettering corresponds to my copy of a perambulation of the boundaries of Holmesfield Manor taken on 25/8/1777, and the reference, in the same document, to 'the new bridge' over the Barbrook, in Curbar Lane, proves that this interesting and unique Derbyshire moorland pack road bridge was not erected in that year.

(3b) A Dronfield Cross-track
This track, still going east, goes to the gate at the junction of Fox Lane and the Sheffield–Baslow highway, and half a mile further up-hill, by some old gravel pits on the skyline (left side of Fox Lane and below the west end of Ramsley Reservoir embankment).

A Stump Cross by Ramsley Reservoir

I have seen a record – in Holmesfield Enclosure Award – of 'Stump Cross piece', and proof that a roadside cross once stood near this point. The old track beyond the embankment proceeded near the line of Fox Lane, which in the Holmesfield 1777 boundary record is called 'the Smilters road or gate', and along a broken causeway. 'Smilters road' means Smelters Road, because it connected with the old lead smelter's Cupola and Slag Mill a little below Barbrook Mill – half a mile W. of Curbar Lane foot – and another in Fox Lane Plantation beside the brooklet.

Fox Lane Guide Stone and Two Crosses

The low guide stone over the wall beside the gate at the junction of Fox Lane and Rumbling Street, marked:

'1710 Bakew' 'Ches–field' and 'Dronfield', is proof of this ancient track which, proceeding N.N.E. on the summit of the war-felled Fox Lane plantation, passed one of the two Fox Lane Crosses and, lower down, joined Fox Lane, above Fox Lane Farm. Then, at the low roadside cottage below Bank Green, it followed the deep trench way (overgrown and going N.) which, swinging east on the low side of Bank Wood, crossed Millthorpe Brook and, turning N.E., on the westerly side of the field wall (beside the path), crossed the road, and after another deep trench way joined Horsleygate Lane.

The more easterly cross (both, I suggest, placed by the monks of Beauchief Abbey) in the war-felled and smaller Shillito plantation, is the indicator to the old Chesterfield bridle road via Cutthorpe or perhaps near Spitewinter Farm. This latter bridleway can also be traced beyond the road junction, on the south side of the more modern roadway, beyond Unthank Lane junction, inside the moor, past a broken 'cross' (in a morticed base), and making towards Spitewinter Lane.

A Harewood Grange Cross

Pegge's learned history of Beauchief Abbey does not refer to a grant of moorland hereabouts; but there are a number of lost charters, and my war-time discovery of the 'stump' or morticed base of a now unnamed cross within 80 yards S.W. of the junction of the two roads – one leading eastwardly to Harewood Grange farm and the other past Slag Mill plantation towards Wadshelf – and also ancient bridle roads which correspond to a boundary of the lands of Harewood granted to Beauchief Abbey – is sufficient for my purpose. Lady Cross is, of course, proven.

(3c) Another Tideswell–Chesterfield Way

This bridle road probably came through Litton and Wardlow Mires to the old four lane ends at the top of Middleton Dale, one (N.N.W.) going to Foolow, one N. of E. (Fieldhead Lane), going to Eyam, and the other keeping the high ground past Dirty Rake by Moisty Lane and Middleton Lane and down High Street into Stoney Middleton, thence possibly from Calver Sough and Kings Gate, over Hare Knoll (589 feet) to a lost ford about 600 yards north of Calver Bridge and beyond the river bending and going eastwardly and discerned in a trench way (now a tip) just short of Curbar New Road and the cartway to Riddings Farm.

At Curbar Gap guide stone the left-hand field (S.) is called Bar Green, a piece of green and open space of a few acres which also 'went in' under the Baslow Enclosure Act. Signs of an old track are seen in the next narrow field going S.E., and at a short (right) bend of the roadside wall a little east of Curbar Gap guide stone. It is then lost, but signs are again observed on the moor of Eaglestone Flat outside the largest second Enclosure Award field and now called the Twelve Acre Field. It appears to have crossed the Baslow Road by a trench way just E. of the first rocks of Gardom Edge and proceeded upmoor (E.E. by S.) to a guide stone 5ft 6in high (and about 600 yards from the road) at a point possibly 500 yards from Clod Hall Lane – where a cross track bends N.E. towards Clod Hall Lane and the milestone which lies full length on the road margin about 200 yards E. of the Baslow Road. From this guide stone the track proceeds S.E. to another guide stone about 400 yards ahead and then towards Clod Hall Farm it is almost lost. Beyond it the course would follow Clod Hall Lane past Bleak House and Pudding Pie Hill (1009 feet), where, on the left hand, although partly covered by tipped rubbish, it is seen in the field approaching the rear of the 'Fox and Goose Inn' at Wigley. There is an old mounting stone on the roadside at Pudding Pie Hill.

Towards Eaglestone and Baslow Bar Road
The course along Eaglestone Flat, at first a little south of west, is a twin trench track which becomes four or five, and one – a curiosity upon a flat Derbyshire moor top – is consistently deep, and another may have been used for wheeled traffic. They were used occasionally by the carters of stone going from the Bar Road Quarry beyond Wellington Monument. Geo. Sheldon, of Baslow, last worked it for a while until 1911, and Samuel Hibberd (Baslow) for quite twenty years previously. The edge-face quarries further east of Wellington Monument may have been unused for quite fifty years.

About half-way towards the unmistakeable Eagle Stone the direction becomes more S.W. The right bend joins the old turnpike along Blackstone Edge (1759 amending Road Act) just beyond Wellington monument, but the original route goes about 60 yards east of the Eagle Stone and, by obvious trench ways across the higher ground, is then almost lost in the now disused Bar Road quarry workings – above the gate, at the top of the Bar Road. It is visible lower down (left side) below the wooden bungalow inhabited by Mr Noton, one of the extra 'keepers' instructed by the new Duke of Rutland last year to 'tent' the disputed way to the Monument and along the drive beside Baslow Edge.

A 'Millstone Road' along Froggatt Edge

The Drive along Baslow, Curbar, and Froggatt Edges, in the early-nineteenth and late-eighteenth centuries, was called a 'Millstone Road' – upon an old rudely drawn map.

Another Millstone Road

There was another 'Millstone Road' marked on the same old map which appears to have proceeded across the moors, from about the junction of Fox Lane and Rumbling Street and continued in the direction of Stanage. It is, however, impossible to trace the course of it upon this rude map, and part may be upon the line of today's Duke's Drives.

It proves that stone and millstones from the Baslow, Curbar, and Froggatt Edges were conveyed, in the eighteenth century along the line of the present Drive known as the Froggatt Edge Drive, but this, in itself, and in view of the rights of 'entail', does not indicate an ancient bridleway. This road is not mentioned in the Baslow Enclosure Award and map.

The Hounds of Gabriel and Eaglestone Cabin

William Gregory, late of Curbar and a Duke's shepherd until 1917, tells me a story. When he was a boy his mother used to say that if anyone heard the 'hounds of Gabriel' he'd be sure to die. One day, many years ago, he was on Baslow Edge, near the Eaglestone cabin – right of the drive from Curbar Gap to Eaglestone – looking for sheep, when he heard sounds like the baying of one or two hounds. He looked down the rough below to see if it was a sheep worrying, but could see nothing, and then, again hearing the hounds, looked up and saw a flock of wild geese flying over in migratory flight. Since then he has heard their cry both by day and night.

(4) THE HOPE–CHESTERFIELD BRIDLE ROAD
Hathersage to Hollowgate

The course of this track may be seen proceeding from the old small hamlet of Hathersage Booths (below 'Millstone Inn') and, crossing the junction of the track from Grindleford Station (which passes Greenwood Farm) to the Hathersage main road – above the 'Millstone Inn' – along the rough ground below the road and Whim Plantation. It crosses Millstone Edge by an obvious trench way on the low quarried edge, perhaps 60 yards N.N.W. of 'The Surprise' view, and going eastwardly across the moor, where the summer-time motorists now stay and desecrate it with waste paper, joins up with Hollowgate. This is the only portion of this old road which remains public, although, as I understand, the Duke's men walled this up on the eastern side, about three years ago, and the public pulled it down again.

A Longshaw Park Guide Stone

Crossing the Fox House–Grindleford Road at the end of the now open wall and at once by Hammerton Cote (this stone 'barn', after leaving S.E. end of Hollowgate, is only a few yards on E. side of the Fox House–Grindleford Road, and was named after a Hammerton family of Grindleford who built it, or for whom it was erected), it is lost in the now called Granby Wood, and goes to a point about 400 yards south of the Longshaw fish-pond, where stands another guide stone. The most curiously planned lettering on the four sides is:

(1) 'SHAFILD 1709 +'
(2) 'TO TIDSWEL'
(3) 'TOHA–THAR–SICH–ANDS–TOCH–APILI–NLEE-FRITH' (eight lines) and
(4) 'TO–CHASTERFILD'.

'To Hathersich and to Chapil-in-lee-Frith' should be understood, and the 'S' after 'and' appears to be an addition. The stone is 5ft 4in x 15in x 11in,and copyists should not make future mistakes about the lettering.

Hollowgate's Old Bridle Bridge
A few yards above the present crossing of Hollowgate over Burbage brook are signs of the base of the old bridle bridge and, in the brook, the keystone of the arch bearing the date '1725'. This and the obviously similar and existing bridge higher up Burbage Brook,under Carl Wark, were probably erected about the same date – the latter being across the old, once undeniable, Dore–Hathersage bridleway.

From this point the track is again obliterated, but, proceeding about S.E., it is again seen in a trench immediately under the drive to Longshaw Lodge – as it leaves the junction of the roads to Froggatt Edge (W.W. by S.), Fox House (N.) and Owler Bar (S.E.).

The Wooden Pole
Few ramblers or motorists leave the road for the charming view from the Wooden Pole which, about 100 yards to the N. of the road junction, stands on the edge, that one hundred years ago and more seems to have been called Black Edge, although, in the generally stated evidence in the 1816 boundary dispute, the name may also have applied to the edge as far as behind White Edge Lodge. My copy of a Totley boundary, taken in 1811, states that they 'crossed the former Turnpike Road (the Froggatt Edge–Owler Bar Road is meant) to a place called the Woodpost, being a post erected as a finger or guide post at the foot of which is a boundary stone of this Manor with a T cut therein and date 1778; this we saw and made it more perfect by fresh cutting'. This proves a bridleway guide before the coach road was made, the earliest being the road from Owler Bar to Froggatt Edge, etc. – 1781 Act.

In the Totley evidence referred to there is a letter 'H' marked on this stone by the Hathersage freeholders in 1801, when Totley perambulated its boundary – *vide* James Dalton, of Totley, aged thirty-two years. Another witness in the same case, Godfrey Dalton, aged seventy-four years, refers to 'going a perambulation of the Commons more than thirty years ago, near forty years ago', and mentions 'The Wooden Pole on which there are several marks LTTWM on the Stone that holds the Pole fast', and 'there is a T' – meaning there was a T – for Totley – upon it. A 'TW' may be for Thomas Willoughby, the surname of Lord Middleton, the then Lord of the Manor of Totley, the first 'T' for Totley, and the 'M' for Manor. The first letter of the five, in the document, is like an 'L'. The present markings on this stone are 'T 1778' and 'TW'. The pole may be the heart of a spruce and has been there for many years.

Decorating the Pole

William Gregory, the ex-shepherd, was there on 'Mafeking Day', when a number of chars-à-banc were going down Froggatt Edge, and one party dropped a flag on the road. So William climbed up the pole, and stuck the flag on the top! The foregoing is sufficient authenticated evidence of the historical value of 'The Wooden Pole', and that it indicated a prominent point near the Bakewell–Sheffield bridle road over White Edge and Totley Moss and also the Chapel-en-le-Frith–Hope to Chesterfield bridle road. This pole should always be replaced.

It is, moreover, significant that today's three-road junction is at the place where the old three bridle roads meet.

From the Three-Roads Meet

Standing at the junction of the Owler Bar–Froggatt and Fox House Roads, and, facing south, there is a gate and drive (S.S.W.) to White Edge Lodge – the shepherd's lodge vacated last year by Mr Sept. Priestley when, for the first time in recent years, there was no winter shepherding of sheep on these moors. Looking towards the end of White Edge (S.) (which, in today's wrongful generalising of place names is two miles long), there is a trench way over the wall which, at first two, quickly became three trenches. The third (left) soon peters out, and the left track is followed – the one to the right going along White Edge summit to Curbar Gap and Bakewell Way. The direction generally is S.S.E., and a branch, going (right) over the brow, eventually joins it again, near Lady Cross. The track follows the drier ground under the right brow and, after a slight bend, is more easily followed. It leaves two trees higher on the right, and, making towards a group of perhaps half a dozen trees, takes the high side of a bed of bracken, at a point about 150 yards west of the road to Owler Bar. The track before and after is easy to follow, and a trench way before and beyond the first dip. Then, in a direction making for Barbrook Reservoir, it becomes four to nine feet deep, and has been worked for stone or clay. (Lady Cross, its square base, and two broken pieces of shaft, is only a few yards on the west side of this deepest part of the trench way.)

The trench peters out and the way swings a little further in the moor and is crossed by the Dronfield-via-Holmesfield track and resumes the former direction. There is a mossy patch, and the course is towards the west side of the reservoir. An almost unnoticed hollow is crossed and the Hurkling Stone wall corner is seen on the (right) skyline. Immediately across the hollow is the old guide stone I rediscovered about fifteen years ago, lying in two pieces in the trench.

The track now makes more towards the centre of the reservoir, and, passing a branch trench way on the left, it descends and reaches the side of Barbrook Reservoir in two trenched ways, the one to the right at about 40 yards from the far, westerly, corner of the western wing embankment.

Broad Sike
Broad Sike is mentioned in the first inch-to-mile Ordnance Map of 1836 and also in the evidence in the 1816 boundary dispute of Holmesfield v. Baslow and Totley, when the former claimed about 300 acres of Deadshaw from Baslow and about 100 acres from Totley. The exact location is not easy to define, but it appears to be the trench way which descends to the Barbrook at a point a little west of the inlet to the Barbrook Reservoir. Sike, in the north, is a marshy bottom with a streamlet in it.

A Public Footway granted over Big Moor
The route is lost through the reservoir and spoil heap beyond it, but, from little below the easternmost bend of Barbrook, below the reservoir embankment, there is an undefined path across the flat moor going eastwardly, to the Owler Bar–Baslow Road. It is awarded in the Holmesfield Enclosure Award of 10/11/1820, as follows:

'One other Public Footway from Totley and Baslow Turnpike Road, near the west end of Carr Road over an allotment No. 169 made to the Duke of Rutland, to Baslow Moor, at Sandy Ford'.

'Sandy' and Salters Ford are the same place – the easternmost bend of Barbrook. The public footway given in the Holmesfield Enclosure Award, as far as the parish boundary (at the Barbrook), was in lieu of the older track, and a path provided for the dwellers in upper Cordwell valley and Fox Lane. It saved a good mile – when crossing the Holmesfield Moor and Baslow Moor, now called Big Moor – on the journey to Grindleford or beyond.

The Bridle Road Continued
The true course of the bridleway to Chesterfield is, to me, still in doubt. It may have proceeded near the line of the green steep Carr Road to Fox Lane plantation past Bank Green, Eweford Bridge, Millthorpe and Barlow, or, scenting a little depression near the southwestern end of the foot of the Barbrook Reservoir, past the ford at the easternmost bend of the stream below the reser-

voir. It may then have gone S.S.E. across the marshy moor top, and crossing the road to Baslow and, beyond it, the pipe track which goes across Ramsley Moor to Ramsley Reservoir and to the guide stone at the junction of Fox Lane top and Rumbling Street. The course would then be towards Spitewinter Farm or Cutthorpe.

(5) THE CARRIAGE ROAD FROM CURBAR TO SHEFFIELD

This is the craziest piece of eighteenth-century moorland carriage road I know, and, if one allows for a few removings of paving stone in odd places, it is, for the greater portion of the three miles between Curbar Gap (Curbar Gap should be, and was, called Curbar Bar Head – bar, a horseway up a slope) to its exit on the road at a point 450 yards almost west of Owler Bar, probably in the same condition as when abandoned as a so-called carriageway – after the 1781 Road Act and making of the first turnpike from Greenhill Moor, Bradway and Holmesfield to Froggatt Edge and beyond. It is referred to in 1816 as the 'upper road', and, to distinguish it from the bridle road down the Barbrook (No. 3) and that along White Edge (No. 6), it might be called the *middle* road over Big Moor.

The sedges and mosses, in many places, have made it into a quagmire and good bootsellers' advertisement, and, were it re-opened, few would care to tread every yard of it during the winter rains and fogs. But there it remains, as I hope it will always remain, to illustrate the trail of difficulty and hardship experienced by our sturdy forefathers when necessity compelled them to take a journey awheel to distant places which, today, are connected by perhaps a half-hour's easy journey in a 'Ford' or 'Morris' car. Square or oblong pieces of rough road metal are to be seen in many places, and an exposed section would probably reveal the original middle-to-late-eighteenth-century pavings – as upon the road along Blackstone Edge to Wellington monument made under the 1759 Road Extension Act.

Curbar Bar Head to White Edge

It leaves Curbar Gap guide stone and, at first, going east, quickly turns northwards, along the wide gap and trenched ways (half a mile long), between Curbar Fields (left) and White Edge Fields. Then, turning sharply E.E. by N., it crosses the marshy hollow and (right) mounts gaily up the slope and bilberry beds to White Edge Lodge. One track keeps close to the wall side. There are four trench ways, one going beside a low group of stones on the edge and three others showing the unmistakeable crinkles upon the skyline caused by an historic track used for general traffic and for going to and from the old Curbar Commons. There is an assumption of an old cairn at the top.

The Sheffield–Bakewell route, along White Edge, from the end of the Fields, is a double trench way half a mile more to the north, and the way to it at first keeps a little to the left, along the drier ground.

From the first summit the double trench track swings more to the N. (left) and, at the next summit, the remnant of flat 'grey wether' gritstones are discerned just short of the flat top (1203 feet) of White Edge. There is also a peculiarly striking view of the rock bastions of Higger Tor, Carl Wark, Millstone and Stanage Edges, and, to the right, of the marshiest, flattest, and most morose moorlands in the Peak District.

Three small stones, in line, are placed on the near right slope, and probably have served to show the way to and from the flat Lucas Fen. The direction onward is generally N.N.E. to N.E. – in line with the air shaft on Totley Moss, or Barbrook Reservoir. There are several deep trench ways and, bending N.N.E. and then N.E., and descending, a plain cartway, along the hard ground, soon gains the east side of Lucas Fen.

Lucas Fen and a Moorman's Story
This Fen, second only to Leash Fen (in the Peak district), reminds me of a story told to me by 'Bob' Lambert, the sturdy sheep farmer and 'statesman', who, already scoring over seventy summers, lives at Cam Houses, within half a mile of the sources of the Wharfe and the Ribble, in one of the loneliest and wildest places in England, and is still tougher than most men at fifty years of age. A landowner, who had more money than knowledge of moorcraft, was going the rounds, and rough shooting, when, suddenly dropping into a mossy place, he sank up to the knees and promptly called out for assistance. 'Bob' looked at him and, enjoying the fun, said (but not in a Sheffield accent): "Yer needn't be freetened abaht it, man. It'll 'owd yo' reight enuf, and anuther on t' top on yer, for ther's been dozens gone o'er t' 'eead i' this place afoor yo' seed it". And then, of course, he promptly pulled the man out.

'The Pile' – an Ancient Landmark
Crossing the end of the moss there is a two-drains meet and a single one, some yards ahead, and, when the men were making them not many years ago, some of the old flat paving stones were uncovered. The way, after going a little to the left, goes through the heather in three alternate, parallel roads. At the top of the faint rise, it turns alternately to right and left, and there are two tracks about 60 yards apart. On the right, near Round Hill, there are a few stones and a now almost imperceptible mound, perhaps 60 yards to the right.

The name of it is 'The Pile'. We say "Go on, pile it on", a "pile of arms" (Shakespeare's *Julius Caesar*), a "pile of stones", and mean a heap. But this old word goes even deeper, and, in the Anglo-Saxon, 'pil' means a pillar. It is apparent to me that here was a heap of stones or cairn and perhaps a tall stone pillar or wooden pole or stake to show the direction to and from this most difficult part of the moor. It may have disappeared in the making of an old cross-shaped sheep lea wall or shelter, etc., over a hundred years ago.

To Barbrook Reservoir and Causeway Ford

It presently descends slightly, but the deepening course is easily traced as it passes within ten yards of a lonely but vigorous birch tree, about 20 feet high. There are obvious parallel trackways, and the course, for the next half-mile, is almost straight towards the inlet of the reservoir, passing, just short of the embankment corner, a waterworks boundary stone. The principal cartway is often swampy and a line of whiskery marsh grasses, but it was never made for a drain.

The Hope to Chesterfield bridleway crosses it at points about 20 and 40 yards beyond the reservoir corner, and there is another alternative further along. The latter may be the Broad Sick referred to in the 1836 O.S. Map, and in the evidence in the 1816 parish boundary dispute. Following close beside the N.E. side of the reservoir it passes the inlet just left of the older and submerged 'still' reservoir – and, about 50 yards above the inlet, comes to a little bend in the stream and a bunch of perhaps a dozen whitey, water-washed stones lying in the stream. They are nearly three feet long and rudely split for the purpose. The bank has been frittered away, but it is abundantly clear that here is the old named (1816) Causeway Ford across the Barbrook which might have passed out of memory. I have never heard anyone refer to it by either place or name. From appearances it may have been a stone ford about three feet wide or a double width of stone causeway may have disappeared and been used for other purposes.

Towards Owler Bar

The Dronfield–Tideswell way crosses perhaps 400 yards up stream, but opposite this causeway ford is a deep trench way going up the bank to the left of the reservoir quarry. It crosses the ensuing marsh (E.E. by N.) in two alternatives, and the plainest passes about 50 yards from (right) the 'L'-shaped sheep lea wall (shelter) which (at present standing) has provided material for a thin tall cairn, and probably was first made for a sheep shelter by a commoner of Holmesfield parish.

A tree is passed twenty yards on the right, and the track ascends to patches of heather and, at the top, joins the Dronfield–Tideswell bridleway. Any old indicator or guide stone has now disappeared. The right branch follows the right bank past today's shooting butts across the ensuing hollow and on to Bucka Hill. The left one goes through a patch of bracken and hugs the left side of the faint hollow, past a few trees, and may be traced to the deep trench way at the side of Saltersitch and a large rowan tree. Then it crosses the brook side wall to the corner of the arable field wall, about 450 yards almost west of the Owler Bar ex-toll bar cottage.

Sea Gulls on Big Moor and Leash Fen

The sea gulls, I am told, began in 1916 to pay annual visits to the nesting grounds around the two shallow small pools on the east side of Leash Fen, and I remember marking these pools on my six-inch map during 1917 on one day when there was a shoot and youths from Staveley Works and school-boys took the place of ordinary 'beaters', who were not obtainable. I am told that the pools were formed by slight subsidences during early war-time.

The gulls first came to Leash Fen and then to Lucas Fen by White Edge, and at the commencement the pewits who claimed the rights of ownership of these solitary places tried to drive away the gulls, and there were many skirmishes. The pewit would fly in the usual fussy, petulant and noisy manner, and the gull would wait patiently until the pewit drew near and then, mounting into the air, allow the pewit to spend his flight. The gulls were not seen to retaliate, and appear to have laughed at their indifferent opponents. Since that time my wife has seen both pewits, crows, pigeons and gulls amicably feeding together, and following the plough in the field above our house.

The gulls come every year during March in the morning period, and on a number of occasions she has seen them flying overhead, unerringly, as though upon two lines of aerial road way, within 200 yards on either side of our house. On one occasion they came through a dense moorside fog, and were only detected by the screeching noise overhead. On numerous occasions my wife has observed them going towards Sheffield and returning in the evening, evidently upon a forage for food. From the nature of their inward flight it would appear that they come from the estuary of the Humber.

The old shallow pool on Lucas Fen is generally called the 'Duck Pond' by the gamekeepers – from the wild ducks to be found there.

The two pools on Leash Fen were drained off some time after the war, by orders of the late Mr Markham, who died last year. The Longshaw moors, until wartime, were let to Sir Thomas Birkin, of Nottingham. Mr Markham gave up the tenancy in 1925. The stories that could be told of breezy Mr Markham, usually referred to as 'Charlie', would, quite literally, 'fill a book', but many of them are too intimate for print.

More people are aware that the gulls are regular visitors to Redmires, but fewer are aware that they frequent the marsh along the county boundary of Friars Ridge between the summit of the road beyond Ringinglow and Stanage Pole. The man who interferes with their family arrangements would qualify for a horse-whipping.

(6) THE WHITE EDGE–SHEFFIELD–BAKEWELL WAY
The forgotten bridleway begins at the junction of the roads from Owler Bar to Froggatt Edge and Fox House, and proceeding along the top of White Edge, for the first two miles, goes a little west of south.

A few yards S.S.E. (right hand) of the gate and cartway leading to White Edge Lodge is a deep trench way going in the same direction and up-slope. It divides immediately, and the correct way is to take the right fork. The other two routes, one bending and going under, and the other over, the top of the hard ground, go to Lady Cross and beyond – from Hope and Hathersage to Chesterfield.

The trench way keeps slightly under the near (right) edge and left of a ruined and roofless watchers', or an older shepherds' stone hut, which, formerly, had a chimney and fireplace and about six-feet square, was a mortared erection. Some of the rock and stone on this small 'Black Hill' edge has been worked away.

In about 400 yards south of the road junction, the track reaches the side of a now feeble game plantation, and, at the end of it, meets a lower, alternative track. A second walled plantation is left more to the right, and at about 700 yards from the road the way crosses the Dronfield–Tideswell bridleway gap on White Edge and in full view of the Lodge. The track keeps just left of White Edge, soon bends a little to the left, and there are several small and rude edge-up guide stones en route. Then the track thins out and crosses a patch of cotton grass over a shallow hollow.

Windlow Hill and Windley Well

The hard ground is soon passed over and the trench renewed in the heather. Presently it crosses a wall (a gap, usually), which, coming from the Hurkling Stone (one quarter mile E.E. by S.), leads in about 500 yards to the clear spring, below the edge, called Windley Well. The summit just crossed, according to old descriptions, was named Windlow Hill and, in one case, Windbow Hill. The track soon leaves the edge of rocks some 40 yards to the right and, crossing the hollow and its peat and stone getters' tracks, affords the first view of the 'Grouse Inn' – and also Sir William Road and Longstone Edge, etc.

The White Edge 1709 Guide Stone

Two features of this bridle track are the elevated and exposed nature of the ground and the number of small stone guides – some of them rudely conical – which still remain beside the way. Hereabouts they are chiefly laid flat. The direction is generally slightly west of due south, and 30 to 60 yards away from the edge. At the next wee hollow is the Tideswell–Dronfield bridleway meet and a stone guide 4ft 9in x 12in x 12in, which fell, or was pushed down, in 1921. The carving on it is:

TIDS–WALL– ROAD 1709
DRON–FEILD–ROAD
BAKE–WELL–ROAD
SHEF–IELD–ROAD

(The Dronfield bridleway going eastwardly from this point is paved for some distance along the flat moor.)

Onwards and slightly descending, the way, for about half a mile is faint but here and there discernible in slight depressions between a patch of heather or in the bally grasses. It is generally about 40–50 yards from the edge. Two low mark-stones are passed slightly to the left, then a third, and a fourth stone 60 yards beyond. Perhaps 20 yards left of the latter stone is a low mound with a few flat stones upon it and half grown over – perhaps an old and once prominent guide cairn or tumulus. Who could tell?

Tony Rowland's Hut
Another mark stone is 50 yards ahead, at the verge of marshy Lucas Fen – perhaps nearly 300 acres in extent (the Duck Pond is away to the left), and the track is nearer the edge. Here is the wee hollow and trickle from the west side of the pen and a few yards short of it the remains of a square piece of rough walling of split grits not above a foot or so high. It is partly heather grown and 12 feet square and, I believe, the site of the 'Tony Rowland's Hut' marked on Hutchinson's 1836 map and on no other map I have seen. The site also corresponds with the marking on the map.

I assume that this shepherd's shelter hut would be built in the eighteenth century by Anthony Rowland, a Froggatt freeholder who had common rights, or by a shepherd man of this name. I have not traced the origin, but there are Rowlands living in Calver and Eyam today.

By the South Side of Lucas Fen
The trenches across the hollow are plain – as also a quarter-mile rearward, between strips of heather. About 40 yards from the hollow the left trench is a strip of heath grass and there is another rudely conical and low mark stone. The track now swings more to the S.E., with Lucas Fen on the left hand and a larger pointed mark stone, probably artificially-placed, shows water pittings perhaps a thousand years old. The track ascends slightly, with White Edge summit on the right. (Mr J.W. Stone, the gamekeeper at Thickwoods Lodge, who died at Stanton Ford farm last year, used to call the summit of White Edge (1203 feet) 'Juggler Venture'. I wonder why, for it sounds like the name for a lead mine.) On the level, the track passes through the outer edge of a patch of bracken. A longer low boundary stone is passed, and a few yards beyond it three deep trenches turn (right, and more southerly) up a shallow hollow to the top of White Edge.

White Edge to White Edge and Curbar Fields
At the top it crosses some amateur quarrying, and after leaving the two trench loops and bilberry briars below the edge a south-southwesterly course is taken for half a mile to the open space and, for another half-mile, along the

trench ways between the walls of (left) White Edge Fields and (right) Curbar Fields.

Moore's Piece and Stanton Ford School

At the S.E. corner of Curbar Fields, just before turning sharply (W.) along the narrow piece to the gate by Curbar Gap guide stone – or Curbar Bar Head – there was a stake and rail fenced field – part walled – called 'Moore's Piece'. It occupied the whole of this narrow piece and from the roadside wall due S of the next (N.) wall corner, went about 50 yards further E. and then N.N.E. to a point about 90 yards east of the next (N.) wall corner and formed a rectangular piece going 160 yards to the N.

It is the stingy piece given by the Baslow Enclosure Award of 10/3/1826 to the Ford endowed school which, no longer used, stood between the Baslow–Calver Road and the Derwent, opposite Stanton Ford Farm and two-thirds of a mile S.S.W. of Calver Bridge. A Mr Moore was the last schoolmaster, and hence the name. This Charity, in Glover's 1829 *History and Gazetteer*, is as follows:

'Stanton Ford School, about half a mile from the village, consisting of a school-room with two chambers over the same, in which the master resides, a garden and field, containing about three acres. The master is appointed by the inhabitants of the chapelry. For the emoluments, which are about £12 per annum, he teaches ten children, appointed by the minister and chapel warden.'

It is stated that there was a 'swopping' of land some twenty-five years ago near the school, and that the then trustees, the late Joseph Moseley and William Gill, arranged matters, and possibly Mr Barber, of Sheffield, who took the place, was concerned in it. The wood fences of 'Moore's Piece' were at once taken to Mr Peat's, the keeper's house, Warren Lodge, under Froggatt Edge, and the 'Piece' went into the moor. The terms of the award were:

'I have set out and allot and do hereby award unto the Trustees of Ford school situate within the hamlet of Curbar and to their successors a piece or parcel of land No. 60 on Plan A part of the said Commons in the said hamlet of Curbar containing 4 acres 0 roods 37 perches, bounded southwestwardly by the Turnpike Road leading from Curbar to Chesterfield and on all other sides thereof by Allotments Nos 58 and 61 made to the Duke of Rutland.

The fences for enclosing this Allotment No. 60 against the said Road and southwardly, northeastwardly and southeastwardly against the allotments Nos 58 and 61 I direct shall be made and maintained by the owner or occupier of the said Allotment for the time being'.

The school got a plot of rough land, then worth possibly £40, and, besides clearing it, had to build the walls around it!

ODD FACTS AND STORIES ABOUT BIG MOOR
The Way to Bakewell
I cannot dogmatise, but from the guide stone and Curbar Gap the way may have gone down to the left and by the three 'The Crimbles' fields jutting out on low side and north end of the nearest 'Elliott's Rough' under Baslow Edge and have gone down to Stanton Ford and Bubnell (or Baslow Bridge) and then to Pilsley, Ball Cross Farm, Castle Hill and Bakewell.

The Mysterious Curbar Gap Guide Stone
I paid at least half a dozen visits before finally deciphering the correct markings on this guide stone which properly, and anciently, is called Curbar Bar Head guide stone – although 'bar' is repeated. No one, gamekeeper or native, or printed reference, could tell me the wording on the only indistinct side of it, and the rambler must accept my rendering as being correct. The lettering on the four sides is:-

SHEFE–ELD.RD (two lines), TIDSW–ALL–ROAD (three lines and a rude 'V' underneath), DRON–FIELD–ROAD (three lines) and CHES-TOR–FEILD–ROAD–HUMPHE–RY GREG–ORY SUPE–RVISOR–1709 (eight lines).

The last complication is 'Chestorfeild Road, Humphery Gregory, Supervisor' and '1709', the date of erection. Humphrey Gregory is the name of the Curbar parish road supervisor, or surveyor, of the year when the stone was erected. It points to the Sheffield Road – along the top of White Edge or the later carriage road (No. 5) past 'The Pile', the 'Dronfield' via Barbrook and Saltersitch (No. 3a), the Tideswell Way, via Curbar and Stoney Middleton 'High Street', and the Chesterfield Road via the two-slab bridge, Fox Lane, or Clod Hall (3c).

The Lost Curbar Bar Green
Beyond the south side of Curbar Lane, and opposite the guide stone, is an elliptical field. It is called today Curbar Bar Green, and appears to have been a piece of roadside 'green' placed very conveniently for the cattle drovers to rest and pasture their animals while 'driving' them along the 1743 turnpike or the other bridleway – and also a suitable collecting place. It 'went in' under the Baslow Enclosure Award.

The Barbrook Reservoir
The Barbrook Reservoir is known to most ramblers. It stands in a dull setting of moorland, at about a mile almost S.W. of Owler Bar, and literally drains the peat bogs of Totley Moss and Big Moor, for I am only aware of one spring

which runs into the Barbrook above the reservoir – at the slab bridle bridge a mile higher upstream.

Mr Colin Clegg, the civil engineer, now in charge of the making of the Ewden Valley Waterworks, and who was chief engineer on the Barbrook Reservoir, kindly affords me the following facts:

Barbrook Reservoir finished in 1908.
Area 30 acres.
Greatest depth 34 feet.
Capacity 100,000,000 gallons.
Length of the two embankments – about 1000 feet. (The wing embankment, however, is not quite so deep as the main embankment.) Altitude, as taken from my six-inch map, about 1060 feet.

I have always thought that the Chesterfield R.D.C., when making the reservoir, should have ordered the construction of a storm pool and filter above the reservoir to prevent silting-up with peat deposits, but only the expert could say whether it was safe to have excavated a deeper reservoir at this point.

Barbrook Reservoir covers the site of a small 'still' or pond reservoir, which had two sluices and, during a dry summer, the still and sluices are exposed, within the reservoir, nearer the present inlet of the Barbrook. There is also a small pond – equally called a 'still' reservoir, but fixed in a more picturesque situation three-quarters of a mile lower down Barbrook. It is not, as may be thought, a fish pond, but, like the higher one, an earlier, infant reservoir and water-supply made for the Chesterfield Rural District Council and finished about forty-five years ago. A pipe track from the lower 'still' goes across the moor and Baslow–Sheffield Road, and empties in the Ramsley Reservoir. The latter, I understand, was finished about the same time; but there was a Ramsley Lodge before 1840. Ramsley Reservoir is about 960-feet altitude and nearly nine acres in area. Ramsley Lodge is one of the best-placed gamekeeper's lodges I know. It overlooks almost every place on this part of the moors.

Buying the Land
Edward Carpenter, M.A., in a critical chapter in his book, *Towards Industrial Freedom* (1917), entitled 'The Village and the Landlord', first published as a pamphlet in 1909 – thus refers to the making of a reservoir on these moorlands:

'A few years ago, when some twenty acres of these very moor lands were wanted for a matter of great public advantage and benefit, that is, for the formation of a reservoir, the ducal estate could not part with them under £50 an acre; and a little later, when an extension of acreage was required, the district council had to pay a much higher price, so that the total purchase, first and last, comes out at more than £150 per acre'.

Mr Carpenter also states that the general farm lands in the parish were then rated on an estimated rental of 14/- or 15/- per acre on the average, and the 1500 acres of moor land in Holmesfield parish, held by the (late) Duke, were rated on an estimated rental of less than 2/6d. per acre; and suggests that either the moor lands were worth a capital value of £150 an acre, or should be assessed at £5 instead of 2/6d. The point raised is that the public paid dearly for the land which, formerly, was the parish common.

Watching the Navvy didn't steal the Grouse

When the Barbrook Reservoir was being made, a cabin – since demolished – was built on the mossy flat of Car Top, a little to the left of the cart track and drive to the reservoir keeper's lodge. Mr William Slack, today's reservoir keeper, also did the work of 'tenting' to see that the navvies did not poach for any feathered or four-footed thing, and the R.D.C., so it is stated, paid the wages. (The navvies employed on the Derwent Valley Waterworks were supposed to 'get the sack' for the offence of poaching grouse or rabbits.).

There was a window in the cabin, and William could see anyone walking along the road from Owler Bar as far as Ramsley Lodge. One day he saw a man coming along from the direction of Ramsley and also noticed that he was potting at the grouse with stones when they perched on the roadside wall. William came out of his cabin and, unseen, 'slived' down the Sampson's Hollow and, under the roadside wall, waited for his man. Then he jumped over the wall and rushed towards what proved to be a little elderly tramp, as though he was going to eat him.

The old man, however, put up the story, true or otherwise, that he had lived in the South all his life and had never seen St Grouse in person. He also stated that he was out of work, and, rather prophetically, and, dimly appreciating the newspaper bouquets of 'economic facts' in 1926, hoped that there would be 'a big war' and 'kill a lot off' so that he could 'get a job'. But it all ended in smoke, for big-hearted William, as one man – who should know – calls him, sent the old man on his way with a present of a little tobacco.

Oat Fields made for Grouse

Many ramblers, when passing by or seeing an enclosure in the middle of a Rutland–Longshaw Estate moor, have wondered why a walled-off field, now barren and perhaps heather-grown, was placed thereabouts, and not in company with others. The reason is that these fields were made about the time of the 'sporting duke', and grand-uncle of the present holder of the title, for the purpose of providing oats for grouse. The silly money and production-wasting fad lasted for a time and was given up, but there are one or two old men who can remember the ploughing of them. These fields are as follows: Bage Field, a rectangular field two-and-three-quarter acres in area, is by the east side of Ankirk Road, over half a mile S.W. of Oxdale Lodge and three-quarters of a mile short of its junction with the main road, above Fox House. Every walker has seen this field and may be interested to know that it cuts across the course of the once undeniable Dore to Hathersage bridle road.

The next field, about three-and-a-half acres, is immediately E. of Flask Edge and W. of the peat-draining of Upper Saltersitch and half a mile N.W. of the 'Peacock Hotel' at Owler Bar – on the Sheffield–Baslow Road. Its name is Flask Edge Field.

The third field, about three acres in area, is on Big Moor, about 60 yards S.W. of the south corner of Barbrook Reservoir embankment, and is called Big Moor Field.

The fourth field, about one-and-three-quarter acres in area, is on the south side of Fox Lane on Leash Fen and about 200 yards S. of the E. end of Ramsley Reservoir embankment. Mr Martin Slack, the present gamekeeper on this part of the Longshaw estate, has for so many years been an institution at Ramsley Lodge that the few natives who are allowed to tread these moors on business are apt to call it Martin Slack's field.

The fifth field, area about 21 acres, is just S. of the Higgar Lodge, which, built for a gamekeeper's lodge and usually inhabited by one, or a week-end 'tenter' – stands so prominently on the high ground north of the Winyards Nick end of Millstone-Edge. (Winyards Nick bridleway gap should be 'Winnatts' or *Windgates* Nick.) There were letters in the Sheffield press last year with regard to the prohibition of making tea for ramblers at this house.

These five fields could be used for growing winter hay for sheep and also contain a shelter shed for sickly animals, and during stormy weather. It is well-known to the few initiated moorland workers that, here and there, on the benty places of the moors, small crops of edible hay can also be cut with the scythe and stacked for foddering sheep in winter.

You Watch Here and I'll Poach There
The name of Martin Slack, of Ramsley Lodge, also reminds me of another story of the moors told by the late 'Tommy Rahndeead' (Marshall), of Totley, and detailed by Mr Horatio Taylor, of Totley.

Old 'Pincher' Hardy, a celebrated Chesterfield poacher, who was selling cottons and basket trifles two or three years ago – a favourite way of 'getting to know a bit' in advance of the job – and may now be receiving his old-age pension, is credited with a fine joke.

He went to George Slack, at Ramsley Lodge (Martin's father), and told him that if he would give him ten shillings about a certain date he would bring a gang of poachers on the Eaglestone Flat, left of the old turnpike (and now 'drive') along Blackstone Edge towards Wellington Monument, and, of course, give the keepers a good 'catch' of poachers. George would not part with the 'ten bob', and possibly was not quite prepared to accept the 'gag'. The story goes that he then went to the late David Peat ('Black Jack') at Warren Lodge, who gave him the 10/- and a night's 'doss'.

Jack Slack, one of Martin's brothers (and the gentleman vagabond who was given a royal funeral at Dore), related how he and other tenters and keepers then spent a night or two shivering like fools, and watching near Blackstone Edge, and how 'Black Jack' would come along with his good overcoat and a flask of the 'holy shpirit' and also look for the poachers who never came. Jack, who, for nineteen years, was a shepherd and 'tenter', then 'did a bit on his own', and, one night, discovered that 'Pincher' Hardy and his gang were having a real night out 'pegging' for rabbits on either side of the road between the 'Toad's Mouth Rock' and 'The Surprise'.

Shortly afterwards Jack Slack met 'Pincher' and, very pointedly, told him that his poacher majesty never came on that drive according to plan. And 'Pincher' quietly replied, "Not likely. Does ta think ah've no mooar white i' mi eye ner that" – only they didn't speak quite so politely as this.

Netting Hares at 'Big Moor Field'
The following is another story told by the late 'Tommy Rahndeead' about an incident which occurred at the walled-in 'Big Moor Field'.

'Tommy Rahndeead' was a good teller of tales who did odd jobs, was 'game carrier' during the 'shoots' on the Big Moor, etc, and a good follower of the hounds – in the days of the Sheffield and Hallam hunts, when a day's 'hunt' and exercise in the open often ended in a good night of 'boozing'.

The late John Silcock, the father of 'Ferdinand', our untameable Holmesfield 'character' – and also of the brother who, before going to New Zealand, carved 'HERE LIES GODFREY' on the northernmost Fox Lane Cross – was a roadman who lived in Fox Lane and had a house and small holding near Bank Green – one of the 'greens' stolen in the Holmesfield Enclosure Act.

On one occasion – not the only one – he left the road and set a net for a hare at the gateway of the Big Moor Field, and then, giving his dog the hint to 'get out' and do the work, sat down, out of sight, to wait for the result. And he soon got it.

Like all poachers, he kept 'quite quiet', and, by and by, he heard the quick rush of feet, and bang came a big wether sheep through the open gate and took the net with it.

So Silcock lost the valuable net, and could not 'bag' the wrong sort of hare which the dog had 'marked' and driven to his master's net.

Sheep Folds and Shelter Walls

Some have been destroyed and others are hidden from sight, but there were probably a dozen collecting places and shelters ('lea') walls on Big Moor alone. Those still identifiable are as follows:

(1) On the north side Barbrook Reservoir – an 'L'-shaped wall at present showing a tall freak cairn. Made by a Holmesfield commoner?

(2) Kitchen Sheep Lea, a double Sheep Fold and 'T' shaped shelter wall about 500 yards W.W. by S. of the summit of White Edge – the fold and shelter for the part of Bubnell Common used by the Kitchen family of Brambley Farm. There was also a stone hut.

(3) West of and under Swine Sty, about 70 yards on the west side of Sandyford Brook, and about 120 yards south of the last of White Edge Fields – called 'Siddalls Fields'. Possibly once a fold and shelter or a double fold.

(4) A 'T'-shaped lea wall, on Ramsley Moor, at a point 880 yards S.S.E. of the junction of Car Road and the Owler Bar–Baslow Road, and made by a Holmesfield commoner?

(5) A lost Sheep Lea called 'Gregory's' or 'Lowe's' (Froggatt and Holmesfield farmers) pulled down before 1816 during the dispute for 'Deadshaw' between the two parishes. The location was called Sheep Lea Hill or the Knowl above the N.W. corner of Barbrook Reservoir embankment.

(6) A Sheep Lea wall on the east slope of Round Hill – about half a mile westward of the small 'still' reservoir below the Barbrook Reservoir, a pre-1816 Curbar commoner's shelter wall.

(7) A 'D'-shaped fold on the N. bank of Blake Brook just W. of the Baslow parish boundary, and situated 600 yards E. of its junction with Barbrook and 450 yards E. of Owler Bar–Baslow Road.

(8) Richard White, of Sheffield, in the 1816 boundary case, remembered two sheep lea walls standing on the lower part of Deadshaw – i.e., on the W. of Barbrook and the small 'still' reservoir. There are also traces of a Sheep Lea S.E. of the Stone Circle on Big Moor which, in turn, is half a mile N.W. of Ramsley Lodge.

(9) Richard White (1816 case) remembered a sheep lea wall of Thomas Worralls, of Froggatt, at a place called 'the back of Robin Hood', about a mile

from the disputed land – of Deadshaw.

Old Keepers or Game Cabins

(1) The evidence in the boundary dispute of 1816 gives clear proof that the Duke of Rutland – as also Mr Shore, of Totley Hall – each had a game cabin or keeper's cabin and tried to preserve some sort of game – probably grouse – before 1816 and the Game Act of 1831 and basis of English Game Laws, which brought the misuse of land which another generation will correct. James Gregory, of Froggatt, aged fifty, and a tenant of the Duke of Rutland for 54 acres, testified to pulling down a 'lea wall' where the 'Game Cabin' now stands. It would appear that this sheep lea wall was used in the making of the Cabin, which in turn has also disappeared.

(2) A ruined stone hut, on the low ridge of Black Hill, about 200 yards south of the junction of the roads to Fox House, Froggatt Edge, and Owler Bar, near 'The Wooden Pole'.

(3) Tony Rowland's Hut, probably a shepherd's roofed hut on White Edge where the tricklings ooze and flow down the Edge from the west side of Lucas Fen.

(4) The Game Cabin or Hut on Totley Moss appears to have been on Flask Edge where the confused ruins of sheep folds are still seen – beside the wall and parish boundary – Totley on the N. and Holmesfield on the south side.

(5) There is another stone hut about 300 yards S.E. of the 1393 feet summit of Ankirk Road and half a mile N.E. of its junction with the Fox House Road.

This hut and also (2) and the one on Eaglestone Flat, were used by the keepers particularly during nesting time and dry weather when watching for fires – at night time. The keepers would do their rounds and meet here – and doubtless use them occasionally when looking for poachers.

Lost Place Names on Big Moor

I have discovered a few, but the following are not known to me:

Cock Hill and *Cock Green* are, I suppose, high or greenish spots where the cock grouse are wont to sport themselves.

Gorsey Knowl or *Fearney* (ferny) *Knowl* – Both names are somewhere on Big Moor.

Back of Robin Hood – This is not near the 'Robin Hood Inn' by the Baslow-Chesterfield highway, but about a mile from the (1816) 'disputed land' of Deadshaw – Richard White's evidence.

History upon Sheffield Corporation's Moorlands

(The ancient Dore-Hathersage to Fox House and Holmesfield-Longshaw Bridleways.)

From S.C.R. Handbook, 1928/29. *Ward's description of the hill fort, Carl Wark, includes his hope that Sheffield Corporation will not make it public – an example of Ward opposing public access. Nevertheless, Carl Wark was made public and remains public, and it does not seem to have suffered unduly as a consequence – certainly less so than in the age of the 'stone-getter'.*

The following pages are a long contemplated attempt to revive and restore a few almost lost moorland place names and some of the fading history and associations of the Houndkirk and Burbage moorlands – and also to describe the route and features of the truly ancient bridle roads which, before the present highways were dreamed of, were the only means of communication between pre-Norman Dore and Hathersage and to Grindleford and beyond – and also from Holmesfield or Barlow to Hathersage. No claim is made that these pre-1800 ways, which, regretfully said, were not mentioned by the Enclosure Awards, are still public. It is, however, contended that the cattle drovers and toll-bar 'dodgers' used them regularly until the middle of last century and that, in due time, an enlightened and more responsible public must have more facilities in return for the complete loss of road walking caused by the ever increasing use of the fast-speeding motor car. The Owler Bar–Longshaw Park and the Dore–Hathersage old bridle roads would save nearly two miles of motor road walking.

The Dore–Hathersage Bridleway

The best way to proceed is from the Dore post office westwardly along Townhead Lane past the last farm (left), called Townhead Farm – 'Townhead', or 'Townend', in a village pointing to the exit or entry of the ancient bridle road. In half a mile we attain the open view of the browny moor slopes of the northeast end of Totley Moss, and a sharp descent leads to the bridge over Redcar Brook. (The lane to the left – S.S.W. – beyond the Redcar Brook and bridge is called Short's Lane, an occupation road which ends at an old quarry beside Blacka Dike. It is named after an old man called Short, whose cottage

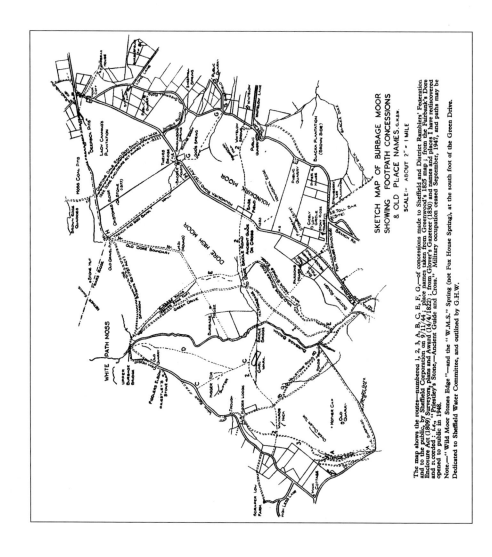

SKETCH MAP OF BURBAGE MOOR
SHOWING FOOTPATH CONCESSIONS
& OLD PLACE NAMES. G.H.W.

SCALE:- ABOUT 2" - 1 MILE

The map shows the routes—numbered 1, 2, 3, A, B, C, E, F, G,—of concessions made to Sheffield and District Ramblers' Federation and to the public, by Sheffield Corporation on 9/11/44, place names taken from Greenwood's 1829 map; from the Fairbank's Dore Enclosure Act (1809) Surveyors, plans and Award (14/4/1822) from Glover's Gazetteer (1830) and names and places I have rediscovered and recorded : i.e., "Priestley's Stone,—Ancient Guide and Cross." Military occupation ceased September, 1947, and paths may be opened to public in 1948.

Note.—" Wild Moor Stones Edge "—and the " W.M.S." Spring (not Fox House Spring), at the south foot of the Green Drive.

Dedicated to Sheffield Water Committee, and outlined by G.H.W.

was removed years ago, says Mr Henry W. Hancock, of 'Rushley', Dore.) The road branching to the north is Newfield Lane, and opposite (S.) is a short enclosed lane leading to the fields. The bridleway on the E. side of it is only faintly discernible in the next field, but, 30 yards down the lane, on the W. side, a winding trench way descends and bends down the grassy slope to a natural slab stone crossing among the gorse and blackberry bushes, etc., a little below the bridge. We cross the bridge, and the trench way goes straight through the field (N.W.) and the next house, High Greave Farm, is almost built over the ancient way.

A spring course and surface diggings are just behind the farm, and, at the first bend of Whitelow Lane, a road made under the Dore Enclosure Act of 1809 and Award of 10 April 1822, to join the Sheffield–Fox House Road of 1816, the bridleway is seen on the opposite side of the road now going westwardly and diagonally across two fields – from a point a few yards short of Whitelow Farm (right) and behind the next farm (left) called Whitelow House. At the entrance to the latter there are two large round stone gateposts which came from the old Stony Ridge toll bar. The slight hollowed way, beyond the second field, has been obliterated by repeated ploughing, but is recovered by a trough and spring, in the top field, at a point about 150 yards S.E. of the junction of Whitelow Lane with the Fox House Road – at the bend of the field wall.

Meg and Jin Hollow

The rough hollow immediately to the left (and south) of the summit of Whitelow Lane, and immediately beside and below the sharp bend of the main road, is locally called Meg and Jin Hollow, or, if you like it better, 'Mag and Gin' Hollow, although the meaning is probably the same. Unfortunately the Ordnance surveyors have not discovered this alluring name. The motorists who, despite the road improvements, cannot go round the corner quickly enough, and occasionally come to grief, call it 'The Devil's Elbow', and have invented the new name of their patron saint which the local pressmen also try to popularise.

I have long known that the name is traditional, and supposed to refer to two sisters and a snowstorm, and, possibly, is also mythological. Mr Henry W. Hancock, (19/8/27), in answer to an article in the *Sheffield Daily Telegraph*, gave glad proof that the tradition appears to go back to, at least, the eighteenth century. The following is from notes left by Mr Hancock's father, who was born in 1819, and wrote them in 1894:

'Meg and Jin Hollow – A tradition, very firmly believed in by old inhabitants, was to the effect that two sisters, Margaret and Jane, were lost in a snowstorm, and that they were found in each other's arms when the snow melted in this hollow'.

A statement, less traditional and which I have also heard from native residents, is that, in the days when it was less difficult to get questionable beef into the city, there were, on occasions, summary executions of decrepit beasts by this place, and that the carcasses were afterwards more or less successfully disposed of in the city.

The fact that two ancient bridleways crossed the 'Hollow' leans to the possibility of an ancient and, maybe, mythological origin for the name, but 'Meggons', used by the Scandinavians for 'The Gods', or other equally interesting explanation, is at present only speculation – although Mr E. Stovin Bramwell (*Sheffield Daily Telegraph* of 16/8/27) may be thanked for his suggestion of 'Meggon Gin Hollow'.

The Dore Enclosure Act Clearances
If the reader could, at the foot of Whitelow Lane, be elevated 300 feet into a stationary balloon, he would probably see that, generally, the old Dore village farms and clearances are behind and east of Newfield Lane and the Redcar Brook, and that the greatest portion of the land now attached to Roundseats Farm (west of the foot of Whitelow Lane), High Greave, Whitelow Farm, Whitelow House, and (old) Whitelow farm lands (near the top of Whitelow Lane right hand) are square or rectangular fields, therefore enclosures and clearances made after the Dore Enclosure Act. Mr Henry W. Hancock tells me that before the Dore Enclosure Act of 1800 there were three squatters' small clearances or farms near Whitelow Lane, and that one was near the top of the lane, only a field away from the Fox House Road.

The Dore–Grindleford Old Bridle Road
The production of old plans would prove whether, from Whitelow Farm, or thereabouts, the Dore–Hathersage bridle road followed the course of today's Whitelow Lane, but, going southwardly across the Meg and Jin Hollow and (S.S.W.) through the top of the roadside plantation, for half a mile, is the nearest old bridleway from Dore to Fox House, etc., which, from Whirlow Hall and Fenny Lane, crossed (as may be seen) between the now disused Whirlow Wheel Dam and Whirlow Bridge (marked 1816 on parapet) and along Limb Lane into Dore village.

This ancient, rude road is easily traceable throughout, and was, possibly, made a rough cart track in the eighteenth century. It crossed the Fox House Road a few yards on the southeasterly side of Piper House, through the next three fields, enclosed by walls and cleared, but, years ago, again becoming part of the moor. Close behind the ruins of Stony Ridge toll bar (abandoned as a cottage in 1914 and pulled down in 1919), it passed through what is now called Stone House – and also 'T'Besom Shop' – and across the short stretch of open moor between the junction of the Fox House and Ankirk Roads. It then followed inside the field above 'Fox House Inn' and, in the 'Bottom

Rough', reached the road to Hathersage, perhaps 100 yards west of and behind the Inn.

Beside Houndkirk Hill

At the junction of Whitelow Lane with the main road to Fox House, the Dore to Hathersage bridleway is seen on the blackened moor slope (across and above the main road and between the two small roadside parish quarries) which, about four years ago, was burnt-out after a spark from a passing steam lorry. The trench track swings to the left, and then right, and the lowest of the well-defined routes has been used by cart or drug when conveying the cracked-up stones from the side of this once rock-girded Houndkirk Hill. The evidence of split-rock is apparent, and stone, possibly from this point, may have been used for the rebuilding of Dore church. Mr Henry W. Hancock also says that stone obtained on Houndkirk Hill (1278 feet) was used to build part of his house in 1852, the year after he was born.

In about 500 yards from the Fox House Road we reach the summit and source of the small, peaty tricklet, and the hollowed track ceases in front of the weary piece of bog land which is part of Houndkirk Moor.

We are at the prosy source of streamlets running (right) into the Redcar Brook and (left) Blacka Brook head waters of the Sheaf, but in late October the red tips of the reedy grasses give warmth to a cold, wet moor which, two generations ago, would have frightened the good townsman walker.

Moor drainage has altered considerably during one hundred years, and there are no adequate traces of a route which would make a long bend by the small rocky edge on the left. I have not found traces of a paved way, but it may be suggested that the straight and obvious way went due west, across the marshy flat and to the two stone gate posts, which, placed in the centre of the broken walls of Bage Field, are beside the Ankirk Road. Mr Hancock has an old map of Dore Township made some time after 1822, which gives the name of this field as 'Houndkirk Bage'. Bage Field was one of several cleared and walled-off pieces which were made on the Duke of Rutland's Longshaw Moorlands about 70 years ago, and, for a short period, planted with oats for the benefit of the grouse. These fields today could be used to produce winter hay and foddering for sheep, and also shelter-places during inclement weather.

We have now walked half a mile across the marsh, and wide Burbage Moor is ahead. Across the old Ankirk Road there are trenchy ways going uphill but slightly to the left.

An Old Guide Stone (or Cross?) Re-discovered

The right-hand track is the correct way, but exactly at the top and about 50 yards away to the south (left) you may see a little stone on the moor which, after discovering it in pre-war days, I have regularly placed in position, and the gamekeepers often removed. (There was a second, smaller, stone, but it had disappeared last year.)

The name of this ancient guide stone is lost, and, possibly, a Cross has stood there. There is a large flat surface rock, and the mortice hole in it is 15in. x 9in.. The remains of the stone post or Cross which I found on the moor a few yards away and replaced now stands 16 inches above the surface rock. The smaller piece was about nine inches long.

It is apparent that this road guide would be seen half a mile away on either side, and was put in a position where guidance would be required by any traveller during snowy and foggy weather.

The direction for the next half-mile is almost due west across the flat moor top, first towards the Higger Lodge and then the summit of Millstone Edge (at Over Owler Tor) and the isolated Mother Cap rock. The summit of Burbage Moor (1431 feet) and the Dore-Hathersage boundary is on the right skyline. (The little nick and bridle road crossing-place on the front skyline, between Over Owler Tor and Higger Lodge, called Winyards Nick on the six-inch maps, should, properly, be named Winnats Nick, and, like the Winnats, at Castleton, means Windy Road Nick.)

A keeper's path goes beside the old bridleway (right of it), and presently there is a small stream source on the near right hand. The track bends a little to the left, and, leaving the stream 100 yards or so to the north, we reach the little depression between the N.E. end of what should be termed Wild Moor Stones Edge and the commencement of Burbage Edge on the right. Wild Moor Stones Edge is not named on the six-inch-to-mile map, and the name, as above, I took from George Sanderson's rare 1836 map of Derbyshire. It is probable that many erratic blocks were to be seen along or under this Edge before the eighteenth and

nineteenth-century quarry-men proceeded so far up the Edge. There are also many large natural stones lying under it today. The north continuation of the Edge, on the east side of the upper Burbage valley, is, on Sanderson's map, called 'Reeves Edge Top'.

Burbage Bridge, October 1945, showing bullet scars from Army training exercises.

A low broken wall comes from the near (left) side of Wild Moor Stones Edge, and is probably a relic of the Dore Enclosure Act Awards. We cross the wall and go down the hollow. The deep trenches, easily followed, bend and bend again in a course roughly W.W. by S., down the heathery bracken and rock-strewn slope, with the tumbling streamlet, now resumed, on our right hand. In nearly half a mile from the broken wall we cross the streamlet, and in 50 yards further the slabbed bridle bridge over the Burbage Brook which, probably, was erected about 1705. A gamekeeper once told me it was made for a late Duke of Rutland and his shooting parties!

Beside the Carl Wark British Fort

There is a rowan tree beside the bridle bridge, which is 5 feet wide, and the rough flat slabs across it about 3ft 6in wide. Some repairs, however, are now necessary, and it is understood that when the Sheffield Corporation make the small Burbage Reservoir which will immerse the valley bottom at this spot, the bridle bridge will be preserved. Across the bridle bridge the way uphill is obvious, first over a rude, exposed paving, and past two trees, and then becoming less distinct, and afterwards guesswork – under the north end of Peakland's greatest British rock fortress – Carl Wark. The crouching rock, prominent on the edge, is Caer's Chair. It is traditionally supposed that the British chieftain, priest, or what not, when trying a case, sat in this chair, and then, at certain intervals, looked at the reflection in the water in the little 'rock basin' above him; and then the prisoner or captive 'went over the rocks' or

Burbage Bridge, before bullet scars.

'went free'. Hayman Rooke, the antiquarian, in 1783, supposed that 'Cairs Chair' was a seat of justice where the principal Druid sat and, contiguous to the rock basin, had recourse to appearances in the water in doubtful cases. Tradition, however, must, in this case, give way to the physical and obvious fact of water-worn rock pittings which, in other places, have also made 'chairs' of isolated gritstone rock. There are also a few taper-edged millstones lying on this side of the slopes of Carl Wark, for the stone-getters have made sad messes here and there in this priceless, and still valuable, British Monument, which, some years ago, should have been made a State-protected Monument. A stone-getter's shelter or sharpener's hut was made on the S.W. side of Carl Wark, probably after the Hathersage Enclosure Act – when this ex-common land became entirely owned by the Dukes of Rutland.

I hope that, without prejudice to any other claims, the Sheffield Corporation will not allow Carl Wark to be made public, but will only permit access thereto by responsible persons or well-led parties. It is too precious to be made a public playground and receive further damage.

Presently we swerve to the left round the N.W. end of Carl Wark, and see the dry, built-up defence wall which is 9ft 4in high and sloping away on the inner, east, side.

There is a plain track at the edge of the heather, but, proceeding somewhat southwestwardly towards today's green swamp and stream source, is soon lost. Here again the drainage of one hundred years ago and now may be totally different, and the signs of a crossing place are obliterated. It is a round-about way, but, from the foot of the swamp, there are gradually improving trench tracks which lead north of west to the deep 20-feet gap on the skyline of Winyards Nick.

The Holmesfield–Hathersage Lost Bridle Road
From the foot of the swamp and stream source there is also an ancient deep track to be followed southeastwardly, on the east side of the streamlet to the road between the Surprise and Toad's Mouth Rock. It comes out on the road at a point about 250 yards S.W. of the Toad's Mouth Rock and about 100 yards short of the roadside trough which is fed by this unnamed streamlet.

The track, in a similar direction, is observed across the road down to the Burbage Brook, and, beyond it are a number of trench ways which approach the west corner of the first walled field, called 'Timothy Field'. The next field, nearer Fox House, is Top Timothy Field.

This track is then lost, but, after crossing Longshaw Park, is seen (when coming on the road from Fox House toward The Wooden Pole) on the right (E.) side of the road about 500 yards S.S.E. of Fox House. It goes S.E., up the south corner of the hundred-odd acres of the huge Nell Croft, across the Old (now green) Branch Road, and, then continuing almost east, just short of the air shaft, on Totley Moss. It is almost lost in the ensuing Moss, or swamp. Beyond (still going S. of E.) it is seen climbing gently up the heather slope and to the bend in the top wall east of the Greengate Hill summit of Totley Moss (1295 feet). The Brown Edge summit of Totley Moss, a quarter-mile E.E. by N., is 1252 feet, but the highest point is a quarter of a mile N.E. of the Air Shaft (1304 feet) on the ridge which, also on Sanderson's 1836 map, appears to bear the curious name of Knaves Hoar Ridge. Thence forward, beyond the top wall, there is a plain trenched way through the heather to beside Brown Edge and, downwards (S E.), are three or four strikingly deep tracks which lead direct to the fields at the rear of the 'Peacock Hotel' at Owler Bar. This old bridleway is from Holmesfield, and possibly Barlow. The Enclosure Act makers knew their business, and unfortunately public opinion had not arisen when this route was not mentioned in the Award. The facts have been hidden too long.

Scraper Low Farm, High Lees Lane, or 'Tin Pot Lane'

The way from Winnats Nick, after a short distance, is rather confusing, but generally it appears to have gone towards Scraperlow Farm and, I think, on the drier land and water-divide between this and Mitchell Field Farm, both farms apparently being made of land cleared after the Hathersage Enclosure Act. A rough farm track leads across this divide – beyond the road, below Higger Lodge – to just N.E. of this curiously battlemented and freak farmhouse, where a path comes up from Mitchell Field. Here there are traces of the old bridleway in the rough grasses. The old way appears to have gone through Scraperlow farmyard and then, going S.W. across the home croft and the next wall, appears to follow the wall on the right hand – going S.W., and, less plainly, to the head of a walled-in bridle lane which is fenced off at the top to keep out stray cattle – or the intruder? Hereabouts is a delightful surprise view across to the Highlow valley and the moorlands beyond.

This now unmistakable bridleway, here natively called High Lees Lane – and a short half-mile long – descends beside a wall, through what is also called High Lees Plantation, and below an old quarry of the same name. The first few yards at the top end of High Lees Lane show signs of old rough paving, but, lower down, there is another trench way to the right. Presently it is also painfully obvious that some of the residents, and others, in the large villa houses between here and the main road, have conveniently made a common tip of the Lane until, to their discredit, it could be called 'Tin Pot Lane'. Perhaps some of the 'countryman' press correspondents who last year were so fond of criticising the young ramblers will write to the newspapers about this mess, and perhaps they will not?

It is, however, a pretty length of typical hillside bridleway, and the exit is at 10 yards above (and S.) of the stone house which, until a few years ago, was known as the 'Hare and Hounds Inn'. There is a stone motor garage on the other side of the exit of High Lees Lane to the main road – which is at a point about 450 yards S.S.E. of, and above, the junction of the road to Hathersage Village and up Hathersage Dale.

I believe that from High Lees Lane and its summit, by the cart lane to the road – one-third of a mile S.W. of Higger Lodge – is still a public right of way.

Longshaw Estate and the Sale of Longshaw Moors

From S.C.R. Handbook 1928/29. When the new Duke of Rutland decided to sell Longshaw Park and Moors in 1927, the Park went to the National Trust and the Moors to Sheffield Corporation. As Ward mentions, the chief purpose behind Sheffield Corporation's purchase was to construct a high-level water supply and reservoir in the Upper Burbage valley. Fortunately for lovers of the Upper Burbage valley, this did not happen.

The following pages are intended to record an important change of ownership – chiefly into the hands of public authorities – of the largest (12,280 acres) single-used moorland estate in the Peak district which, until the Hathersage, Holmesfield, Baslow, Barlow, Dore, and Totley Enclosure Acts of 1808, 1816, 1823, 1817, 1809, and 1839 respectively, were almost wholly the common sheep pastures and summer cattle grazing lands for the farmer-freeholders of the several parishes and their labourers. The several boundaries are taken from the sale plans.

The Longshaw Lodge Estate
The boundary of this estate of 747 acres is as follows:

From the Surprise, on the right side of the main road to Toad's Mouth Rock, Fox House, Wooden Pole, and Froggatt Edge as far as, and then by the brooklet which runs down White's Moor and the foot of Oak's Wood, to Grindleford Station. From the station, the boundary, for almost 300 yards, is Burbage Brook, then, almost due north, the top of the Bole Hill late Derwent Valley Water Board's quarry, to a few yards below the Surprise View.

The Lock Off Padley Woods
The average altitude of the Park estate is about 1000 feet. There are about 315 acres of woodland and 270 acres of moorland, the remainder being chiefly grass and heathland. It is five miles round the estate, and, when opened, it will give the public some of the choicest walking – and relief from motor-stricken roads – in the Derwent valley area. The lock will no longer be upon the charming Padley Woods and the rocky restless Burbage Brook, and the several drives across the Park will afford welcome saunters during a sweltering summer afternoon.

Local Generosity

Sheffield, during the last two years, has welcomed an outburst of generosity, and the present of Graves Park (Norton Hall and grounds) and £10,000 towards the purchase of Ecclesall Woods, by Alderman J.G. Graves, the ex-Lord Mayor, and the same sum granted by the Town Trust, will gratefully be remembered by the citizens and those, who, more particularly during war-time, tried to buy the (Roman) Templeborough Camp for a little over £2000 and could not raise publicly one fourth of the amount!

Froggatt Edge Drive

The effort to purchase Longshaw Park began in the early part of 1927, upon intimation of the intended sale of the great Longshaw Estate by the new Duke of Rutland. The Agent would not separate the Froggatt Edge to Curbar Gap Drive from the moor – although it could not spoil the grouse shooting – or Froggatt Edge would have been purchased for the nation at once.

Longshaw Purchase, Burbage Drive – Open At Last!

The committee were thus compelled to look to the next best, and the fact that already in January 1928, over £9000 of the £14,000 required to complete the purchase, and hand it over to the National Trust to be a piece of beauty unde-filed and for the use of the public for ever – is proof that a wise choice was made. The Sheffield Corporation were intent upon Burbage and Houndkirk moors, and completed the transaction; the Longshaw committee taking the park and the corporation the moors. The latter, subject to one day's closure each year, have undertaken to give public use, for the first time on record, of the green drive down the east side of the multi-tinted Upper Burbage valley, from the upper bridges to just below Fox House, and the several old and suc-cessive 'trespass' boards and built-up wall will no longer deter the innocent, timid walker.

The corporation also will not allow any building between Toad's Mouth and The Surprise view, and also will have power to take the water supply from the springs in Longshaw Park and to pump it into the reservoir, etc., when required – possibly from small, and obscure, receiving tanks. Corporations, in catchment areas, usually, are criticised by ramblers for unnecessary attempts to prevent reasonable access, but, in this case, the first duty of ramblers is to thank the water committee and Mr Wm Terrey, the general manager, in ridding the Burbage green drive of the 'instructed' gamekeepers. We hope that the 'bus holiday' crowds will not be allowed to become so thick, or so foolish, as to require the paid services of a wheelbarrow trundler of waste paper.

A Ramblers' Committee

The Longshaw Committee is, in effect, a ramblers' committee; for the names of Mr J.E. Doncaster (Chairman), Mrs E.B. Gallimore (Secretary), Sir William Ellis, Douglas Yeomans, W.W. Chisholm, Mr S. Osborn (Treasurer), P. Barnes,

S.E. Morton, Dr Abercrombie, Mr Pye-Smith, Miss Tozer, Mr H. Boulger (Peak District & Northern Counties Footpaths Preservation Society) bring to mind the doers of many doughty deeds and walks, and one is proud to be associated with them. It now remains for the Ramblers and Rambling Clubs to collect at rambles and social gatherings, and to fill the 'Shilling' collecting books (of 25 receipts), which, for clubs, are obtainable from S.E. Morton, 47 Victoria Street, and, for individuals, from the Secretary of Longshaw Committee at 84 West Street. A collecting book should go into every office and workshop. The 'Clarion' has promised £100 during 1928, and it is hoped that some club will 'go one better'.

Bits about the Park

The long strip of apparently natural woods north of Grindleford station now called Padley Woods may, properly, be called Yarncliff Wood (from its millstone quarry) and to have stretched from Burbage Brook to the top of the eastern edge of the lower valley. Bolehill Wood, N.W. of the station, is derived from the eighteenth-century lead-burner's 'bolehill', below the south top of the Water Board's late quarry.

Sheffield Plantation, to the east of Yarncliff Quarry and Lodge, takes us back to shortly after the Hathersage Enclosure Act, when a Sheffield plantation company attempted to make profit and also adorn some of this previously common pasturage. The detective reader can declare that Ebenezer Rhodes, in page 17 of his *Peak Scenery* (1824 edition), was standing near the Wooden Pole when he referred to the building of walls (following the Enclosure Acts) and to the site of Sheffield Plantation which, with other suggested purchases of moorland, were to be planted by a Sheffield society and committee and shareholders of £50 minimum, and £500 maximum. This company's plantation, for some reason, would be purchased by the Duke of Rutland about 1840, and the Longshaw Lodge and estate (however neglected since the war) began to be beautified and the Drives to be made.

Granby Wood, named after the Duke's heir, and situated west of the Fish Pond, would probably be planted more or less simultaneously. The 15 square fields on the north of White's Moor, like others south of it, and on either side the 'Grouse Inn' (Mrs White), are a monument to this old Tedgness Farm family, who cleared this land eighty to one-hundred-and-ten years ago.

Little John's Well, the spring on the drive about 450 yards S.S.E. of Longshaw Lodge, and Robin Hood's Well, about 200 yards E. of it, are probably two of the many fanciful place names which are given to these – presumed – mediaeval celebrities.

Timothy Fields, 200 yards W. of Fox House Inn, are post-Enclosure Act cleared lands. The wall in the 'Bottom Timothy' is almost gone, and merges into

Longshaw Deeds Handover 1933.

Middle Timothy, but Top Timothy Field is intact. Did Timothy somebody clear this land?

Lawrence Field, the moorland on the south-east side of the road, between The Surprise and Toad's Mouth Rock, is also a mystery, and the same remark applies to the big Nell Croft, a large rough piece just S.E. of 'Fox House Inn'.

Fox House: The only reference, I know, to the origin of this much extended inn, is in Bernard Bird's *The Perambulations of Barney the Irishman* (W. Ford, York Street, Sheffield, 1854, p. 20), where he says: 'Fox House, originally built by Mr Fox of Calley [it is Callow Farm] near Highlow Hall'; and that it had lately been much improved by the Duke of Rutland; was then much frequented by Sheffield parties; and that the then landlady was Mrs Furniss.

Old Roads and Guide Stones: The old roads across the Park are shown on the map. The continuation of the first coach road up Sharrow Lane, Psalter Lane, High Lane, Ringinglow, and Ankirk Road to Grindleford Bridge, Sir William, Great Hucklow, Tideswell, Wormhill and Buxton (1757 Act), was across the front of Longshaw Lodge and pastures, down to the Yarncliff bottom gamekeeper's lodge. Near the N.E. end of the Park, just N. of the brooklet, is an original milestone marked 'Tidfwell-8 Buxton-15'. On the other side is 'TO . MILE(S) Sheffild' – and some too-wise person, not knowing that to Sheffield via Ankirk Road is eight miles, has obliterated the figure '8'.

A bridle road guide stone, now about 400 yards S. of the Fish Pond and Rhododendron Walk, is marked: (1) 'SHAFILD . 1709+' (2) 'TO . TIDSWEL' (3) 'TOHA–THAR–SICH–ANDS–TOCH–APILI–NLEE–FRITH' (eight lines), and (4) 'TO–CHAS–TER–FILD'. The directions are Sheffield to Tideswell, and Chesterfield to Hathersage and Chapel-en-le-Frith. This guide stone, I think, stood near the Fish Pond, and was removed when it was made.

Another guide stone which, possibly for quite fifty years, has stood in the drying ground behind Longshaw Lodge, has these markings: (1) 'SHEIF–FEILD–Rode' (2) 'Tid3WALL–RodE' (3) 'DRO–NFELD–SidE' and (4) 'HOPE–Rode–1737'. It refers to Sheffield–Tideswell and Dronfield–Hope Roads, and may have stood near the Wooden Pole. If any living man can swear to the exact location of these guide stones, let him declare it, for the time is short. The '3' is for 'S'.

The Earliest Reference to Longshaw – 1722

A 'long' natural 'shaw' (or wood), from near Grindleford station, towards the Toad's Mouth Rock, could be the obvious, but, as yet, unproven origin of 'Longshaw' but I, and all nature lovers, are indebted to Mr Edward Greaves Bagshawe, solicitor, of 63 Norfolk Street, for a conversation, and then the loan of a copy of a 1722 document in his possession which gives the first known reference to 'Longshaw'. The name does not appear upon the first (1836) Ordnance Map. The document is as follows:

September ye 11th 1722 Hasleford.

Much Honored Sir,

Since I dated my last Mr Froggot of Carrhead was at my house and tould me yt the Duke of Newcastle Steward sent for some of ye freehoulds within ye parish of Hathersage to meet him at Nottingham Races And he further told them that the Duke would be at one halfe of chardge to trye with Yorkshire men about Moskar if ye freehoulds would try ye other And further if ye freeholds wtin Hathersage parish got ye better of Yorkshire ye Duke would allow yt inclosed which is now Inclosed And to Inclose more of ye comon there towards their expences Now there is notice given for all freeholders within ye sd parish to meet & consult about the matter on Monday ye 24th of the instant September And soe give theire answers speedelie to the Duke Steward.

I thought it proper to acquaint your Worship for I could not give noe account to then until I receive your answer I feare yt Both yor Worship & Mr Ashton will loose your sheep walke in Longshaw but by leave for Dore Claimes as far as Burbadge and hath produced a writing concerning there bounds which ye claime there from Henry the Eight time Although there is no hands betwixt noe Lord: perhaps yor worship may find out some good title for youe grandfather kept a great flock of sheep there every summer: it will be very hard to loose sutch a walke belonging to soe antient family. I rest yor most Humble & Obedient Servant
to command   GEORGE COOPER.

Addressed to William Archer Esqre at his house in Sohoe Square London and readdressed from thence for William Archer Esqr. at the Bath in Somersetshire.

A Hathersage–Sheffield Moscar Common Suit-at-law

The document, as will be seen, can be connected with the final contention for

Moscar Common or Moor and the verdict in 1724 for Hathersage against Sheffield in the long-running Moscar land dispute.

The explanation is as follows: The Duke of Newcastle's steward invited some of the Hathersage farmer-freeholders to meet him at Nottingham Races, where, perhaps, 'they backed some winners'! He also said that if the free-holders would fight the Manor of Sheffield for Moscar Common, the Duke would pay half the cost of the hearing, etc., and, if Hathersage won, he would allow what was inclosed (some of today's Moscar House fields?) to remain inclosed, and to help them further, in the matter of their expenses, allow the freeholders to inclose more of the common – into grazing land, I suppose. (Little if any more land hereabouts seems to have been inclosed until after the Hathersage Act of 1808 and Award of 23/6/1830.) The Hathersage freehold-ers were to meet on 24/9/1722 and give their answers, speedily, to the steward of the Duke of Newcastle, who, at this time, was Lord of the Manor of Hathersage.

A Fortune with a Name and a Lady
George Cooper, of Haselford Hall, in Highlow's small manor, was, in this document, writing to William Eyre, of Highlow Hall. The latter, says Mr E.G. Bagshawe, was left a fortune by a man called 'Archer' on condition that he married a Miss Wrottesley, and took the name of 'Archer'. He took both the fair lady and the fortune, and afterwards seems to have spent little time in Derbyshire, and Highlow Hall was gradually abandoned as a residence. It will be noted that William 'Archer' was then in Bath, the eighteenth-century spa, where, like today's Harrogate, many go to regain good health, and others to lose it.

A Dore–Hathersage Common Dispute
The other part of the letter indicates that the Dore freeholder-farmers are claiming the Eyres' (or Highlow's) 'sheep walke' in Longshaw – unless they give or rent it to them 'by leave', and that Dore claims to go as far as 'Burbadge' (Brook?), and to support the claim by producing a writing or document of Dore boundaries dating from the time of Henry VIII – although there is no signed agreement between the Lords of Dore and Hathersage Manors to this effect. George Cooper also says that William Archer's (late Wm Eyre) grandfather kept a great flock of sheep there (at Longshaw) every summer, and it would be hard to lose such a (sheep) walk belonging to so ancient a family – as the Eyres of Highlow.

These ancient land battles took some curious turns and quite possibly the Dore freeholders and Lord of Manor could have urged population and farmers' needs (who knows?) for a boundary which, today, goes over the natural watershed boundary, N.W. of Parson's House (not Burbage House), above Fox House, to Burbage Brook (at the east bend just below the under

Carl Wark bridle bridge and, in one-third mile up stream, turns N.E. direct to the edge and the summit of Burbage Moor, 1431 feet – a curious anomaly.

Mr E.G. Bagshawe, who himself is descended from one of the old Forest of the Peak families and landowners, also says that when the Archer and other estates were sold, about 1800, the Highlow farmers still exercised these rights of pasturage in Longshaw.

A Supposed Boundary of Longshaw Sheep Walk

One can only guess, and hope that the guess is approximately true, that Longshaw sheep walk was, apart from the 'Shaw' itself, the ground north of the brooklet on White's Moor to the Wooden Pole, then almost due N.W. to Burbage Brook (where, to the E. and N.E., a stray (Enclosure?) piece of Derwent comes in – from Fox House and Parson's House to Burbage Brook), and, possibly, the moorland from Millstone Edge to Higger Tor and then down to Burbage Brook. The land between the streamlet down White's Moor to Heywood Brook and Grindleford Bridge is in Nether Padley.

The Great Longshaw Moorlands

The public and ramblers will become more interested in the use of the moorlands, and the next generation may see further changes. The remarks of an older Sheffield rambler, whose name is a household word, after attending the Longshaw and Stanage Moor sales on 5/7/27 – that "the days of moorlands for exclusive grouse shooting in the Sheffield area are about over" – at present are only a little more prophetic than true. The prices offered at the sale are proof that their inflated local value, as grouse moors instead of all-year pasturage plus sport, has declined appreciably since 1914. Some of the reasons are the proximity to the extending city; that some of the younger generation prefer more than a few days costly 'sport' per year; and the great expense attached to modern grouse shooting.

The Longshaw Moors were sold for the Haddon Estate Company, a form of name which has developed among landed estates since the Death Duties became heavier. The vastly greater portion of these moors became part of the entailed ducal estate, after the Commons Enclosure Acts of Barlow, Baslow, Brampton, Holmesfield, Dore, Totley, and Hathersage, by means of 'allotments' 'awarded' to the Lord of the Manor for his 'manorial' and other rights, leading landowners, and smaller freeholders under these Acts and Awards; by purchase from other landowner or freeholder 'allotment' holders who quickly sold small unsatisfactory 'lots' for 'the old song'; or in later exchange with other owners – to link up the various estates, etc. Some moorside farms, such as Clod Hall and the Peacock (Owler Bar) are the direct result of these Enclosure Acts, but it will be seen that other portions of enclosed and cleared land are now part of the moorland.

The area of Longshaw Estate was 11,553 acres, plus the 747 acres of the Longshaw Park. 9270 acres were sold as grouse moorland. With it were 'sporting rights' over 2200 acres of adjacent farm lands. The customary statement is that (where a farm or house and lands, such as the Cupola Cottage, on Baslow Hill – in this case 5a. 1r. 9p. – was sold separately) 'The Grouse and Black Game shooting over this lot is reserved *in perpetuity to the owner for any time being* of lot 22' – meaning the owner of the adjacent Clod Hall Moor. (A friend informs me that despite this clause a neighbouring owner can shoot game on his land, and that in law the owner of the shooting right can only claim the additional right to shoot over it – Q.E.D.) The italics, however, are not in the printed particulars and sale plan. The high water mark of shooting over this estate appears to have been 1893–4, when 3633 and 3354 brace of grouse were 'bagged', although 3282, 3224 and 3002 brace were shot in 1914, 1915, and 1921 respectively. Since the latter year, however, the highest total (in 1923) was 2231 brace. Since 1924 the wintering of sheep on these huge moors (except a few on Burbage Moor) has ceased, and, as we say, when the sheep go off the moors, the grouse also decay.

The principal divisions of Longshaw Moors and the rough boundaries and outlines are as follows:

Houndkirk and Burbage Moors, 2407 acres. The general boundaries are from The Surprise, and, including Millstone Edge and its quarries, the right side of the road past Higger Lodge and Tor, to Burbage Bridges, and forward, only excluding Ringinglow hamlet and Mr Priest's Moor Cottage, but including Lady Canning's miserably wizened Plantation. This moor, after following the W. side of Ankirk Road, also includes the heatherlands on the S.W. side of Jumble Lane and on the west side of Sheephill Road. Then forward – from its junction with Sheffield–Fox House Road – it includes the moorland on the right side of the road to Stony Ridge toll bar site, and then the right side of the Old Branch Road, and at its junction with New Branch Road the boundary turns northwards and follows the right side of the road past Fox House, to the Toad's Mouth Rock and The Surprise. The Ankirk Road runs through this huge acreage. This 'lot' also carries 'sporting rights' over another 580 acres of farmland, including Sheephills, Barber Fields, Owlett House, Whitelow, Old Whitelow and Copperas Farms, and Gill's Lands – of 46, 78, 38, 37, 41, 18 and 11 acres.

These moors were purchased for £21,000 by the Sheffield Corporation for the chief purpose of a high level water supply and reservoir in the Upper Burbage valley, which, possibly during the next ten years, will immerse the old bridle bridge at the foot of Carl Wark.

The Meg and Jin Hollow field and one E. of it were 'thrown in' the Corporation purchase.

The Hathersage Water Dispute, Fox House Spring

Hathersage, during recent years, has sadly neglected its water supply. The supplies from up Hathersage Dale have been inadequate during any dry period, and its quality the talk of the users – or rather 'boilers' – of it. The village 'natives' and the Sheffield 'foreigners' should have agreed together and taken a supply from the Derwent Valley Water Board's pipe line years ago. During the last two years a controversy arose with regard to taking water from the beautiful, clear, and abundant spring between Fox House and the Toad's Mouth Rock – a spring for which, curiously enough, I have never been able to find a name. Sheffield's purchase of this moorland ended part of the controversy by an undertaking that, if Hathersage cannot obtain water from the D.V.W.B. on reasonable terms, or from other sources, Sheffield Corporation will provide Hathersage and Outseats with 40,000 to 50,000 gallons per day from the Burbage source, or, failing agreement, the source of the said supply will be determined in conference with the Ministry of Health. During recent years the builders of villas and houses in the higher parts of Hathersage have been compelled to sink private wells or tap springs – hence the need for a high level supply.

I understood at the second meeting (August 1927) between the Water Committee and the Sheffield Committee who are acting on behalf of the National Trust, that the bridle bridge under Carl Wark will be preserved. The writer pointed out that this bridge was on the old Dore–Hathersage bridle road that was legally omitted and then stolen after the Hathersage Enclosure Act and that the date of erection of this bridge could probably be connected with the 1725 date-stone in Burbage Brook, a few yards above the Hollowgate old bridle bridge crossing about a mile below.

Sheffield's Purchase

The Corporation, it is hoped, may consider the renewing of sheep-grazing upon this moorland, and it is gratifying to note that Mr 'Sep' Priestley's sheep were grazing on Burbage valley moor sides in December. (Some 'wintering' of sheep on Burbage moors has been allowed since the general prohibition on Longshaw moors after 1924.) Last year the shooting rights were let to Sir Charles Clifford (of the *Sheffield Telegraph*), Major A.J. Gainsford, and Messrs H.T. Bradbury and H.H. Reed, and a short lease is under consideration. They added it to the Brookfield Hall Moors of White Path Moss, which adjoin this moor near the Cowper Stone end of Stanage Edge and continue towards Stanage Pole.

These now Corporation Moors, to which odd pieces of more valuable land were added (below Millstone Edge), were bought privately by Sheffield Corporation, the total acreage of 2407 being increased by about 56 acres.

Big Moor, of 3111 acres, also includes sporting rights over another 366 acres –

to wit 152 acres under Curbar Edge and 122 and 21 acres of Pewit Farm and Sharp's Land. The shooting rights on the 123.5 acres attached to 'The Peacock Hotel', at Owler Bar, are divided between Big Moor and Totley Moss.

This great moor was entirely carved out of the Baslow, Curbar, Padley, Holmesfield, and Hathersage Commons. It is perhaps the best chunk of the Longshaw moorland estate, and, apart from two trifling Enclosure Acts paths awarded across it, is free from public rights of way – although, in pre-Enclosure Act days, five bridleways went across Big Moor.

The outline of Big Moor, from the junction of the Froggatt Edge–Fox House–Owler Bar Roads, near Wooden Pole, is the right side of the road to Owler Bar (excluding the two last fields), the right side of the Owler Bar–Baslow Road to the junction with Clod Hall Lane, and then the right side of the latter, to Curbar Gap. From Curbar Gap, Big Moor includes Warren Lodge, below Curbar Gap, the long stretch of 'rabbit warren' fields under Curbar Edge, the whole of Froggatt Edge, and just below it. The boundary, excluding the fields attached to the 'Grouse Inn', is then the right side of the Froggatt Edge Road to its junction with the Fox House and Owler Bar Roads.

The bidding only reached £15,000, and it was withdrawn, and then, with Totley and Ramsley moors – a total of 4868 acres – sold privately to Chesterfield Rural District Council, for the small sum of £25,920. The 'R.D.C.' already owned Barbrook and Ramsley Reservoirs and the 'still' reservoir, lower down the Barbrook and Big Moor. The price of Big Moor and Totley Moor alone was £22,000 – for 4230 acres.

The 'R.D.C' then let the shooting rights of Big Moor, Totley and Ramsley Moors to Major Wm. Wilson, of Horsley Gate Hall, Holmesfield, the Master of the Barlow Foxhounds. One facetious native said: "There'll be no more game-eating foxes shot on Big Moor now", and the answer was that the same native might later on be able to run after the hounds on this moor. Some of the hunt horsemen, on Tuesday, 29 November, rode on the roadside footpath above and below the Totley Brickyard and then up the hill on the Duke's Drive to Totley Moss.

Totley Moor. 1119 acres. The boundary of this once truly sheep-moor is, roughly, from just below the Totley Rifle Range up the old Totley Moss walled-in bridle road, but not including Bole Hill and Bole Hill Lodge, the wall just north of the Totley Moss Road across Totley Moss and of the 'Drive' to the right which leads to the green Old Branch Road. Then it follows the left hand of the Old Branch Road, and from the west end, and exit, of Totley Moss bridle road, the right side of the road to Owler Bar, excluding the fields on the north side of the 'Peacock Hotel'. It includes Thickwood Lodge, and, excluding the two fields above the Totley Brickyard, ends just below Totley Rifle Range.

Totley Moor also includes shooting rights over a further 131 acres of which the 72 acres of Mooredge Farm is the largest piece. Totley Moor was 'withdrawn' at £4750, and was purchased shortly after the sale by Chesterfield R.D.C..

Ramsley Moor, of 638 acres, also included sporting rights over another 160 acres of Birk's Farm (47^1/$_2$), Fox Lane Farm (90^1/$_2$), and Unthank Farm (24 acres). The boundaries exclude fields attached to the Owler Bar 'Peacock Hotel', and, roughly, are the land on the left side of the Sheffield–Baslow Road between the top of the green Carr Road and the foot of Fox Lane – short of the foot of Clod Hall and Curbar Lanes. Then it follows the left side of Fox Lane to the length of Fox Lane's ex-Plantation, to the foot of Carr Road, and the south side of this latter road, to its summit.

The auctioneers (J.D. Wood & Co., of London) failed to get a bid for this lot, but the parts properly called Greaves' Piece (a Holmesfield Award allotment to George Bustard Greaves), on the north side of Carr Road, with Smeekley and Bank Woods (the nearest to Major Wilson's present boundaries), in all 204 acres, were withdrawn at £2500. I understand that Major W. Wilson afterwards purchased the above three pieces privately. Ramsley Moor was also sold privately to the Chesterfield R.D.C. for £3500.

Leash (Fen) Moor and Blake Brook. 681^3/$_4$ acres. The boundaries are the right sides of Fox Lane (from its junction with the Sheffield–Baslow Road), along Rumbling Street and Buckleather Lane, but excluding the fields W. of Buckleather Lane, and including the second field south of the junction of Spitewinter Lane. Then it goes beside Leash Fen drain to opposite Clod Hall Farm, and the right side of Clod Hall Lane, to the Baslow Road, and so to the foot of Fox Lane. Leash Moor or Fen is the biggest bogland in Derbyshire. There were no bids, and this moor was purchased privately by Chesterfield Corporation for £2000 – for water supplies. With Leash Fen are also included the sporting rights over Freebirch (134), Hare Edge (51), Hare Edge (Hancock 20), Clod Hall (41), Farms and Slate Pits Land – in all 271 acres.

Clod Hall Moor. 866 acres. The boundary is from the Sheffield–Baslow Road, the right side of Clod Hall Lane, excluding Clod Hall and Newbridge Farms and their grass fields. It misses a narrow northwardly patch of about nine acres at and behind 'Robin Hood Inn', includes Moorside Farm (£50 per annum rent), Nelson Monument, Birchin and Gardom's Edges, and the rough land on the N. side of Chesterfield–Baslow Road, to half a mile W. of the 'Robin Hood Inn', then goes northwardly, but it excludes the Baslow Far End Farm and Baslow Golf Links, and the two Cupola and Toll Bar cottages – under Gardom's Edge. Thence it goes on the right side of the Sheffield Road up the 'Baslow Hill' to the foot of Clod Hall Lane.

This moor also includes sporting rights over another 424 acres, i.e., $51^1/_2$ of Clod Hall $164^1/_2$, and $153^1/_2$ of Newbridge and Yeld Far End Farms – chiefly farm lands under Gardom's Edge, Baslow Golf Links, and near 'Robin Hood Inn', etc.

This lot was bought privately, and probably precautionarily, by the Duke of Devonshire, and, after the sale, quickly turned over to Chesterfield Corporation for £4500.

Blacka Moor. 448 acres. This is the short, steep 'rough' N.E. of the Blacka Brook feeder of the Sheaf and the ex-plantation and moor – chiefly on the S. and S.W. side of the brook and Cowsick, including Strawberry Lees, late-lamented and once monastic farm, the two brooklets (Cowsick is northwest of Strawberry Lee) which flow downwards on either side that once good cattle-feeding farm, to the stone wall on the right of the Duke's Drive from Totley Moss to Stony Ridge. The top boundary is then on the right side of the Fox House–Sheffield Road, beyond the roadside narrow plantation and the Meg and Jin Hollow.

This moor carries sporting rights over another 201 acres – including 55, 28 and 41 acres of High Greave, New Whitelow, and Roundseats farms.

It is observed that the new owner has placed a trespass board and locked the gate at the Fox House road end of the drive to Strawberry Lee. Dr G.H. Froggatt, a Froggatt lad, who became a dentist and 'made good', became the purchaser for £6000, and it is hoped that he will carry out his promise and not allow this plot, or the 103 acres of lots of land he purchased under Froggatt Edge (on either side the 'Chequers Inn'), and other smaller lots at Curbar, to be vandalised by freak post-war villas, or forty-years-and-fall-down property. The Press announcements were carelessly made, and the rambling fraternity were led to believe that the public had probably obtained the right to walk along Froggatt Edge top as far as Curbar Gap.

A 'Chequers Inn'–Curbar Path
There is a demand for the removal of the alleged ban on the ancient and stiled path from near 'Chequers Inn' (Froggatt) towards Curbar, and, save for the fact that the natives were chiefly ducal tenants, it is difficult to believe how this path could have been placed in jeopardy. I hope that the new owner will have greater regard for this medieval right of way.

Froggatt Edge Drive. The present Duke closed Froggatt Edge Drive in 1924. It is not a public pathway, but, in 1909, after Mr John Derry's, etc., campaign in *Sheffield Independent*, I secured a written promise from the then Duke's agent that it could be used by parties of not more than six persons, but not during the shooting and breeding seasons. The agent, however, would not allow publication, or agree to my request to define the two 'seasons'. The present agent, however, did not formally repudiate the 1909 arrangement in 1924, when the gamekeepers and 'watchers' were ordered to keep pedestrians away, and the closure caused another hubbub of criticism of the Duke. The then walling-up of the entrances to many Longshaw 'drives' was not accompanied by one much-wanted concession to the members of the public, who are morally entitled to use them.

The Chesterfield R.D.C., it is hoped, will dedicate a public path along this Drive, and so give full and, though not legal, a rightful and long overdue access to one of the most beautiful walks and views in the Peak District. The agitation which began quite twenty years ago will cease when the claim is granted, and the previous argument of exclusive 'grouse moor' cannot now be raised as under the former ownership.

Eaglestone Flat, of 394 acres, was purchased privately by Baslow Urban District Council for water supplies and the use of the several springs. The rough boundaries are from the top of 'Bar Road' (behind and north of Baslow's 'Hydro'), the rough piece under and west of Baslow Edge, and along to Curbar Gap. The boundary is then on the right side of Curbar Lane to its junction with the Sheffield–Baslow Road, and downwards to Cupola Cottage. From the latter it crosses the Barbrook and old bridge and up the path and wall side under Wellington Monument – to the top of Bar Road. This moor also includes the sporting rights over another 506 acres, chiefly on land south of the Wellington Monument and west of Baslow Edge and south of Curbar hamlet. These 'sporting rights' are pointers to the fact that unless owners compelled the farmers of adjacent lands to sell the shooting rights or made it a condition of tenancy, the farmers would quickly reduce the game to reasonable proportions, and obtain better crops at higher levels.

The Drive and Road on Eaglestone Flat
This piece includes Wellington Monument, Eagle Stone, the 'Duke's Drive' along Baslow Edge top, and the once coach road from Wellington Monument, along Blackstone Edge to Curbar Lane foot. During 1926, I addressed, by invitation, a private meeting of Baslow residents in regard to the public usage of this 'Drive' and road, and the U.D.C., afterwards, and in view of the impending sale of the moors, decided to await developments. There is no doubt that Baslow as a whole was a big critic of the Duke of Rutland, the late owner, and Mr Noton, the 'watcher', up Bar Road, in closing the access for visitors and residents. It is now hoped that the U.D.C. will dedicate these two picturesque routes to the public and allow the latter, so to speak, 'to get their own back'. The Enclosure-Act-omitted Sheffield to Baslow bridle road is easily traced between (and beyond) Eaglestone and the Wellington Monument.

Other 'lots' sold during this sale included Overstones Farm (185 acres), bought by the tenant, Mr Ernest Priestley (the sheep-dog trial winner and judge); Mitchell Field Farm (82 acres); Callow Farm (16); 'Fox House Inn' and its $9^1/_2$ acres (bought for £5500 by Carter, Milner & Bird's brewery) and Hallfield Farm, Totley ($63^3/_4$ acres). 'The Peacock Hotel' and its $123^1/_2$ acres were bought by the tenant, Mr John Brougham. Holmesfield Park Wood (90 acres) was sold (and is being slaughtered, up to Hob Lane); also the $25^3/_4$ acres of fields behind Totley Brickyard, the Cupola Cottage, and old Toll Bar on Baslow Hill (of 51 and 3 acres respectively), and 44 acres of enclosed land between Rumbling Street and Buckleather Lanes. 'The Chequers Inn', at Froggatt, and 112 acres were sold to S.H. Ward & Co., brewers, for £3600; and several small plots at Froggatt and under Froggatt Edge also changed hands. In every case it appeared that the sporting rights go to the purchaser of the adjacent moorland.

The Wooden Pole is within Longshaw. This four bridleway guide, on the base stone, is marked 'T1778' and 'TW'. The first represents a Totley parish boundary 'riding' of the 'bounds' and 'TW' is Thomas Willoughby (Lord Middleton), the then Lord of the Manor.

'T'Owd Pole', as is it also called, is at the boundary of Totley and Hathersage parishes, and, if it could, would tell many stories of pre-Enclosure Act days.

Stories about Owler Bar
and 'The Peacock'

From S.C.R. Handbook 1929/30. Ward's local pubs were The Peacock at Owler Bar and The Robin Hood at Lidgate, and probably a lot of the anecdotes in this article were picked up in these pubs.

This story, like many others, is the result of a chance conversation with a (Froggatt) countryman, and then correspondence with his uncle, Mr James Wragg of Oldham Road, Warrington, who now (January 1929) is approaching his seventy-eighth birthday, and has vivid memories of the days of his youth spent at Owler Bar on the road from Sheffield to Baslow and seven-and-a-third miles S.W. of Sheffield. These and other gleanings and editings of anecdote, fact, and story, as near correct as I can make them, are part of the half-forgotten records of two and more generations ago.

The centre of the story, now known to thousands of Sheffielders, is the road-sides round about breezy Owler Bar. The setting is not long after this portion of the Holmesfield common lands of 9650 acres (area of parish is 4600 acres) had been enclosed by the Act of 1816 and Award of 10/11/1820, and the fields were first enclosed between walls between Moorwoods Lane end and 'The Peacock Hotel', and towards the Pewit Farm and Holmesfield's high and historic hamlet of Lidgate.

Ancient Lidgate and Moorwood
The latter hamlet, in the Holmesfield Manor Court Rolls of 1491, in these words is, 'a parcel of land abutting on the common on the west, and on the land of Thom Robynson, of York, on the east, and lying between the highway leading from Holmesfield chapel as far as Chapell Lydzatte on the north' – Kerry's transcription. Owler Bar, by comparison, is young, and the nearest cultivations, half a mile or so N.E., were those of 'Tho Morewodd' (1481–2) or 'Will Morewode', holding a croft called 'Morewode' (1486–7), while, in 1576, 'Thom Heley' had 'destroyed the hollies in Morewood', and was fined for the offence.

The name Lidgate, wherever I have found it in the local moorland area, always seems to occur at a point where the old village cultivation and fencing ended and the old road or 'gate' opened out to the waste lands and common pasturage.

The 'old' Owler Bar Toll Bar (1)

The 'Wraggs' homestead, two stories lengthwise (with a third stuck to it in the manner of a child building houses), whitewashed, stone built and flag slated, with two high and thin brick chimneys, and a dwarf one beside them, is the old, original Owler Bar toll bar built when the Gleadless, Holmesfield, Froggatt Edge to Calver Road was first made a turnpike, in or about the year 1781. At that date there was no neighbour less than half a mile away. There is also a blue-slated stone shed and a forlorn garden on the Holmesfield side of the house, and, between the house and garden, an old parish pinfold. The three small windows, including the tollkeeper's projecting, peep-eye window, nearest the 'Peacock Hotel' (about 140 yards to the W.) remind one of the Moslem woman's veil, and also of today's acceptance of the injunction of let there be light inside the house for the housewife.

'The Peacock' and the New Toll Bar

The new toll bar which stole the old name, and stands by the road junction at the foot of the 'Peacock Hotel's' open yard, shows two squarely projecting windows, and also the progress made in toll bar housing about 1816 to 1818, when the Sheffield-Baslow road was made and the imitation eighteenth-century 'Peacock Hotel', with its wind porch and small-paned and pointed windows, stables, and baiting shed, was added to the list of stone-built moorland roadside hostelries. The altitude of the hotel is about 1010 feet. 'Fox House Inn', however, is 120 feet higher, and 'The Barrel' at Bretton exceeds it by about 240 feet.

Today's 'Developer' at Owler Bar

Today, however, marks a third change, for 'good-bye toll bar, welcome motor-car' has brought the developer and advertiser. The last and youngest brother, Mr Fred J. Wragg, who, to a non-rackrenting Duke, paid £3 a year for the cottage and three acres between the two roads, and purchased it at the Duke of Rutland's first sale (1920), agreed to dispose of part, and then, to the regret of all the natives, sold the whole of the small but proudly esteemed family home and holding. Thus, today, we have to thank the uninspired rural authority for 20 yards of unlovely roadside hutment and an infant petrol station, to which is added (1928) the glaring yellow box-like roadside advertisement, while the former rent of £3 p.a. is raised nearer to the fourth power of the number.

A Night at Owler Bar Seventy Years Ago

"I well remember," says Mr Wragg, "my first glimpse and night at my grand-mother's cottage about seventy years ago. My father always led his own coals at this period to the Baslow Toll Bar. He usually hired a horse and cart from a friendly farmer, but later bought his own pony and cart. It was a sunny morning, and I begged and fretted until dad said to mother: 'Wrap him up warm and I'll take him'. The trembling horse, however, slipped so much on

the icy road way that father got out to walk. But he had difficulty in walking and sticking to the roadside, and the horse followed him wherever he went. I got a proper knocking about over the exposed stones and boulders in the road, but at last we saw the old Owler Bar cottage, and dad said: 'That's your granny's'.

"I was lifted down and left in the house until dad got the horse 'sharpened', and loaded with coal from Dronfield Woodhouse pits. But the day became wild, and the snow fell fast and deep. And so I was persuaded to stay the night and sleep with my father's oldest brother, James.

Owler Bar original Toll Bar.

Driving t'Rats off t'Bed

"When supper was over, uncle read a chapter from the Bible and I went to bed. There was a long stick on the bed, and I asked why it was put there. Uncle said, 'Why, it's to drive t'rats away. Tha wain't be freeten'd, will tha, when ah 'it 'em?' I didn't say much, but thought a lot, for I hadn't seen a rat before. The tallow candle was still burning when I heard a squeaking and scuttering and two rats were soon upon the bed. Uncle beat them off, but as one lot went, another seemed to come. I popped my head under the blankets and stayed there, but the stick kept going 'plomp', as it seemed to me, nearly all night. The wind howled and rattled the diamond windows in the lead casement and roared up the old wide chimney", in a way that, often enough, my old friend, it roars in my old windows on the wild and windy Moorwood Lane, so beloved by every blast that blows across the Ramsley moortops or the hollow from Ringinglow.

"Father came for me next day, and I remember Granny saying: 'Tha' munna bring that lad ageean, as 'e's bin rooarin' an' whimperin' ommost all neet.'"

Dodging the Owler Bar Toll Bar Keeper

Says Mr James Wragg: "I am not a rambler, but if I was younger I soon should be. I am taking great interest in those Clarion Rambler booklets you so kindly sent me, and there is much therein I never knew before. I took one up, and the first thing I saw was in relation to Toll Bar Dodgers. Yes! there have always been dodgers, but never so many as in the last five or ten years before the final finish up of Toll Gates.

"Every succeeding year it became better known what a splendid drive it was to get round Stony Ridge, 'Fox House Inn', Grindleford, Calver, Baslow, and return to Sheffield by Owler Bar. The drivers or parties on the longer route

were liable to tollage on their return journey as they were using two lengths of road – and this is where the trouble came in. Some parties, in all innocence, drove through until they were pulled up by the Toll Keeper, and, of course, they paid. Others thought it a grand freak to 'slip' all the Bars on the new lengths they had travelled on. These 'dodgers' also knew there wasn't one Toll Bar keeper in fifty who could chase them to Sheffield ($7^1/_2$ miles) and take their names and addresses. The whole thing got to an excess, as your little book implies. What was to be done?

How one of the Dodgers was Caught

"A Mr Rodgers, a magistrate, used to call at Owler Bar sometimes for a chat with my father. I think he was a Commissioner of the Roads, and, as luck would have it, one of these toll-dodgers smote through, before his eyes, with a carriage and pair, and refused to draw up. Dad told him that was the sort of thing he had to contend with very often.

"'Oh!' said Mr Rodgers, 'Get hold of half a dozen of 'em and summon 'em to Hemsworth, or Eckington Petty Sessions. We'll make examples of 'em, and it'll get in the papers as well.'

"This is where I came on the scene. Father was too old and stout to give chase, but I was a strong young man, used to running in sports, and with the harriers. Although I could relate others, I will only mention this, my first chase.

"A gig with two men appeared about 100 yards away, but, on approaching the Toll Gate, they whipped up the horse. I made for its head and received a cut across my cheek (with the gutta percha end of the whip lash), that made it bleed for about three inches. Dad said 'Follow them up if you can' – and I did. I reached Moore's livery yard in Eldon Street, off Sheffield Moor, before they got the horse (which was 'all-of-a-lather') out of the shafts.

"Mr George Moore, the horse and cab proprietor, came up and, seeing me in shirt sleeves, and with my cheek bleeding, wanted to know 'what it all meant'. I told him they had defrauded all the Toll Gates from Owler Bar and I wanted their names and addresses. Moore then called us into the office and made the two men put down their names and addresses. Then he let me go, and said: 'I shall want a reckoning with them for bringing this horse home in that state'. So, in the end, they had to pay heavily at Hemsworth and also to the proprietor, for, as it turned out, the horse and trap was hired to Grindleford and back, but, actually, had been driven to Monsal Dale and back – or twice the agreed distance!"

Catching the Pony and Trap Dodgers

Mr James Gregory, a Holmesfield octogenarian who spent some of his early

years in service at 'The Peacock Hotel', at Owler Bar, tells me that the original 'Jack Young', the horse slaughterer, of Pond Street, Sheffield, who, by virtue of his trade, was as well known as the Mayor of Sheffield, had a novel way of catching the 'dodger' who hired his horses and traps. The landlords and ostlers at 'The Peacock' (Owler Bar), 'The Chequers', 'Red Lion' (Grindleford), and Baslow inns, etc., had a standing order to give his horses a 3d. refresher of meal and water whenever they called. The bill was regularly posted to 'Jack', and he often discovered that the 'party' for Owler Bar or Fox House, etc., had been the round journey to Baslow and back.

The Old Publican's Sunday Afternoon Parade
The hiring of 'pony and trap' for a 'drive' into Derbyshire was a common practice until after the opening of the Dore and Chinley Railway (1894) and the advent of the motor car. The Sheffield publican's 'parade' and Sunday afternoon drive (with his wife) to Fox House or Owler Bar, was perhaps the first intrusion and Sabbath breaking upon our Derbyshire-ward roads – and before the day of the bicycle.

The Life of a Toll Bar Keeper
Mr James Wragg continues: "Many people imagine that a Toll Keeper had a nice, easy-going life. Certainly he had plenty of fresh air at Owler Bar. The truth, however, was that he had to be prepared for a very small but regular wage and no commission, and have something else with which to fill in his living, and be a shoemaker, tailor, stone-breaker, or road mender, etc. – and, usually, he had a rent free house and a garden. At the call of 'Gate', he was obliged to get up at any hour, and, in many ways, to bear endless insults from the public. He was tied in for seven days a week, and, unlike today, had no chance of overtime, at 'double time', or 'time and a half'. I have known my dad not to have twelve hours bed in a week. This was long before the Dore and Chinley Line was made, and also in the days, as I well remember, when the Dronfield miners used to run their 'snap dogs' in Hyde Park, Sheffield, and would sometimes work only three days a week. They often caused the over-moor carts and their drivers, who came from Bradwell, Castleton, Edale, and other places, to the Dronfield, Stubley, Oxclose, and Dronfield Woodhouse pits, to spend two days and one night in getting and delivering a load of coal. Then there were the calf-carts which came on their way to Sheffield from the farms at Bakewell, Monyash, Flash, and neighbouring villages."

The Pewit Farm, still the first house on the right side of the road between Owler Bar and Lidgate (Holmesfield), was also a small fire (good) brickyard and a depot for the coal which was led from the small pits, mentioned by Mr Wragg, to await the over-moor customer who, to obtain an early 'cale', would oft-times arrive there considerably before 6am, and leave home sometimes before midnight. This elevated brickyard, worked by Mrs Brown, of the

'Robin Hood Inn' at Millhouses, was stopped about sixty years ago, but clay from this site was carted to Pearson's pottery at Brampton, near Chesterfield, until about twenty years later. I also remember that, when I was a boy, forty odd years ago, Bellamy's carts – Cricket Inn Road, Sheffield, behind 'Cricket Inn' – and many others in the Park district of Sheffield, would often leave home at about 4am to obtain an early 'turn' in loading coal at the Birley Pit, which then stood at the foot of Birley Hill, beside the Sheffield–Eckington Road.

The farmers, in those days, often put up for the night at 'The Peacock Hotel', at Owler Bar, and Mr James Gregory informs me that on Thursday nights, in the sixties, the 'hotel', often enough, was, despite the law, 'open all night'.

The Last Toll at Owler Bar
Mr James Wragg took the last toll at Owler Bar. The gate was to be thrown open at midnight, and this is his story: "A trap was heard coming along Baslow Road at five minutes to the hour, and Dad asked if I would like to take the last toll. Of course, I was fussy enough to do it. 'Gate' was 'hollered out' in the usual way, and 'Coming' was the reply. I was paid 6d., and the men demanded a ticket. I said I would give them one, but they would not need it. 'Why?' was the quick reply. 'Because', said I, 'this, with all other gates, will be thrown open for ever at 12pm.' The driver then said he would have 'taken damned good care I should not have had that tanner if he had known that before' – and drove away cursing like a 'backer' after the 'bookie' had sloped with his winnings".

And the Ghost that Followed
"Just half an hour later I noticed that Dad was looking rather strange and that he kept going to the door. Then he called mother and I 'to see the Ghost'. It looked like half a church, its spire, and all white, standing on a wall. Then it moved and hove in full sight round the bend of the road coming from Holmesfield way with a lot of men about it singing and shouting. Soon they reached the Toll Bar and deposited their precious cargo of straw on the grass. Then a short 'nominy' was said, and a torch was lighted and placed to the bottom of what was my dad's effigy. There was a blaze, I can tell you! When it was burnt to ashes they said another little 'nominy' and then disappeared on the same way, singing as they went. Of course we all laughed away the Ghost."

The Intruder in the Lonely Toll Bar House
Mr Wragg continues: "I have always wondered why so few robberies occurred at these lonely places, and chiefly because there was always a certain amount of money in the Toll Bar house and the keeper must always turn out at the call of 'Gate'. Before there were any 'puffing Billies' or cycles to my aid (the Chesterfield to Sheffield Midland direct railway line was only opened in

1870?) I had to tramp it to Joseph Rodgers & Sons, cutlers, Sheffield, every day, 15 miles a day for six days a week! Those work days were twelve hours, and often I was very tired. One night, however, I was roused by a loud call of 'Gate'. 'Coming' was the reply, and so soon as father got in the porch a rough fellow rushed past and spread himself down on the hearth rug. He was informed that he could not be allowed to stop there, but, in reply, merely told dad to mind his own business, for neither fair words nor foul would move him. Nothing but abuse came from his lips. Just then mother, who was greatly alarmed, called out to me to come downstairs, for 'there was a man in the house who was going to strike father'. But I had heard all, and quickly got half-dressed, and jumped on the floor, heavily. This did the job – for the man was on the road before I could see him."

The Petitioner who Repented
"I may here state that the clergyman, Mr James Hurst, the then vicar of Holmesfield, who took round the petition for abolishing the toll gate, afterwards petitioned again for their reinstatement, the reason being, this time, because the rates had doubled and trebled. It was, of course a waste of time. Lord Beaconsfield, I think, was the chief member to defend the Toll Bar system in Parliament, he saying that the only people who contributed were the users of the roads."

"My grandmother and Uncle James became very ill and both died within seven days. The cottage was closed a short time until the toll gate was thrown open. My parents then moved in to the old Owler Bar homestead again. All honour to my parents, who insisted on giving all their lads good trades. My sisters are both dead, also a younger brother, age nineteen, who died at the Toll Bar."

The Vicar and the Road Surveyor
Mr James Gregory informs me that the Rev. James Hurst was a regular attender at the Road Commissioners' meetings at the 'Peacock', Owler Bar. He regularly had a good feed and a bottle of sherry to himself, and often got merry. Mr Bland, of Barlow, the road surveyor, who conveyed him in a trap, regularly dined off a basin of milk and 'pobs!' Mr Roberts, of Abbeydale Hall, was a prominent road commissioner, and at that time, in the sixties, the Rev. J. Hurst would be delighted with a bumper collection of 15 shillings on Sundays.

The Runaway Brewery Horses
Before the Dore and Chinley line was opened, beer was always transported over the moors in brewery wagons driven by two and, on occasion, four horses. The practice only died since the war, with the increasing growth of the motor and petrol wagon. The roads, in those days, were more like hills and holes than billiard boards, and there was usually more splash than side-slip between Owler Bar and Baslow.

Rawson's, the Pond Street brewers, had a bonny pair of chestnuts – mother and daughter – and the youngster loved to get home in a hurry. On the return journey, after leaving the Wooden Pole, she would feel the breech band (going down hill) and set off at a gallop, and force her mother to keep pace. Says Mr Wragg: "Father never closed the toll gate until he knew Rawson's wagon had returned. The firm did not approve the galloping business, and tried fresh drivers. One, I believe 'got the sack'."

At length, Rawson, junior, decided to test matters and do a journey with the driver. The runaway tried her game on him, but means were taken, on this occasion, to stop her gallop, and, shortly afterwards, a cure was effected by parting the daughter from her mother.

Twenty-four-hour Journeys with Beer

Mr James Gregory reminds me that Rawson's brewery wagonners at that time made regular journeys from Sheffield to Longnor and back (50 miles) within the twenty-four hours. These four-horse wagons passed Broadfield Toll Bar (near today's Abbeydale Picture Palace and $1^1/_2$ miles from the centre of Sheffield) a few minutes after midnight. They would leave one load at Bakewell (16 miles), and take the spare horses to pull up the steep hill to Monyash, and, after leaving part of the second load there, proceed to Longnor via Crowdecote Bridge. The tolls on these broad-tyred wagons, which carried probably two tons of beer over these rough, steep roads, are stated to have been as follows: Broadfield 4/-, Green Oak (Totley) 2/-, Baslow Bridge 4/-, Monyash 4/-, and Crowdecote 2/-; the half-tolls being for toll bars on the same length of road. It was therefore necessary to complete the return journey within twenty-four hours and avoid double tolls – or twenty-five hours from Pond Street Brewery.

Tennant's, the Sheffield brewers, also had a beer stores at Taddington (21 miles from Sheffield), which, 'kept' by a Mr Stones, supplied Flagg and Chelmorton and the local farmers. The Longnor beer stores was kept by a Mr Bradbury.

Mr Gregory says that on one occasion the wagoner and his assistant were asleep and omitted to put on the slipper, near Hurdlow Plain. One of the horses slipped on the hill and was killed, and the men 'got away' with the yarn that they had lost the horse – a 40 guineas animal reared at Woodthorpe Hall, near Totley.

The Coal Carter gets a Thrashing

There was a Joseph Bingham at Cowley, who owned two horses and carts, and often led coal or slack to Stoney Middleton and the New Engine and Ladywash lead mines, etc. His stepson, Sammy, a somewhat illiterate young man, usually went with the horses. On the return journey, says Mr Wragg, he often 'put up' at the 'Chequers Inn' at Froggatt, stayed until he was 'put out' at turning out time, and, as I heard from another source, sometimes stayed all night. Many times the horses started for home 'on their own' and, on occasions, when the Owler Bar toll gate was left open, they arrived home first. Usually, however, they were stopped at the bar until Sammy had reeled across the five miles of moorland road, and Mr Wragg, more than once, has seen the first horse asleep and nodding when the gate was opened. One night, 'Sammy' must have fallen asleep or taken off the 'breech band' when coming up Froggatt Edge with two loads of stone, for, says Mr J. Gregory, one horse came crashing down the hill into the toll bar gate, and he came outside the 'Owler Bar Inn' in time to turn away the second horse from even greater trouble. The horse 'stuck' in the broken toll gate, but, fortunately, was not hurt.

Young 'Sammy' got his 'benefit' eventually, for, one night, 'old Bingham' called at the toll bar and had a thick stick in his hand. He was tired of waiting until past midnight sometimes three or four nights a week, before the horses had 'suppered up', and he could go to bed. There was, he thought, 'just about time enough to get to the 'Chequers Inn' before 'turningout' time', and, if he found young Sammy there, 'he would break that stick over his damned 'eead'. The wayward dissolute was there 'right enough', and there was some squealing when 'Sammy got the business end of the stick on his body', and, says Mr Wragg, "each had a cart and horse to himself when they came through the toll bar that night."

The Ordnance Surveyors levelling up the Roads
"I was at home one day when Sammy came through the gate with his carts. The Ordnance surveyors were at work (in the seventies), standing on the grass margin, and, with poles in the ground, planning out their work. Sammy drew his horses to the side, and, going plump to the men, said: 'What's yo' chaps after wi' them sticks?' They looked at Sammy, but did not reply. 'Then', quoth Sammy, 'are you gooin' to see if th' world's gooin' rahnd?', and one of the men replied, 'No! we're going to have these roads levelled up and make it so much easier for your horses.' I cracked out laughing, and that ended the fun".

The Old Road Coaches
"When I was a boy", says Mr Wragg, "I distinctly remember two stage coaches which passed Owler Bar for Matlock and Buxton. The yellow one, called 'The Enterprise', driven by James Ashmore, went through Bakewell, and the horses were changed at 'The Peacock'. The red coach, for Buxton, was called the 'Lucy Long', and, driven by George Sims, changed horses at Owler Bar. I often marvelled that, during snow time and pitch dark nights, neither of these coaches ever got off the road". The vehicles, in those days, did not light up the moorsides for miles with their 'searchlights', but, on the contrary, carried candles in the side lamps.

The Roadside Stone that Wept and Smiled

Mr Hoyland, the tall, strong, merry and still pranksome lithographic printer (Sheffield), of seventy-eight summers, who now lives at Hathersage, says that he also remembers George Sims. Hoyland, in his youthful days, often walked to Edensor, and, on his first journey by this coach, George Sims, after leaving Owler Bar, pitched his driver's yarn upon the stranger after this manner.

"Ther' wer' an awful murder done on this rooadside a long time sin', and yo'll see a 'eead sticking aht o' t' moor on t' right side o' t' rooad. When it rains yo'll see it wi' tears i' its eyes, and when t' sun shines yo'll see it smilin' all o'er its face".

This 'eead' was a low stone, shaped like a human head, which formerly stood on the right of the road, a little on the Baslow side of the gate and drive (left of roadside) which leads to the Ramsley gamekeeper's lodge.

Mr James Wragg also remembers this stone, but (like the old millstone which, until the war, stood by the cart road to Parsons House Farm, at the junction of the Fox House and Ankirk Roads) it was a target for the boys and passers-by, and much disfigured.

My informant also reminds me that Samuel Ward, of Holmesfield – the roadman who used to mark the roadside walls with whitewash, to measure off the yards of stone road metal to be broken up by the parish stone breakers – was also accustomed to whitewash this stone 'eead'. "And", says Mr Wragg, "it didn't look nice when you passed it on a dark night."

Basket Making at Owler Bar

Mr Wragg believes that his family of Wragg, which today is represented in Holmesfield, Totley, Dronfield, Woodhouse, Froggatt, and elsewhere, came originally from the east, about two hundred years ago, and settled in Crich, as basket makers. They chiefly made the sower's basket commonly in use forty years ago. The material principally was hazel, riven oak, or ash, and the same as used for the old-fashioned coal and coke baskets, which only differed in shape. Then they turned their hand more to the coal basket, which, by the old Derbyshire folk is called 'whisket'. His grandfather, Thomas Wragg, and his family, born at Crich(?), carried on the same trade in Dronfield. Thomas Wragg married early, and moved to the little Owler Bar cottage or toll house, which then had a whitewashed front, two rooms, green shutters, and a thatched roof. He worked at Dronfield until he built the little shop adjoining the house, and then commenced the basket trade at Owler Bar on his own account.

The 'Rough Country' at Owler Bar One Hundred Years Ago

Mr Wragg's father and uncle often remarked about the rough country about

Owler Bar nearly a hundred years ago. There was bracken, gorse, rushes, heather, and blackberry bushes all around, and although the fields were enclosed and cleared after the Holmesfield Enclosure Award of 1820, some of it was finished during Mr Wragg's boyhood. He well remembers gathering blackberries and bilberries on the roadside between Owler Bar and Totley day school, but today, thanks to the Fearnley Corporation motor buses, the blackberry gatherers from Sheffield will almost take them out of our moorside gardens, and the roadside blackberries have almost vanished from every main road.

The Family and Besom Making
Thomas Wragg had three sons named, in order, James, John and William, and three daughters named Mary, Charlotte and Letitia. His wife died before the children were 'able to do for themselves'. This Thomas Wragg married a second time, a woman from the old-fashioned but now ruined and partly demolished and scarcely recognisable farm house and buildings near Dore and Totley station. (I remember when a boy that this farm house – which had swings near the house – was a centre for Sunday School outings and also the playing field stretched to behind today's post-war garage and to the wood on the steep bank beyond the two sets of Dore and Chinley railway lines.) The daughters were neglected by their step-mother and pushed out in service all too soon. James, Mr Wragg's uncle, and John, his father, were kept at home with grandfather at basket and besom making for shops in Sheffield. His father, John Wragg, left home, and first started toll-collecting, alone, at Slate Pit Dale, about a mile from Holymoorside and Walton.

File Cutting in Moorwood Lane
The other brother, William, was put to file cutting, and, about seventy years ago, was cutting files in the brick cottage 300 yards N.W. of the house where I now live and 'Pinders Farm', properly known as Moorwoods Farm (Moorwood Lane), and occupied since 1921 by Mr Creswick, a descendant of the historic family who lived at Ewden Lodge. All the Wragg family, except the three daughters, are buried in the corner of Holmesfield churchyard, nearest to Cartledge Lane.

The Origin of Owler Bar and 'The Peacock'
The land round about, at the time Mr Wragg's grandfather moved to the Owler Bar Toll Cottage, was all moorland, and the Toll Bar, at that period, was, says he, nothing more or less than an Owler pole stretched across the road. This, according to my informant, is the origin of the name of Owler Bar, and also the explanation of this mystery name. Mr Wragg's father was born on 11 February 1811, and when a boy, as I have heard previously, played among the stones when the 'Peacock Inn' and the new toll house, just below, were in course of erection. (The Rutland Estate records would prove the date but it is apparent that this imitation eighteenth-century inn was built after or

about the time of the opening of the present Sheffield–Baslow Road, and possibly not earlier than 1818. 'The Peacock' (Rowsley) and 'Fox House Inn', built in similar style, are also Ducal whims which give the idea of age to comparatively modern buildings.) It was, he says, a great improvement setting the main Sheffield Road further back and bringing the Toll Gate front to where it is now. The two sets of the old toll bar stone stoops were bought or taken by the late Mr George Crawshaw (died 1928) and fixed in Moorwood Lane when improving his newly acquired three-farm estate.

Mr Wragg's uncle James was always very delicate, and had to stick at basket and broom-making along with his father. His dad, however, was strong, and did all the heavy work on the land. He was also the carter who took the work from home to Sheffield. He was, like all good country men, fond of horses and a young and daring rider, whether on bare-back or otherwise – and, by the by, one of the distant relations of the Wraggs (Harry) 'has just won the Derby'.

Frightening Thieves with a Hatchet at Stony Ridge Bar
Mr Wragg's father moved from Slatepit Dale to the Stony Ridge Toll Bar (destroyed during war time), which was then a rough and lonely place for a bachelor. It was there he held at bay two violent tramps for over two hours, and said they must have caught a glimpse of him behind the door holding a woodman's hatchet ready to chop the first man who got inside. They went away, however, before daylight, and did no harm.

His 'dad' tired of single blessedness, and, looking for a suitable mate, soon found one. His courting was seldom and sweet, for it was necessary to arrange with his brother at home (Owler Bar) to go and mind the Toll Bar in his absence, while he went courting Mary.

A Stony Ridge Toll Bar Wedding
His parents were married at Dore church (4/9/1844), at the time it was made a separate parish from Dronfield – 1844. (The old Dore chapel of ease was rebuilt in 1828, and the new church chancel in 1896.)

It was rather romantic, for his dad, unlike his brother James, 'was a bit shy', and 'didn't want to see a lot of curiosity-mongering and skylarking at his wedding'. So he arranged with the Rev. Richard Martin, an Irish clergyman (the first vicar of Dore, from 1844 to 1849, and curate-in-charge of the parish – then under Dronfield from 1840) to mumble out the banns each week. His father said that the parson did this job very successfully, for there was scarcely anybody in church when the party turned up fully an hour late, and the parson and those present were shivering.

The reason was that his father had directed the bridal party of his mother and the best man to turn through the stile opposite Wing's Farm (the ruins by

Dore and Totley station) and follow the footpath until they met him. They reached the stile all right, but it was already ankle deep in the fast falling snow. They then lost the track and wandered about until the bridegroom found them.

However, they got properly wedded, and then plodded homewards, knee-deep, up the road to Stony Ridge Toll Bar. It was a cold reception for his mother, for the moment his uncle set his eyes on her, he walked out and went home to Owler Bar. His mother 'began housekeeping with a downright good cry'.

Half a Cart Wheel for a Fender
There was half a cart wheel for a fender, and not much furniture, but the house was scrupulously clean. More than once that day his mother wished herself at Sheffield again. However, she settled down to make the best of it, and "I can tell you that never a couple, up to their golden wedding or after, lived a more comfortable and happy life."

How the Parson was Offended
On the Sunday after the marriage, Mr Martin, the clergyman, appeared at Stony Ridge Toll Bar house for the purpose of presenting a bible and prayer book to the newly married couple, this being, I think, the custom in former times. His father, however, grievously offended him by saying, in a joke, that "He had better brought a good pair of blankets". Mr Martin was an Irishman, and he never spoke to him afterwards.

The Poor Parson of Dore
This first, and early-Victorian, vicar of Dore, according to Mr C. Gill (Totley) and Mr Gregory (Holmesfield), would go to the 'Hare and Hounds' or 'Devonshire Arms' (Dore), and, crossing his legs, to hide one knee, place his hat over the other one to hide the holes in his trousers. I am also told that he would, similarly, place his hands over his elbows, and that his clothes were patched like those of a road tramp. He, like the famous Parson Aldred, liked his 'drinkin'.

Mr Wragg's father, in all, had forty years of Toll Bar work, as follows: Slatepit Dale, Matlock, Calver, Baslow and Owler Bar (1st time in charge), Mosborough, Intake, Owler Bar (2nd time), Stoney Ridge (2nd time) and Owler Bar (3rd time).

Bitten by an Adder on the Roadside
"One summer night, about 11pm," says Mr Wragg, "a man called at our house. His thumb was tied up, and he was white and trembling like a leaf. He wanted the nearest doctor, and father recommended him to go to Dronfield, five miles away, where he would have two chances, Dr Bolton or Dr Rooth. It

appeared that he had sat upon a large stone by the roadside to have some 'snap'. He put his stick beside the stone, but it slipped and fell on the ground. Then, when he was picking it up again, he felt something pierce the end of his thumb, and saw an adder sliding away. Fortunately, he pulled off a boot-lace, tied it tightly on the proper side of the first joint, and stopped the venom from travelling further into his system."

The Lady Lodger at the Toll Bar

Mr James Wragg tells an interesting anecdote about the lady lodger at the Owler Bar old toll bar house. It was a dark December evening, and a heavy mist lay over Owler Bar and Brown Edge. Presently, there was a gentle knock. Father opened the door, and was confronted by a tall, thin, but very lady-like person, who appeared too agitated to make him understand beyond the fact that she wished to see the lady of the house. So mother sent, and found that her visitor was well-educated, and very respectably dressed. She invited her inside, and soon made her a cup of tea and some toast. Then, in conversation, it appeared that the lady had started to walk from Bakewell (nine miles away) to Sheffield, and became frightened in the mist. She tried to run, but couldn't, and even the flutter of a grouse wing made her heart leap to her mouth. She was quite exhausted, and 'Could mother find her a bed for the night'. She couldn't promise this much, for her son, who was expected home at 11pm, would require the only spare bed.

Then father chimed in, and suggested that she might go to 'The Peacock Hotel' close by, where they always had spare beds. But, oh dear, the lady had a perfect horror of public houses, and she had lost everything since leaving home – watch and seal, and purse and satchel, and 'God knows what', says Mr Wragg. She would 'sit in the chair all night'. But this couldn't be granted, for, being a toll bar, the keeper had to sleep downstairs, and also, there was no upstairs to the house. "Then father suggested a rough bed for me on the floor of the little back room, and he was sure that Jim wouldn't mind when he knew the position the lady was in."

"Then", proceeds Mr James Wragg, "the gold-fingered guest had retired when I got home, and, having to walk to Sheffield [Joseph Rodgers & Co.], and be there at 8am, I never got a look on her fair face.

"The lady arose at daybreak, and mother made her another nice cup of tea and some toast, and, with a load of thanks and promises to repay all her kindness, she pittapatted down the road towards Sheffield, and 'the very first thing she would do, would be to post something off to mother' – whether she wanted it or not. But when I reached home next night, mother had spread the sheets, quilts and blankets all over the house, for this sparkling lady had left a thriving colony behind her. The landlady of 'The Peacock' had been called in, and soon told her what the lady had left (in the way of bugs and lice), and that she must put everything in boiling water at once and, as mother said, 'They did get a boiling'.

"The fine lady lodger's promises were like pie crusts, and so mother had to be content with what the lady had left behind her."

'Jonty' Pinder's Grouse Shooting

Mr Wragg remembers the men who, at grouse shooting time, came near the old toll bar house, waving flags and shaking rattles, and even firing guns at random, and it always seemed a silly and costly proceeding. There was, however, some fun mixed with the farce and expense.

It was perhaps about 1859 or 1860, and Jonathan Pinder, of Moorwoods Farm, on the lane where I reside – and a farm about whose transfer into the next hands was the subject of local stories – was for a time 'a bit of a teaser' to the grouse preserver (who solved many problems, such as Pinder's, long ago, by the only safe method of obtaining the sporting rights over the adjacent land) and also the corn-poaching grouse.

Jonathan (or 'Jonty') seldom 'let a chance go by', and, although his brother Thomas let his brother do most of the shooting, there is no doubt they got most of the game they required. One of Jonathan's fields adjoined the land attached to the old Owler Bar toll bar, and, at shooting times, or just before, the two Pinders would place about a dozen sheaves of oats in the middle of the field to attract the birds from the moor.

Then the fun would commence. Seven or eight 'tenters' (or assistant keepers) were always engaged during the shooting season to drive the birds back to the moor, and also to watch for poachers. These men were supplied with flags, rattles, and even guns, to frighten the grouse away from the fields, and says Mr Wragg, "I have seen 'Old Jonty' on one side of his wall and seven tenters on the other doing sentry duty, waving flags and rattling, and shouting themselves hoarse. These tenters sheltered and lunched in my uncle's basket shop, adjoining the house, and sometimes left him precious little room in which to work." It appears, from another source (Mr J. Gregory) that the Duke of Rutland, according to Pinder, would not pay sufficient for the shooting rights, and Pinder, for a period, shot over it himself or let it to a Mr Dobbs. The Duke's beaters and watchers, therefore, were also engaged in the extra task of spoiling 'Jonty's shoot'. The difference, however, was solved after a time, and the sport of grouse-shooting 'safeguarded'.

How Judgment fell upon an Unorthodox Sportsman

There was a certain John Stone, a Totley horsebreaker, who had, or thought he had, perhaps sixty years ago, a private shooting range 'of his own', not far from today's military shooting range at the foot of Totley Moss. John fixed his own times for gun practice, and (like another local resident in much later years, who successfully went beside the roadside walls popping off grouse with an air gun), his targets, which he generally aimed at soon after dawn, were four-legged or feathered ones. 'John' had a few of the Duke's grouse in his day, and the so-called 'Sporting Duke' was no particular benefactor to the countryside and the 'safeguarding' of production of food and meat.

However, judgment appeared to fall upon him one day, for, in scrambling over a wall, the gun 'went off', and nearly blew off his arm. He was taken to the Hospital, and, although the doctor said that his arm was doomed, he would not have chloroform. He told the doctor to 'get on with the job and he wouldn't give him any trouble', and, although, as he admitted, he 'grew rather shaky towards the end', he watched the operation throughout.

The Poachers borrow another Poacher's Dog
Stone had a somewhat slow sheep cur dog called 'Wag', and Mr C. Gill, a Totley mason, declares that "he could send him out for a rabbit any time and he'd bring one back". Some of the Totley or Dore poachers on occasions loosed this dog, and unknown to Stone, had the use of him for a night's poaching.

Stone lived at the little farm at the corner of Stable Lane – going towards Totley Moss and the cricket ground. The house higher up, almost opposite the present Rifle Range house and ex-farm, was once a 'one up and one down' erection with a cheek-by-jowl stable attached, and 'Fatty' Coates, a well-known character, built a chamber over the stable.

'Fright Healing' at Thickwood Lodge
"Now," says Mr Wragg, "let me give you a miracle that happened at the gamekeeper's Thickwood Lodge," the gamekeeper's lodge S.W. of the junction of Moorwood Lane, and the Baslow–Sheffield Road, 600 yards N.N.E. of the 'Peacock Hotel', at Owler Bar. "You have read about 'faith healing', but – here is an example of 'Fright Healing'. The then gamekeeper, Henry Peat, uncle of the late David Peat, of Warren Lodge, at Curbar, had a daughter, a nice young girl far in the teens, who, taken very ill and bedfast for thirteen weeks, was given up by everybody – and also the doctor. Her father, unfortunately, became very demented, and it was unsafe for the mother and daughter. All knives and firearms were removed, and someone had to sleep with him. This little job fell to me for a time. However, an improvement took place, and I went home."

"One night, however, Peat found a revolver, and pointed it at his daughter. She was terrified, and, somehow, struggled out of bed in her nightdress, and, although pitch dark, she found the way to the main road and into Andrew's (Mooredge) farm yard, 300 yards nearer Totley. They took her in for the time being, until her father was removed to Mickleover. Later on, she returned to her mother at Thickwood Lodge, and was a complete cure and wonder to all who knew her. She was, literally, a dying girl who was 'fright-healed', and afterwards married, but died under an operation in a Sheffield hospital.

A Keeper's Treasure on Big Moor

"Here's a job for seekers of Treasure Trove," says Mr Wragg, "but all the clue I know is that the prize is somewhere on the Big Moor. I related previously how the gamekeeper Henry Peat fright-healed his bedridden daughter, but all this has its sad side. Henry Peat often called at our house on Sunday mornings for a smoke and a chat. One Sunday, however, he seemed to be trifling with his pipes and pouches. I never saw a set exactly like them. The pipe had a large, ornamented, tapering head, and was blackish-brown in colour, apparently the result of much smoking. His pouch, probably of pigskin, was beautifully marked, and his tobacco box looked like silver, but we were most puzzled by the fact that we never saw him use them.

"The poor fellow was 'going wrong' then, and the Sunday morning after he made no attempt at smoking, and when Dad spoke to him about it, he said he had 'buried all the lot on the moor'. I have an idea they lay not far from his little hut, or near where poor Hodkin, the herbalist, was found after one year and ten months' exposure."

The hut was in an ideal place, not 100 yards inside Big Moor, and there used to be a stone seat under the wall next to the moor, between Bucka House and the 'Gypsy Lane', now called Occupation Lane – where gypsies no longer camp and steal the rabbits and grouse. Here Peat would sit and soliloquise, and have an expansive view, and, if it rained, he could pop over the wall to his sod-built hut, which was roofed over with heather.

The Miser at 'The Peacock Hotel'

There is said to be hidden money buried somewhere in Bucker (Bucka) Field, or in the walls, but this intimation will not increase the number of trespassers or make a 1929 rush to the Big Moor 'Klondyke'. A man named Thomas Coates, uncle to the then landlord of the 'Peacock Inn', at Owler Bar, came to live there for a time. He was known to have money, but, not unlike some of today's Derbyshire and other farmers, he would, when possible, never use the Bank, but preferred to have his money handy at all times. (This was a practice not always so 'simple as it looked', for it could also be useful in 'dodging' the income tax man. This method, however, is also known among agriculturalists in many countries in Europe and even in India – Punjab etc. – where, despite all criticism of 'British Rule', the native hides his money, the taxes cannot all be gathered, and some of the required improvements cannot be made.) Mr Wragg says that he must have been approaching eighty years of age. He was rather slovenly in dress, and I am also told that he swore like one of

Wellington's troopers during the privations of the Peninsular War.

He often could be seen wandering about the walls of Bucka Field and Lindley Piece (second field left, going roadwards, from 'Peacock Hotel', towards Wooden Pole – cleared by a Lindley?), but one day he went 'Holmesfield way' with a cart, and it upset on the way.

He returned home on the top of a load of coals, with a broken leg. No one could persuade him to go to the Hospital, and the broken leg was set at home. He would not lie in bed until the bones were set or healed properly, and some years afterwards he died without revealing the whereabouts of his 'hidden treasure'.

Mr James Gregory, however, says that on one occasion, in the sixties, he was in 'The Peacock' at Owler Bar, and quietly examined Coate's pockets. He found that the 'treasure', in his inside vest pocket, was only a roll of the old-time packets of paper in which the 'pennyworths' of pipe tobacco were wrapped.

A Belted Knight (1564) has a Fourpenny Feast
"You know more about the old pack-horse roads, but," says Mr Wragg, "if you take a spade and dig a trench about 18 inches deep, one end pointing to Bucka Field, the other to Smeekly Lane (Carr Road), you will find some deep-worn flags. I think you mention this bridle road in one of the Clarion books. Suppose we leave the corner of Calver Field – that is the field which from Owler Bar divides Baslow Road and Froggatt Road – and follow the Salters Brook about 200 yards down, we come on the spot."

This was perhaps the main pack road from Sheffield to Baslow, the route being from Holmesfield, Lidgate across Salterbrook, Big Moor and Eaglestone Flat to Baslow.

It is also the route travelled by Sir George Vernon, of Haddon Hall, when, in 'The Steward's Accounts Preserved at Haddon Hall', a pamphlet and selection published by the late Mr W.A. Carrington, there was an entry of: 'payd for bread and cheyse and drynke at holmsfelde as my M(aste)r came from shefeld the xxviijth of september (1564) iiij' – or 4d. – and it was apparent that, on this visit, nine days earlier, the steward had given him 10/- for playing at dice with 'homffrey ffulwood'.

The Lost House on the Baslow Road
Mr Wragg refers to the cottage which formerly stood inside the Bucka Field near to the Baslow main road – at the corner of Bucka Field, and near the Occupation Lane which connects with 'Cordwell' Lane. It must have been built by the first Thomas Hattersley, about one hundred years ago, and it is

said to have been pulled down for the double reason that it was a decrepit erection and that the houses of semi squatters close to the moor were not popular with the shooting fraternity. The first Thomas, who was also a pot-seller, died, and his son ('Moor Bird Tom'), also named Thomas, lived there many years, and, says Mr Wragg, "I just remember him." The third Hattersley died some six years ago, at about eighty-three years of age.

Thomas 'No. 2' was the parish 'pounder' or 'pinder', who 'pinned' or 'pounded' stray cattle or horses in the little pinfold adjoining the garden of the old Owler Bar toll bar, and waited until the owner appeared on the scene. There was often a good 'row' about the charges made for his trouble and expense in feeding the lost animals.

Hattersley's house, in the later stages, was allowed to get into a disgraceful state. There was no whitewash on the outer walls and no paint on the woodwork, while the windows were filled with the old-fashioned bull-eye green glass, and the broken squares with rags. The occupant was, on several occasions, remonstrated with by Mr Nesfield, the Duke's agent, and, more particularly, on the approach of the shooting season, when the 'parties' would be able to 'see the sight'. But the warnings were unheeded, and finally the house was condemned, and, despite Hattersley's rage, pulled down in 1866, and he removed to Lidgate. Hattersley appeared to believe that the house was, or should have been, his own, but somehow or other the Duke's representative, 'knew better'. The exact site, going from 'The Peacock Hotel' towards Baslow, is the first field beyond Saltersitch Bridge and 20 yards inside the (Bucka) Field. The roadside wall is built upon 12 feet of the projecting foundation wall of the old house, and from the evidence of mortar at the foot of the wall, it was two stories 'lengthwise' – left side of the road.

The story, taken from the oldest inhabitants, is that the first Hattersley 'cleared' some three fields about the time of the Holmesfield Enclosure Award (1820) and built the little cottage from the surface stone he found hereabouts. He is said to have 'signed a paper' and, for the first few years, paid a nominal acknowledgment – and to have believed that the house was his own. It is also admitted that, in later years, the house, in bad repair, was an eyesore to the Duke and his shooting parties, and that the then landlord, Mr Coates, wished to add the land to his Peacock Hotel Farm.

'The Peacock Hotel' and the Hosts
The older generation will often declare that the palmy days of the moorside farmers and coaching inn were before the advent of the motor, and when, although the day's work was long and money less plentiful, there was generally time to stop for a drink and a chat during the journey. 'The Peacock Hotel' is companion to 'Fox House Inn', although its history (dating from about 1818) is less prosy. A list of hosts, not guaranteed to be exhaustive,

begins with a Mr Green, and includes William ('Humpy') Hattersley (a fifteenth-century Holmesfield family); Mrs Hattersley, *née* Pinder; William Wall Coates, of Dore Moor (1861–7) who married this lady, Mrs Coates; and Mr F. Armitage, who wedded the latter. William Hutchinson Brougham was there in 1884–1903, and his widow, Anne Eliza, 1903–23, and, since that date, her son, John Hutchinson Brougham, who, two years ago, purchased the house and farm at the Duke's second sale of moorlands and adjoining properties in 1927.

The majority of the recorded incidents centre from a little before to shortly after the time of the well-known but short-lived Coates (1861–7), a member of a Dore Moor and Dore family, who have given dozens of anecdotes to the 'natives' of the village which is rapidly being smothered by the quick march of Sheffield southwestwards.

The Trotting Matches at Owler Bar

It is tolerably well known among the 'ancients' of Holmesfield and Totley that sixty and more years ago there were many trotting matches between Owler Bar and towards Ramsley Moor top – one to three miles length – and 'with big guns too'. Mr Wragg says: "I don't think my father ever drove the horses in a race, but he trained some for the events, and, though still only a boy, his management of horses reached the ears of the principals of the Duke of Westminster's stables. The then Duke sent one of his stewards or trainers to try and arrange with my grandfather to allow him to take up a post at the Duke's stables, and, of course, promised good pay." This would have just suited him, but his father, a good Wesleyan, would, under no consideration, give consent. Moreover, there would be no one left competent to work outside the home and do the carting, or go in the woods at felling time (chiefly Ecclesall Woods and Smeekley) and pick and measure the pieces suitable for their work. His father, although so young, and never having a day's schooling, was a master of the slide-rule. Any woodman could cheat his brother James, or his father, but they couldn't cheat 'Jack'.

The Celebrated 'Blazing Bob'

His father trained a horse called 'Ling Cropper', which won a good few trotting matches, but the horse called 'Blazing Bob' won more. Until 1885, in the little parlour in the 'Peacock Hotel' at Owler Bar, there was a large painting of this wonderful trotter, but the Broughams gave it to George Lowe, at the Monsal Dale, Headstones, inn. These trotting matches, usually, were held early in the morning, and once, Mr Wragg was gathering mushrooms in Bucka Field when the second 'Blazing Bob' flashed by. One day it was driven from Owler Bar to Manchester and back, and when his father opened the gate it was 'all of a lather'. It was taken into the stable, and, in ten minutes, 'dropped down dead'. The 'boozy' landlord-owner (Coates) then received a 'wigging' from Wragg senior.

Shifting the Mile Stone before a Race

The following story of one of 'Blazing Bob's' victories has been verified from one who remembers the event. The horse, in the sixties, was backed to trot a measured mile in three minutes, and the hotel owner, Mr W.W. Coates, and Messrs Jack Young, James Boothroyd, Mr Eastwood and others, backed it heavily. The course was between the eighth milestone, two-thirds of a mile S.W. of the 'Peacock' and the seventh milestone, nearer to Sheffield and opposite Thickwood Lodge. Tom Hattersley ('Moor Bird Tom'), who still lived in the long-lost 'Bucka House', had a good fund of racing man's wit, and, on this occasion, demonstrated his ability. The horse ran its course and won, but, during the previous night, Tom moved the eighth milestone a good hundred yards nearer to Sheffield, and 'Blazing Bob' obtained a useful bit of what is known as racing man's 'Sammy' or start.

The landlord and owner, Coates, in commenting on this (for him) successful trick, declared that: "If it only cum off once in twenty times it reckoned when it did." The secret did not leak out for 'quite a long time' afterwards.

Mr Charles Gill, a Totley mason, declares that, possibly, the last 'trotting match' in this district was about 1898, between 'Fox House Inn' and 'Whirlow Bridge Inn', and the participants' horses owned by Messrs 'Jack' Gilmour ('Porter Cottage Inn', Sharrow) and the late 'Jack' Atkinson, the well-known carting contractor, of Brightside Lane. The 'match' took place in the early morning, before the air was breathed over. The result in this instance was another 'case' at Dronfield or Eckington and a fine for, I presume, furious driving or, to the danger of the public.

Prize Fighting near Owler Bar

Another feature at and near Owler Bar, in the old days, was prize-fighting with the 'raw uns'. Mr Wragg says that he always knew, when, perhaps an hour before dawn, his father let through the bar one or two conveyances, followed by a crowd of several hundreds on foot, there would be another brutal exhibition down Cordwell Lane, in the Smeekley Field (half a mile lower down on the right), which his ancestor had allotted to him in lieu of the piece taken from the toll-bar land when the Sheffield Road was diverted and 'The Peacock Hotel' was built. This field, however, was too near the wood, and, being infested with summer flies, the cattle rebelled, and jumped the fences, and the land was disposed of.

A Forgotten Road Diversion

The old cart road from Sheffield, which formerly went from Dore and by Oldhay Bridge and Totley Bents, can still be traced. It passed behind the small plantation on the flat, beyond 'Cross Scythes', where we have the windings of the present highway and the only windy and PROPERLY named 'Devil's Elbow' in the district. Then it followed the present road and, by today's Totley

Brickyard, through the yard and buildings of the modern Mooredge Farm (corner of Moorwoods Lane), and, still on the left, to the side of the old (1781) toll bar, and a bifurcation turned to the right, behind the site of the 'Peacock Hotel'. It is also observable in the first moor field beyond the hotel, on the right side of the road to Froggatt Edge.

The Holmesfield Enclosure provided for the present diversion past the Hotel, and for which the toll bar beside the hotel was built. A slice of land was taken from one of the small fields connected with the old toll bar cottage, and the small Smeekley Field, about half a mile down 'Cordwell' Lane (Horsleygate Lane) on the right, was given in exchange – in the often, to small holders of land, inconvenient Enclosure Act method. There was plenty of bracken for bedding, and an abundance of blackberries, wild roses, cowslips, and rabbits in this field.

Another Feature of the Past
'Fatty' Coates, another brother of the landlord of the 'Peacock', was a saw grinder, who lived at Lane Head, Totley, and, like a sheep-dog, was supposed to eat one meal a day.

One day, probably over fifty years ago, he engaged with a Sheffielder to eat a leg of mutton. The 'match' took place at the 'Peacock', and it was agreed that whoever failed to eat his 'leg' should pay for the feast. 'Fatty' soon put away his own portion, but, whether designedly or otherwise, the Sheffielder's 'leg', like fashionable venison, was somewhat 'high', and he failed to consume it. 'Fatty', however, came to the rescue and ate the lot.

Happily, these once popular public house 'contests' and exhibitions of gluttony, practically, passed away with the Victorian era.

The Man She Would not Love
There was once a suicide at the 'Peacock Inn', about 1863. A coal carter, named Richard Gregory, from Calver, who generally came with two horses and carts, used to bait his horses at the 'Peacock' at dinner time. Richard, his father and brother, worked the small lime kiln at Calver, Richard being the bad lad of the family, who gave way to drink. At the 'Peacock', he fell in love with one of the servants, but she didn't fall in love with him. Still he followed and pestered her in the hope that, eventually, she would make him happy. But the more he tried the more she refused, until, one day, he said he would make an end of himself before he got home.

He stayed in the tap room, singing and drinking, until William Coates, the landlord, told him to 'supper-up' his horses and get to bed, for "there was one made for him", and he must get off home next morning. The morning dawned, but no Gregory came downstairs, and it was found that he had cut his throat in the stackyard.

'Kess' Green, the Moorland Shepherd

The series may fittingly be closed with a story of a well-known shepherd. Kess (or Kester – for Christopher) Green was one of the Duke of Rutland's shepherds for wintering of sheep on Longshaw Moors, who, in later years, retired to Curbar. I once met the late 'Jake' Green, his son, and the keeper at Piper House near Strawberry Lee Farm, perhaps about 1912, after doing some researches on the site of the ancient (Beauchief Abbey) monastic farmhouse which stood by the three decaying trees on the horizon, known locally as 'The Three Ships'. (I was informed that most of the old shaped and dressed stone from the ruins of Strawberry Lea Farm were carted away, many years ago, by Mr Coates, and used in some of the houses, etc., in the Dore New Road. There is, however, one large shaped corner stone on the site, and two or three smaller ones in or near the field walls.) Later on 'Jake Green' met a friend, and, after referring to the encounter, and my statements and questions, he said: "That bugger knows more abaht t'moors nor ah do, and ah've bin on 'em all my life".

Says Mr James Wragg: "I was in the 'Peacock' tap room (Owler Bar) one day, getting a toll from a man who had omitted to pay at the proper place. 'Kess' Green was there, boozing, and, while the shepherd was away from the flock, they also went 'trespassing', and some entered the landlord's (Coates') garden and ate all the parsley."

"The landlady came into the room and 'set about' Kess in fine style. I was coming out when I heard Kess reply for the first time, after he had listened to a good deal of the landlady's clapper." Kess then said, quite suavely: 'Well, Polly [Mrs Coates], I never knew afore that parsley would harm my sheep'.

It was very provoking, for, in those early-Victorian days, it was not all 'booze' and 'bar' work, and the landlady never knew when somebody in a carriage and pair, etc., might be calling for a good meal.

"However", says my informant, "Polly calmed herself down when she was told that we had plenty of parsley in the toll bar garden".

The Story of 'Fox House Inn' and Callow Farm

History, Incident and Tales of the Moorside

From S.C.R. Handbook, 1930/31. *Fox House Inn is now a large restaurant incorporating a small bar area, and its Disneyland pub sign and large car park would probably not earn the Ward stamp of approval which he gave to the new owners of 1927.*

The persistent rambler may expect to grow old and grey, but, before he reaches the armchair stage, he will remember those who guided his earliest walks and adventures into the near unknown which is removed from the brick and mortar, or the most recent, concrete, or 'coke-breeze slab' masses and surroundings of his everyday life. The incidents and scenes on his first walking tour, and the recollections of the warm welcome at the inn, or farmhouse, in which, after a marathon day or a buffeting on the hills, he ate three meals at one sitting, or found the finest bed in which he ever slept, will always remain in the honeyed treasure house of his memory.

But, perhaps dearest of all, is the house or inn which was the calling or dining place during his earliest walks with his parent or elder companion.

Such is 'Fox House Inn' to myself and to my generation and older ones who fared forth and moorwards, before the opening of the Dore and Chinley Railway (1894), and when a walk over Totley Moss, Ankirk (Houndkirk?) Road, The Cupola, Stanage, or to Hathersage, Eyam or Baslow and home, was the usual good day's exercise, and one could tread the highway without fear. And such will 'Fox House Inn' be to many young ramblers who, thanks to the newer and brighter opportunities and planned routes can 'stand on the shoulders' of and excel the older brethren.

'Fox House Inn', despite today's increasing nearness to Sheffield, the senseless suicidal rush of the motor car round its awkward corner; and necessary provision of an 'A.A.' road 'bobby' and ambulance box for those who make a shambles of the King's highway, will probably continue to be, during this generation, the best-known inn on our local moorside roads. The new reason is because it is nearest to the 747 acres of the People's state of Longshaw Park, and the newly-opened 'green drive' up the beautiful Burbage valley – also, and alas, because another reservoir, to cover up the site of the bridle bridge under Carl Wark, and part of the Burbage valley, may be commenced by Sheffield Corporation during this year – if the Bill is carried through.

'Fox House Inn' suffered a rebuff during the transition from the waggonette and carriers' carts to the motor car and lorry, but, as a calling place for tea-drinkers, or beer-drinkers, it is again 'coming into its own'.

The history of 'Fox House Inn' has been obscure and, although the many con-versations with friendly 'countrymen' resulted in the giving as well as the getting of information, the usual and only knowledge was that 'Fox House' was originally built by a Fox of Callow Farm (Highlow) and that the sign of Reynard the Fox over the entrance door is deception, and like many wrong names on Ordnance Maps, a hindrance to those who might enquire into its history.

The Roads near the Inn
'Fox House Inn', approximately 1132 feet above sea level, is one of the highest in Derbyshire. Its situation, $7^1/_8$ miles S.W. of the centre of Sheffield, is at the junction of the Sheffield–Hathersage Road (opened about 1816) and the 'New Branch Road' which, near and beyond The Wooden Pole ancient bridleway guide, links up 'Fox House Inn' with the Owler Bar to Froggatt Edge Road opened in 1781. The 'New Branch Road', I think, was also opened about 1816, and, although I have not obtained proof, it may be reasonable to suppose that the license would date from about 1816 – '1816' is carved on the top of the parapet on the side of Whirlow Bridge. The old Dore to Grindleford bridle-way, however, passed behind 'Fox House', which may have been a beer-house before 1816. Who can tell?

The Ankirk ('Houndkirk'?) Road dates from the 1757 Road Act, and the Old Branch Road, green and deserted and a camping ground for gypsies quite fifty years ago, is now being converted into a motor road by Sheffield Corporation, and straightened out. Thus poetry leaves another old road during 1930.

The Features and Growth of the Inn
'Fox House Inn', like Longshaw Lodge, 'grew in penny numbers', and a student would have difficulty in finding the oldest part of the house and out-buildings. Appearances, however, are deceptive, and when the Duke of Rutland's representative improved and extended it, possibly in the forties of the last century, he obeyed the Estate whim of making this lonely inn fit in with its surroundings.

The new owners, Messrs Carter, Milner & Bird, Hope Brewery, Mowbray Street, Sheffield, who purchased 'Fox House Inn' and 9? acres of land (for

£5500) at the sale of Longshaw Moors, etc., in 1927, and their architect, Alderman W.C. Fenton, have not desecrated a pleasing inn and replaced it with an up-to-date, and, out-of-place, 'hotel' for the dandy and butterfly fraternity. They have changed the interior to an extent, but the principal alteration is probably the

Stony Ridge Toll House.

merging of the comfortless, oblong two top rooms into the previous public bar-room and the making of a more cosy 'public' room.

This late small 'top room' was built in or about 1895 and the bottom (S.W.) room probably in the late forties. Bernard Bird, in his book *The Perambulations of Barney the Irishman* (1854) stated that 'Fox House', originally built by Mr Fox, of Calley [Callow Farm is meant], near Highlow Hall', had been lately much improved, was then much frequented by Sheffield parties, and that the landlady was Mrs Furniss.

Dr T. Spencer Hall, M.D., in *The Peak and the Plain*, pages 336 and 343, refers to his visit in the autumn of 1852, and to 'the large parlour of Fox House Inn, said to be one of the most complete rooms of its kind in all England'. The large bottom room in the old days was known as 'The Duke's Room'. The Duke of Rutland and his young sons used to sleep at 'Fox House', and Mr Peat's mother used to put the candles at the bottom of the stairs in the early 40s, there being no sleeping accommodation at Longshaw. It was used for sleeping accommodation as late as the eighties by Archibald Stuart Wortley and his valet.

Some of the Landlords

It would be difficult to obtain a correct list of landlords and dates, but Mr William Peat, of Stone House, informs me that in 1837 his mother, then Alice Pixton Marsden, at seven years of age, was at 'Fox House Inn' with her aunt, Mrs Anne Walker; that she left her aunt (to be married) in 1850; and that Mrs Walker died at 'Fox House Inn' a few years later. The licence, says Mr Peat, was then transferred to Mr Thomas Furniss, who had been farm man for Mrs Walker – 'Mrs Furniss' appearing in Bernard Bird's book of 1854. The 'Mrs' may have been contemporary with the 'Mr' in each case – and the Walkers are said to have come from Ringinglow and were coal-getters or wire-drawers. *White's Sheffield (and District) Directory* of 1833 says that 'A. Walker' was the landlord of 'The Fox and Goose' (i.e. 'Fox House').

The next in order, John Thompson, a Bakewell butcher who 'reigned' from 1858 to 1892 and died that year is perhaps the best known host. He was followed by his son, Thomas, who died in 1895 (his widow keeping it a short time longer until 10/12/95) and Mr Benjamin Thorpe (now of Grindleford) who, the next in order, in January, 1913, gave way to the present landlord, Mr Thomas Rowarth, a son of Isaac Rowarth, the host of the famous 'Snake Inn', who married Miss Dorothy Wain, one of an equally well-known Upper Derwent family – the Wains of Grainfoot Farm, near Derwent hamlet.

When the Horse was King of the Road

'Fox House', before the advent of the motor, and more particularly, before the opening of the Dore and Chinley Railway, was a famous calling and baiting place for the drivers and passengers of the coaches and carriers' carts, which, on market days, plied between Eyam, Stoney Middleton, Tideswell, Hathersage, Bradwell, Castleton and Sheffield, and also for the brewers and flour millers' wagoners, and the coal carters, who came from the Derwent valley villages to Dronfield, Dronfield Woodhouse or the Pewit Farm coal yard, near Owler Bar, etc. On one occasion, the Eyam coach turned over in a snow drift, at the corner of the Hathersage–Grindleford Roads, just below the Inn (1886?). Sometimes there was a long row of coal carts at 'Fox House' (often two carts to one man), and sometimes the drivers were served with liquid refreshment in the 'small hours' when travelling to obtain an early 6a.m. 'cale', or 'turn' at the Pewit coal yard. The Inn, during Thompson's days, was famous for its 1/6d. ham and egg teas, and my father and many of the old brigade made it their objective after an afternoon walk across the Totley Moss, etc.

The Landlord asks for an 'Extension of Time'

John Thompson, on one occasion, was reminded of the 'open hours' at 'Fox House Inn'. He was providing for a special dinner party and applied to the Bakewell magistrates for an hour's extension – to midnight. The chief magistrate (Mr Nesfield, the Duke's agent), after hearing the application, observed that Thompson 'already had twenty-four hours a day in which to serve his customers', and that 'he couldn't very well grant him any more time' for that purpose. It reminds me of the story of Enoch Lenthall who, before I worked at James Jackson's, in Mary Street, Sheffield, was the locker-up and once 'made' 172 hours in one week, and assured 'Jimmy' Jackson, the 'boss', that 'he had worked 'em all!' There was no overtime rate in those days and, in this case, the story told to me while Enoch was employed there, was that 'it cum off', and 'Jimmy' Jackson (who, at that time, was 'making money for dust' out of the crinoline boom) paid Enoch the seven days and four hours he had 'made' during the week.

The Old Sideboard and Strawberry Lee Bull's Head

During Mr John Thompson's time the pride of the house, seen by thousands of visitors, was an old richly carved and panelled sideboard of black Spanish oak, put together with wooden pegs, which, the family believed, was made in Saragossa. It came from North Lees Hall, Hathersage, where, according to the widow of Mr T. Thompson, it stood fully seventy years ago. It was sold after the death of the latter and although one of the family bid more than £8300 for it (and failed to buy it), it was afterwards sold at a Sheffield auction room and the sideboard left the district. It is now said to be at Southport. Mr 'Ben' Thorpe did not secure it and Mr Rowarth, similarly, has failed to bring back the old attraction which, in the large bottom Duke's Room, was in keeping with its surroundings. The family, I understand, do not credit the rumour that, despite the carving of the crucifixion and 'cock-crowing', and other scriptural items on the panels, the sideboard was a fake which, previous to its sale in an appropriate old farm house, had been conveyed there by a Sheffield second-hand dealer for the purpose of 'catching a mug' buyer of antique furniture.

The feature of the interior is now in the top improved tap-room, and is the stuffed head of a fine bull which was reared and fed on the once excellent pastures of the Strawberry Lee ex-monastic (Beauchief Abbey) Farm, by Mr Thomas Mottram, the gifted 'handyman' and steward for George Sampson, of Beauchief, before the Pegge Burnells sold the farm to the Duke of Rutland and the Sampson's left it to go derelict – about 1910. The then Duke and Duchess admired the bull and, when it was killed (about 1886), the head was stuffed and presented to the Duchess by Mr Sampson. It reposed in Longshaw Lodge until 1927, and was purchased by Mr Rowarth at the sale.

It was hoped that Councillor G.H. Froggatt, the new owner of Strawberry Lee and Blacka, would have been able to restore the lost prestige of Strawberry Lee's pasturage, and it is hoped that the current rumours that it was intended to build another plot of suburban villas on this moorland site, beside Totley Moss, are baseless. It is also hoped that this large plot will be scheduled by the local authority under the district planning scheme and be preserved from the builder. Strawberry Lee, at the moment, is again open for sale. May the attractive way to it soon be open to the public which, by moral right, is entitled to a direct path between Totley and Stony Ridge.

Sleeping in the Snow all Night
Mr Benjamin Thorpe, the last cheery landlord, tells of a man from Stoney Middleton who, on one occasion stayed at the Inn until 'turningout time' and then started for home, over four miles away, in a snow storm. He was found next morning by the landlord and ostler, in the garden opposite the Inn, covered with snow, but still alive. They carried him inside and, after attention and refreshment, he walked home little the worse for the experience.

Stone House or 'The Broom Shop' occupied by Mr Wm Peat
Stone House is the first house on the left at the top of the hill from 'Fox

House', on the way to Sheffield – altitude about 1260 feet. The workshop beside it is the 'Broom Shop' for the making of the 'besoms', or brooms which, until more recent times, were used in every stable and most Sheffield factories and rolling mills, etc. It is interesting to record that the making of 'besoms' from ling was commenced by Mr Henry Peat, the grandfather of the present occupier, since the erection of the house, by Mr Hancock, of Dore, in 1826, and has continued without interruption.

Mr Henry Peat began this trade a short time before the house (since extended and outhouses attached) was built, and he cleared the nine acres of adjoining land which were 'awarded' to Mr Hancock in the Dore Enclosure Award of 10//4/1822 – Act of 1809.

Longshaw Dog Trials started at Fox House
The Longshaw Sheep Dog Trials originated at 'Fox House Inn' from an argument between shepherds and farmers as to who owned the best dog. Several shepherds and farmers challenged each other and prizes of a pig and a sheep were subscribed by the local farmers and Duke's tenants.

The first official trial was fixed for 24 March 1898, on Totley Moss, but on account of a severe snowstorm, was abandoned, and held on the following day, in 'Timothy' Field, a little below and across the road from Longshaw Lodge gates.

Mr Ernest Priestley (White House, Hathersage, but then at Overstones), the late Samuel White ('Grouse Inn'), Ben Thorpe ('Fox House'), and Joseph Crossland (of Hathersage) were the founders of the 'Trials', which, today, are perhaps the most important local event in the country. The late William Bocking (Hathersage), father of the present secretary, was the first secretary, and Joseph Crossland, the first Chairman. These Trials already have contributed over £1600 to the Derbyshire and Sheffield Hospitals Blind and Nursing Institutions.

Mrs Thompson, the widow of the late Thomas Thompson (of 'Fox House') informs me that although the 'first official trial' began in 1898, there were several more elementary trials between the strictly local farmers, who had sheep on Longshaw and Burbage Moors, and the Duke's shepherds, and that the first contest was in 1894. The object was to prove who owned the best sheep dog, and the stakes were quarts of beer, or a similar simple prize. She remembers the names of Samuel White, Ernest Priestley, Thomas Mottram and T. Gregory (Curbar) among the earliest contestants.

Another aspect of the 'Trials' – apart from the value of the prizes and judging – is shown in the speech of Mr Benjamin Thorpe, at the annual dinner of the Hope Valley Dog Trials Association, at the 'Peak Hotel', Castleton (*Sheffield*

Telegraph, Monday, 26 November 1928) wherein he observes that:

'Twenty-six years ago a sheep dog could be bought for half-a-crown and a pint (laughter), but today a puppy commanded at least £5'.

Another Hope valley farmer has stated to me that as much as £500 has been earned by the 'sport' of sheep dog 'trialing' in one year. Celebrated dogs have been sold for as much as £150 each, and a favourite dog has also been poisoned, presumably by envious persons.

The Rambling Instincts of Sheep

Many stories could be obtained about the doings of shepherd, sheep and dog at 'Fox House' and Longshaw Moors. A recent one, in July 1926, is in regard to an ewe and a lamb driven in a flock of 400 from Mr T. Rowarth's pasturage in Longshaw Park, via the 'Snake Inn', Glossop and Crowden to 'Pickness' (Peaknaze) – Moor on the Derbyshire side of Longdendale. The ewe and lamb returned to Longshaw Park and were rediscovered at 'Wooden Pole Piece', near the junction of the Owler Bar–Froggatt Edge and 'Fox House' Roads nine days later. They had 'scented' their return journey to the better pastures, for a distance of about 25 miles.

During Isaac Rowarth's time at the 'Snake Inn' (1879–1923) one ewe sheep which came to Longshaw Moors to 'winter', repeatedly found its way back to its summer quarters before lambing time and the March 'gathering day'. Other sheep have been known to return from Grainfoot Farm (near Derwent) to Longshaw.

Some days before the farmer was ready to 'drive' them by road, and perhaps forty years ago, it was a common occurrence for teens of sheep to arrive on Longshaw Moors from different farms in the Ashop and Derwent Woodlands, a few days in advance of the main flock, in early October. In these days, however, good breeding ewes were allowed to live seven or more years, whereas, since the War and today, with the smaller family and joint, there is greater demand for lambs and smaller, younger sheep.

Sheep Gatherings and the Use of the Moors

The Duke of Rutland, or his agent, provided free food and liquids for the shepherds and farmers during the annual sheep 'gatherings', and the March gathering, about forty years ago, would probably occupy two or three days. Two memorable gatherings (in 1886 and 1893?) were held during a heavy blanket of snow, and a number of farmers came to 'Fox House' in horse-driven sledges.

The sheep were examined for 'scab' early in the new year and sometimes in rough weather, the taproom of the Inn was covered with straw and the sheep were 'salved' indoors. And, on more than one occasion, farmers and shepherds have 'slept off the booze', all night – on the straw.

Some thirty to forty years ago the 9000 odd acres of Longshaw Moors provided the best sheep pasturage and grouse preserves in the district, and the Duke of Rutland used to take as many as 9000 sheep for winter pasturing. The sheep came from all parts of northwest Derbyshire.

The wintering of sheep on Longshaw Moors, with the exception of Burbage Moor, was stopped by the Duke in 1924, and, with the exception of Burbage Moors, is still discontinued, although the moors are now chiefly owned by two public authorities. There was a period of about ten years (1901 to 1911) when, on the senseless assumption that the pasturing of sheep adversely affected the feeding of the grouse, there was a similar ban on the use of the moor for the wholesale production of flesh meat. They ultimately discovered that with no sheep the grouse were rapidly decreasing or leaving the moors. It was eventually realised that the sheep in winter time scratch for food and leave some picking for the grouse, as also keep open the sheep tracks and provide shelter for the birds during stormy weather. Another shepherd's argument is that when heather is not grazed by sheep it grows too rough and strong and is unsuitable for the grouse – and also that the heath is smothered by the long grass and bracken and dies because the sweeter, short grass is not grazed.

When the sheep were allowed to return for 'wintering', and some young cattle were again taken for 'summering', it was found that, owing to the closing of other Derbyshire moors against the sheep, the farmers had been compelled to reduce their flocks and it was impossible to provide anything approaching the former total. The same farmers and natives are now saying that since 1927 a large portion of the Longshaw Moors are being provided with foxes for hunting purposes, and that the number of grouse on Big, Ramsley, Leash and Eaglestone Flat Moors are further reduced and also the farmers' and cottagers' fowls, for miles around those moors.

The Shepherd 'Gets his Legs in a Raffle'
An interesting true story is told of an old head shepherd, Mr Peter Priestley, about fifty years ago. The head shepherd and his assistants had the task of branding the sheep with the letter 'R' before they were turned on the moors in October, and because, whatever the farmer's private mark, they were in charge of the Duke of Rutland for six months. The sheep were branded on any part of the body, but being an additional marking, chiefly on the rump.

Priestley, like many men, had a habit of 'platting', or 'crossing' his legs when he sat down. On one occasion, after branding a few hundred sheep and spilling pitch on his trousers, he went into 'Fox House Inn' for his 'drinking', and fell asleep before the fire. Then, when he awoke, he discovered that the pitch had melted and that his legs were stuck together. Priestley required assistance before he could 'unplat' his legs and walk home to Mitchell Fields farm.

The Fox Family and 'Fox House'
The key to the history of 'Fox House' is in the word 'House', and I interviewed Mr Robert Fox, of Foolow, who, born at Callow Farm in 1861, is a sprightly representative of the eldest born of the Fox family. Until recent years he lived at Shepherd's Flat, near Eyam. He, like most sons of Derbyshire yeomen fathers, knows much of the family history and also he could say something of the training and doings of 'boxing men' and their 'promoters'. He traces the family heirs to the farm down to an Ursula Fox in the seventeenth century, and, referring to his grandfather, Robert (1780–1863), thinks that 'Fox House' was built by his great-grandfather George (1728–1821), or the latter's father, William (1684–1773), and about the middle of the eighteenth century. The family belief is that these ancestors had the grazing of what today is the public's Longshaw Park Estate, and, on the north of the road from the Surprise to the Toad's Mouth, as far as Higger Tor and part, or all of, the opposite side where the Burbage 'green drive' runs today.

First a Shepherd's Cottage
'Fox House', he says, was first built as a 'two-roomed' cottage, 'down and up', and was tenanted by a shepherd, or one of the sons who tended the flock of over 500 sheep, which in those enlightened days of moorland usage, had pasturage all the year round – apart from the 'summering' of young beast and horses. One of the Thompson family informs me that, before 'Fox House', it is said to have been known as 'Shepherd's Rest.' The pasturage rights of Longshaw at that time belonged to the manor of Highlow, and the Foxes, he believes, were stewards at one time.

The Beginning of 'Fox House'
The original cottage first known as 'Fox House' is supposed to face the open yard, immediately behind the Inn, to the left of the five stone steps in front of the rear entrance – and west of the long, projecting southwest 'Duke's Room' having the diamond-paned and mullioned windows. Standing in the yard, and looking at the line of outbuildings left of the stone steps, it is the first mullioned window on the ground floor. It was apparently one room 'up and down', and the living room was about 18ft x 11ft. The bedroom window appears to retain the original leaded, small window panes. The front wall of this cottage was projected three feet from the original, presumably during one of the alterations made by the Duke of Rutland. There may have been an outhouse attached, and part of the stables and outhouses on the left may have been built at the same time, or soon after the 'House' became an 'Inn'.

Messrs Carter, Milner & Bird Ltd, inform me that Alderman Mr C. Fenton, the architect, found three additions to what is called the old tap room, in this part of the original house, and the approximate guide to the date of erection in the stone window frames. The architect fixes the age of these window frames to approximately a period of fifty years and, saying that they were not made after 1780, refers to the 'frames' of a house at Ashopton, built in 1758, which had a common peculiarity with those of 'Fox House'. We shall, however, obtain further evidence from the wills of the Fox family, of Callow, who built it.

Mr Robert Fox believes that the house and sheep walk were sold about 1810 to the Duke of Devonshire for about £200, and Mr Sam Priestley, of Hathersage Booths, who died last year, says that his father John, and grandfather, J.S. Priestley, of Overstones, had the sheep walk from 1817 to 1887.

A Fox Family Sheep Mark
The family papers were destroyed during the time of Robert's father, but one treasured relic I saw at Foolow, is the sheep-mark (used for marking the horns) used by Robert Fox (1780–1863), his grandfather, the last Fox, of Callow, who had the Longshaw pasturage. It bears the letters 'R F' and is let in the shank by the ordinary 'V' slot.

Although Mr Robert Fox refers to an Ursula Fox in the seventeenth century, the earliest record I have seen is a 'W. Fox of Callow, tenant of Mr Eyre, of Highlow, 1670'.

The 'Toughness' of the Fox Family
Some idea of the toughness of the first-born of the family may be gathered from the information I took from two of the three plain upright family gravestones on the southwest side of Hathersage churchyard:

William Fox died 18/1/1773, aged eighty-nine years (1684–1773). Sarah, his wife, on 23/12/1771, aged eighty-eight years.

George Fox died 24/2/1821, aged ninety-three years (1728–1821). Mary, his wife, died 18/12/1788, aged forty-nine years.

Robert Fox died 19/3/1863, aged eighty-three years (1780–1863). Mary Ann, his wife, died 14/3/1845, aged fifty-seven years.

The last Fox at Callow, born in 1820, who left about 1890–2, finished his days at Shepherd's Flat, near Eyam, and died about 1903 (?). His eldest son Robert (now at Foolow) was born in 1861.

A Fox's Will gives Evidence
Further evidence from two family wills is as follows:

William Fox of Callow near Hathersage was also a Butcher in 1764 and on 24 April 1769 when he made his will he bequeathed to his daughters Mary, wife of Joseph Hall; Ellen Goodwin, widow; Martha, wife of Joseph Oliver; Margaret, wife of William Oliver; and Sarah Mosley, widow, a guinea each. To the two daughters of his late son Robert Fox he gave a guinea each. To his son, William Fox, he left an estate called 'Newitt Field', at Hathersage Outseats, for life; and then to his (testator's) son George Fox. The Residue went to his son George Fox, he maintaining testator's wife Sarah. Will proved 29 April 1773.

George Fox, then residing at Callow, made his will 9 September 1815. The farmer mentions his sons William, Robert, John, Nathaniel and his daughter Deborah, wife of Henry Middleton. He gave land at Newitt Field and Hathersage Lane to them in equal shares.

To his son Robert Fox he bequeathed the cottage house or tenement at Longshaw held under the Duke of Devonshire Lord of the Fee.

The value of a silver tankard now on the premises was to be equally divided between his children.

George Fox died 26 February 1821, his daughter Deborah Middleton having died the day previous. His will was proved 26 April 1821.

George Fox's son William was living at Abney Low in July 1825, and his other sons Robert, a farmer, John, a joiner, and Nathaniel, a publican, were living in 1823.

The words in bold type above would appear to prove that in the absence of any mention in the will of William Fox, the 'cottage house or tenement' was not erected until after his death in 18/1/1773, and that it was erected by his eldest son George at any time after January 1773. Until the contrary is proved, I incline to a period shortly after 1773.

The Fox Family Legend
William, the second brother of the George Fox who died in 1903 (Robert being the other brother) had a remarkable memory, but the greater portion of his unrecorded knowledge of local folk-lore has passed away. During the intervals between hoeing turnips or hay making, etc., he told local stories and also 'quoted the Bible by the yard'. He strongly adhered to the persisting family legend that the first Fox came with William the Conqueror, and also the first of the most notable Derbyshire family of the Eyres of Highlow, etc., who flourished exceedingly in the fifteenth century. The mixed version he gave to Alderman R. Ibbotson, of Hathersage, and others, was that the Eyres were participating in the grim entertainment of the battle of Win and Lose Hill, near Hope Bridge, when one of the 'Princes' was surrounded by the enemy.

One of his faithful soldiers then 'jumped in among 'em and those he didn't kill he made take to their heels'. The 'Prince' then rose to the occasion and said, "What is thy name?" and the humble 'Tommy' of those days answered: "My name is Truelove." "Then," said the Prince, "it shall be Truelove no longer, and if we win this battle today thy name shall be Eyre, and thou shalt be 'heir' to the whole of this valley."

The Eyre Family Legend
The Eyre tradition, however, is given by Mr A. Bemrose, junior, in an article on North Lees Hall, Hathersage, in 'The Reliquary' of April, 1869, and is copied from an old pedigree then preserved at Hassop (Hall), as follows:

'The first of the Eyres came with William the Conqueror, and his name was Truelove, but in the battle of Hastings (14/10/1066), this Truelove, seeing the king unhorsed, and his helmet beat so close to his face that he could not breathe, pulled off his helmet and horsed him again. The king said: "Thou shalt hereafter from Truelove be called AIR or Eyre, because thou hast given me the air I breathe". After the battle the king called for him, and being found with his thigh cut off, he ordered him to be taken care of, and being recovered, he gave him lands in the county of Derby in reward for his services, and the seat he lived at he called Hope because he had Hope in the greatest extremity; and the king gave the leg and the thigh cut off the armour, for his crest, which is still the crest of all the Eyres'.

The Fox becomes Steward to the 'Eyre'
The battle, of course, was won by this unnamed 'Prince', and it transpired that, according to William Fox's version, the lucky young Eyre and also 'heir' to the Hope valley, had a 'pal' in the army whose name was Fox. And so Eyre, who quite appropriately, wanted to share a little of this thick stroke of luck with a good hefty pal, sought out Mr Fox, and said to him: "I shall make thee my steward" – and other things to similar effect.

This first Eyre decided to reside at Highlow, and placed this faithful steward, Mr Fox, at or about the site of the present Callow Farm, which, 520 yards north of Highlow Hall, is situated immediately east of the cart track which, from about 70 yards N.E. of Highlow Hall, leads to Offerton Hall and first crosses the hollow of the replanted Dunge Wood and its Brook.

"And", said the first Eyre, Esq., of Hope valley, "We'll call this place the Call-o'er, for we'll call thee o'er when we want thee." So ends Wm Fox's story of how the Foxes came to Callow Farm.

This William Fox was possessed of much interesting history, true or legendary, and, unfortunately, much has been lost in the destruction of the family records. He firmly adhered, however, to the statement that the Fox family gave their name to 'Fox House Inn' and resided at Callow – in the present nineteenth-century built farm house and previous erections there – without a break in the male line since the eleventh century! The Fox tradition is also believed by the living representatives of the family.

When George Fox, the last of his line, owing to, we may say, financial reasons, was obliged to leave the ancestral yeoman's house of Callow, in or about 1890–2, there was general regret throughout the Hathersage district at the passing of a virile Derbyshire hillside family which, in tenacity, strength, and probably worth of work and production, had more reason for pride of ancestry than many of our noble families.

A 'Fox' Dinner and Bed Story

William Fox was a powerful man and a worthy specimen of Derbyshire's rough, yeoman farmers. He once attended a Court Leet at Highlow Hall, and there was a merry time after the feast. On one occasion, he was reaching across the table when someone took his chair away. And so, when he sat down on something which wasn't there, he grabbed the tablecloth and brought everything off the table. Said William: "A custard puddin' 'it me in th' chops, an' a pease pie 'it me in th' belly."

On another occasion William was well lined with jolly good ale and strong, and perhaps not fit to go home to The Holt, near Callow Farm. So they put him to bed – in a fashion. He woke up, dazed and drunken, and, thinking it was morn, tried to get up, but "summat 'it 'im such a crack on th' yed, 'at it knocked 'im dahn ageean." Then he tried again, and there was "another hump on his noddle." However, said he, "Ar'n't ah th' strongest man in th' Hope valley?" and tried again, until he was rather sore and also somewhat sobered. Then he discovered that he had been sleeping under the bed, and not upon it.

The Fox and the Fighting Man

William was 'a bit of a bruiser', and he heard of the fame of a 'fighting man' at Hayfield who was 'kept' at, or 'helped to keep' (by attracting customers) a certain pub in that village, and by repute thrashed everybody he disliked, or dared to sit in his favourite chair – when told to come out of it. So, one day, quietly, William walked to Hayfield and sitting in the fighting-man's chair, asked for beer and bread and cheese. The landlord, or waiter, told 'Bill' he'd better not sit in that chair as the 'bruiser' was expected very soon, and so-and-so would happen – just what 'Bill' wanted.

So 'Bill' sat, in the sense of 'everything comes to him who waits'. The 'bruiser' duly arrived, and, in reply to the peremptory command and threat, Bill merely asked him to wait 'until he'd eaten his bit of bread and cheese, and supped up, and then, perhaps they'd see about it'. The natives gathered round, expecting to see 'Bill' get the usual 'dose', but, instead, he gave the

Hayfield bruiser all he wanted and a little more and, afterwards, stayed at the pub for a few days and became the pride of the place. The amount of ale he 'supped' is not recorded.

The Lost Holt Farm
'Bill' was a 'fish tenter' for the Derwent, and, in early life, he had a few closes of land, a few sheep and lambs. His cottage called 'The Holt', now in ruins, but still visible, is on the near, low side of the cartway path between Callow Farm and Offerton Hall. He died at Fall Cliff Farm.

Another Fighting Fox and his Lady Wife
The Fox's are supposed to have come into prominence after a historic fight, and this characteristic seems to have persisted through the last three generations.

Robert Fox (1780–1863), known locally as 'Bobbling Bob', was a fine strong man and a fighter. He is said to have fought Alfred Shaw, an English 'champion', near the long lapsed 'Bell Inn' at Hathersage, and, in the first round, to have broken (or bruised severely) his shoulder blade, but, nevertheless, to have persisted for 15 rounds until he gained the victory.

His wife was a London lady of high degree who is said to have come to the Ordnance Arms mysteriously and, meeting 'Bob' there, to have married after a brief courtship of a few weeks' duration! The story goes that she had recently lost her rich 'young man' because she was told not to meet him in Hyde Park wearing a certain dress of which he did not approve. The young man then said: "If that's your disposition, I'll say Good Morning and we'll part."

It is, however, possible that she was the 'chance' child of some aristocrat and that the family, after educating her, wanted her out of the way.

Robert, being a fine piece of manhood, quickly 'took her eye', but it was a case of fashion marrying work. She seems to have tried to tame 'Bob', but he was no lover of 'visiting', 'afternoon teas', and the like, and eventually she became a somewhat lonely, if queenly woman, who loved her children and left her mark on the features of later generations. The farm wives of Hathersage talked for years of her beauty and breeding, and of 'how two extremes had met'.

More Anecdotes
One of the stories about the wife of the said Robert Fox is that one day she spent the butter money upon a new bonnet, and didn't tell 'hubby' about it! So, next day, she set him hand-churning the buttermilk with, of course, no result. Robert then 'chucked up the job'. Then, later, when telling a neighbour's wife about the 'hard job e'd 'ad, churning for nowt', she gave it away, unconsciously, by saying she'd "seen t' missis go down wi' th' butter yester-

day" – and then, I suppose, there was a domestic explanation which most husbands and wives can understand.

The Goose at Callow

I have heard the story of the late Joseph Townsend, the last occupant of Bretton Clough Farm (once two dwellings), beside today's well-known footpath – who, due to arrive at Offerton Hall Farm rather early one December morning, was rather late, and, in explanation, said: – "Ahve bin chasin' a gooise at Callow for mi Christmas dinner."

Mrs M.I. Porritt, of Shepley Hall Farm, Audenshaw, near Manchester, however, reminds me of a more famous goose at Callow, and of some old doggerel about it. The only lines she remembers are:

'Not all the coal from Staveley Pit
Could roast the goose from Callow'

and I wonder who could complete this old rhyme and story.

How the Longshaw Moorland Pastures were 'Awarded'.

The Hathersage Enclosure Award of 23/6/1830 (Act of 1808), under which, 'by estimation, ten thousand acres or thereabouts' of waste, moorland or common, 'went in' (as the native says) gives ample confirmation that the Duke of Devonshire had obtained the Highlow estate of the Eyre family, and its 'rights' before 1810. A piece (No. 18 on the Award book and plans) of 641 acres, on the westerly side of Burbage Brook and from the Surprise to the Toad's Mouth Rock, going north from the Brook and including Millstone Edge, was awarded to the Duke of Devonshire 'in lieu of tithe'.

A Parson's 'Award' pays part of Enclosure Act Expenses

The stretch of 139 acres from Fox House to Burbage Brook, to its most easterly bend (near the old bridle bridge, under Carl Wark), and thence to just below Parson's House (now, called Burbage House), and thence down the road to the Inn is, curiously enough, placed in Derwent parish. This piece seems to have been 'awarded' to 'Bingham, Rev. Thomas', whose name and 'clerkship' in holy orders I have not unearthed from clerical records. This latter portion is called 'Wildmoor Stones Edge'. This well-named Edge is the first half-mile of quarried top on the right of Burbage valley and of the green drive going from below 'Fox House Inn'.

The same reverend gentleman was 'awarded' the most northeasterly part of Burbage valley (2341 acres) as far as the Dore boundary along the road to Ringinglow, and to the summit of Burbage Moor (1431 feet) – many casual walkers do not know that, although Higger Tor is 1421 feet, the flat-topped Burbage Moor, one mile E.E. by W., is ten feet higher, and the actual summit is a small mound on which, I suppose, a stake or pole was probably fixed.

Reverend Thomas Bingham's awarded piece also is fixed in Derwent parish but, as a matter of fact, he purchased both 'pieces' (373? acres) from the Enclosure Act Commissioners for £537. 14s. 'towards defraying the charges and expenses of the said Inclosures' under the Hathersage Act.

'Parson' builds Burbage (Valley) House?

The Rev. Thomas Bingham is also credited by the members of the Priestley family with the erection of the long deserted sheep farm house in Burbage valley – which, it is said, was never inhabited, half a mile S.S.E. of the Upper Burbage road bridges, and also the walling of several field fences which, apparently, were not completed, or were taken away later, when the Duke came into possession. The old house is falling into ruins, and some of the woodwork was taken to one of the houses at Hathersage Booths many years ago.

It is possible that he also bought, or was 'awarded', the curiously intrusive patch of Dore parish which, in the centre of the Upper Burbage valley, comes over Wild Moor Stones Edge to Burbage Brook and, between the today's named Burbage Rocks (Reeve's Edge Top further north) and the Brook, occupies about 120 acres of the east slope of the valley.

It is also possible that, if old map names and memories are reliable, he also caused the building of the once-named 'Parson's House' (Burbage House) farm house, half a mile N.E. of 'Fox House Inn' (altitude of a little over 1250 feet), which is now owned by Sheffield Corporation. Other rare local memories are that the Rev. Thomas Bingham came to grief over money matters and was compelled to sell out to the Duke of Rutland, or whoever had the land for a short time before him.

A Duke's share of the 'Award'

Other proof that the Duke of Devonshire had 'rights' in today's Longshaw Park Public Estate (747 acres), is that the southerly part of this estate, which includes Yarncliff Top (98 acres) was (No. 8) also 'awarded' to the same Duke for 'tithe'. Another piece of Longshaw Park Estate (No. 5) from Burbage Brook to the Fox House–Hathersage Road (also 98 acres) was 'bought' by Joseph Trickett, and also the piece No. 4 (102 acres) which lies between the Fox House–Wooden Pole and Grindleford Roads, and is the part in which Longshaw Lodge was built.

No. 7 'piece' of 170 acres, which lies east of the Fox House–Grindleford Road, was also 'bought' by Charles Brookfield – of Hathersage? A further 'piece' of 189 acres (No. 1) going to White Edge and Windley Well (under White Edge), to the Hurkling Stone parish boundary mark on Big Moor, and then to White's Moor, also went to the Duke of Devonshire, for 'tithe'.

The reader will now understand that, before the Duke of Rutland obtained the 9000 odd acres of Longshaw Moors, he purchased, or exchanged, several lumps of moorland from the Duke of Devonshire, or other owners, before the early extension of Longshaw Lodge – about 1840.

Nell Croft is 'Noll Croft'

This is a curiously named large field. The N.E. wall is now well inside Totley parish, and the S.E. part of the field, on the E. side of the Fox House–Owler Bar Road, is within Hathersage Outseats. The grazing of the field is usually attached to 'Fox House Inn' and the 33 acres of it, within Hathersage Outseats, was bought from the Enclosure Act Commissioners by Dewes Cook, of Totley Hall. The more N.E. portion of the land between the Fox House–Sheffield Road and the old (green) Branch Road, of 45 acres, and now called 'Blakelock Moor', after one of Sheffield's Victorian grouse shooters who shot on this once pasturage, was also bought by Dewes Cooke.

It might now be assumed that the previously unexplained 'Nell Croft', which, on the Award, is called 'Noll Croft', is named after the Knoll, or higher ground of Stony Ridge which is east of it and inside Totley Moss Moor.

The Name of the Spring near 'Fox House Inn'

No one knew the name of the gushing and famous spring which flows from the south end of Wild Moor Stones Edge, on the north side of the road, between 'Fox House Inn' and Toad's Mouth Rock. I have discovered, after twenty years of searching, that (in the Hathersage Award) its correct name is not Fox House Spring, but 'Wild Moor Stones Spring'. Hathersage Parish Council lamentably failed to take water from the Derwent Valley Water Board before the War, but have now made arrangements with Sheffield Corporation to take 40,000 gallons of water a day (at 3d. per l000 gallons) from this spring, and will probably 'pipe it' along the roadside and make a storage tank just beneath Millstone Edge.

Longshaw and its Lodge

The earliest reference I have seen in regard to Longshaw place name is in a document of 1722, and the earliest reference to the first edition of the several times extended Longshaw Lodge is on p. 425 of *White's Sheffield (and District) Directory* of 1833, as follows: 'On the hills about 2 miles from the village (Hathersage), the Duke of Rutland has a shooting box'. The Duke is also one of the 729 inhabitants, and his place is given as 'Longshaw'. This shows that the first part of the Lodge was presumably built soon after the Hathersage Enclosure Award of 1830 – assuredly not later than 1832.

And now my three years' task is done and as good as I can make it. My thanks are due to Messrs E.B. Bagshawe, D. Beresford (Leadmill), R. Fox, the Misses Greaves (Offerton Hall), R. Ibbotson, the late Samuel Priestley, Mr and Mrs W. Peat, and Mr and Mrs T. Rowarth, for the information or clues which they supplied.

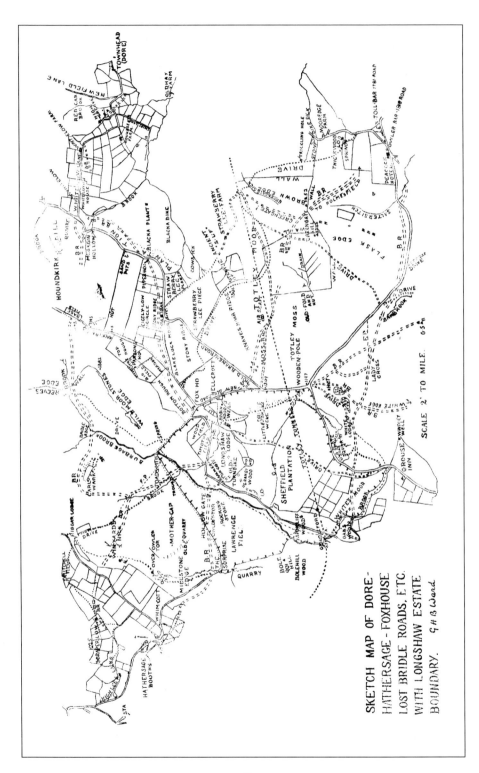

SKETCH MAP OF DORE-
HATHERSAGE - FOXHOUSE
LOST BRIDLE ROADS, ETC.
WITH LONGSHAW ESTATE
BOUNDARY. *G H Ward.*

SCALE 2' TO MILE.

Facts and Records of Blackamoor and Monastic Strawberry Lee Grange (Sheffield Corporation Public Moorland)

From S.C.R. Handbook, 1937/38. Like Big Moor, Blackamoor is just half-an-hour's walk or so from Ward's former home from 1915 to his death in 1957. The name 'Blackamoor' apparently originated from the Duke of Rutland's sale in 1927, when the estate agents coined the name in the hope of selling off the area as a grouse moor, as it had been under the Duke. Locals still know it as 'Blacka', though 'Blackamoor' seems to have caught on more generally. The area is now managed by Sheffield Wildlife Trust, and how much longer it will be yours and mine to go across freely and at length has been a matter of much recent debate.

I intended to collate and add to the gatherings of a quarter of a century and print this article two years ago but the intervention of a speeding cyclist at the foot of the hill on the road adjacent to home (in the dark, 5/1/35), and a long 'knock-out' is a good part of an excuse.

I love these wild places. This area is one of the many moorside associations of the greater part of a life-time, and I would that others could love them, and work for them in equal fashion. My father George Bridges Ward, first took me, when a boy, to Strawberry Lee Farm (in Tommy Mottram's time), with his young men's class, on New Year's Day, forty-nine or fifty years ago, and, in his way, he was a pioneer and lover of the things of the free and open air – and a connoisseur in the art and knowledge of gathering, and of growing, a collection of rare Derbyshire ferns.

Blacka Moor is now yours and mine to go across 'freely and at length' and, equally, to respect and to protect for the benefit and good health of our fellow citizens. It is the chunk of 448 acres included in the 3864 acres of Derbyshire moorland now wrested from the unsocial Grouse King – plus the Sheffield-owned Burbage Moors 2407, and Longshaw National Trust Estate, 1009 acres.

This 'freeing' of Blacka Moor is due to the purchase and gift to the City of

Sheffield of Alderman J.G. Graves, J.P., in 1933. We are not adulators and we want no favours, but it is one thing to 'make money' in one's own way, and it is quite another to spend much of it in a manner calculated to benefit those citizens who live today and will follow after.

Therefore, this article is dedicated, by this pen, to the man who gave freedom to our feet in going across Blacka Moor and Strawberry Lee. Brethren upstanding! Here's to Alderman J.G. Graves, J.P.!

The Blacka Moor portion of the Longshaw Moorland Estate, was purchased at the Duke of Rutland's sale, of Longshaw Estates (12,300 acres), on 5/7/27 by Councillor Dr G.H. Froggatt, of Sheffield, for £6000 and, immediately, certain necessary repairs were made to Strawberry Lee farmhouse and out-buildings. It is feared, however, that an early scheme of sheep farm develop-ment in those years of severe price depression did not meet with the desired success, and the feared possibility or intention of 'developing' the estate, or making a line of villadom beside the road from Meg and Jin Hollow to the site of Stony Ridge Toll Bar, was met by the decision of the Sheffield Corporation not to 'develop' the frontage on the opposite side of the road – on their Burbage Moors estate. The Norton Rural District Council, in close co-opera-tion with the Sheffield C.P.R.E., also got to work and, before the R.D.C. area of Totley, Dore, Beauchief and Norton, Greenhill and Bradway was swal-lowed by Sheffield city, this R.D.C. did the preliminary work for preventing development on this land under the provisions of the Town Planning Act for scheduling areas to be earmarked as undeveloped. In this manner, and a work in which our friend Coun. R.S. Wells participated, 'Blacka Moor' was pro-tected in advance. It was stated in the *Sheffield Clarion Ramblers' Booklet* for 1931, that 'Strawberry Lee, at the moment, is again open for sale'. The estate was, as stated, sold two years later.

During 1933 the rambling public of the Sheffield district were delighted to learn that, in addition to the giving of parks, playing fields and art galleries, our Sheffield Graves Trust, founded and financed by Alderman J.G. Graves, J.P., of the old 'Let's talk of Graves' fame, had decided to deliver Blacka Moor from the grouse monopolist and give it to Sheffield at, we understood, a cost of £9000. From that occasion, and not until, the public date their full freedom to walk across Blacka Moor Estate, which includes Strawberry Lee ex Monastic farm and buildings. The gamekeeper's 'words', or the gun produced, but not used, against the members of our S.C.R. Club at Strawberry Lee, near the house door, during 1929, are records of the past.

We will now detail some of the forgotten or dusty facts of the history of this part of the moorland area upon, and adjacent to, our people's piece of moorland where no grouse are shot and, we trust, their eggs will not disap-pear.

TOTLEY MOSS IS MONASTIC PASTURAGE IN 1263

The connection of the greater Moor of Totley Moss, and also Blacka Moor, with the monks of Beauchief Abbey can be traced to a grant by Matthew of Hathersage, the lord of the manor, who, according to a reference to his widow named Anora (*née* Meynil, of Barlborough Manor) in 1263, died in, or before, 1263. He ensured his translation into future happiness and compounded for stealing the king's deer (by fixing a buckstall – to attract deer on the Sheffield side of the Derwent) and other peccadilloes, by the giving of 13/4d. a year from the proceeds of his corn mill at 'Haversagge', and the 'grant' of the 'common pasture', as described in the following boundary:

'From Fulwode [Fulwood] to the head of Burbache [Burbage] and so descending to the water of Burbache [Burbage Brook] thus to Hyggehose [High-House?] and from Hyggehose descending to Lightokford and from Lightokford thus to Paddely [Padley] and from Paddely ascending to Levidicros [Lady Cross, about 400 yards W. of upper Barbrook Bridge] and so from Levidicros by the boundaries of Totinley [Totley] and Dore to the boundary of Halumshire'.

THE BOUNDARY OF THE MONASTIC PASTURAGE

The extent of this grant of several thousand acres of moorland pasturage, which, in those far off days, before grouse-murdering was known as 'sport', was used for the all-year-round production of sheep and summer grazing of cattle, can be appreciated by a perusal of the Ordnance Map.

We can commence six miles S.W. of Sheffield Town Hall; at the summit of the road (1361 feet), between Ringinglow hamlet and the two upper Burbage Bridges. Here, if the unsociable gamekeeper does not intervene, we follow the county boundary in a straight line, going almost N.W. for one mile past the boundary stakes (if they still remain) and, in one-third mile, we pass the ruins of an old stone butt, or hut, 11ft x 10ft, where, today, no traces of roof or slates are seen. I have no record of the origin, or of the purpose it served.

At the end of this mile-long walk, along a route of cotton grass and semi-swamp beloved only by the gamekeepers' tormentor (the active, well-seasoned and well-shod, innocently-minded trespasser), the healthy investigator would turn due south. Here he is at Friar's Ridge, along the proper and ancient boundary line of Derbyshire and Yorkshire, and of the 'Fulwood' side of Hallamshire (N.E.) and Hathersage (S.W.). Both sides of Friar's Ridge were also Monastic boundaries in 1263 and, on the Fulwood and Rivelin side, there are records of grants and confirmation of grants in 1218 and 1238.

The Burbage Brook rises and flows southwardly in a swampy mess which continues halfway to Upper Burbage Bridges.

BURBAGE BROOK TO PADLEY

We follow down the Burbage Brook and wonder whether Hyggehose (High House) was an ancient, and long lost, shepherd's dwelling in the upper portion of Burbage valley. Then we cannot decide whether Lightokford was the bridle road ford across the Burbage Brook (1) below, and east of Carl Wark (2) across the same stream at the ford of Hollowgate, or (3) possibly, beside the old Padley Saw Mill, a few yards N.W. of the railway bridge at Grindleford station.

The three foregoing are probably pre-historic bridleway crossings. The date of the bridle bridge under Carl Wark may be suggested from the date of 1725 on a keystone of the old pack bridge at Hollowgate's (now) wooden plank crossing, a few yards N. of the plank – in the stream bed.

PADLEY CHAPEL TO LADY CROSS

Padley Chapel, and the lately revealed site of the thirteenth-century known manor house of the Bernac family, requires no description, but the old boundary line of Padley Manor is lost. The pre-1867 one-inch-to-mile Ordnance Map shows 'Padley Common' on the south side of the streamlet course down White's Moor and between it and Blacka Sick, the upper feeder of Haywood Brook – on the easterly side of the 'Grouse Inn'. It therefore may have proceeded to the source of the former at Windley Well on White Edge, then to the Hurkling Stone on Big Moor, and thence to the head of Blacka Sick. But this must be regarded as guess work. We can be sure that Lady Cross, however approached from Padley, is a Beauchief Abbey boundary cross fixed beside the ancient bridle road from Dronfield and Chesterfield to Hathersage and Hope, etc., at a point on Big Moor one-and-two-third miles almost S.E. of Padley chapel, and about 1000 yards S.S.E. of the Wooden Pole bridleway indicator, north of the junction of the roads from Froggatt Edge, Fox House and Owler Bar.

TOTLEY MOSS TO RINGINGLOW

The 'common of pasture' defined in the boundaries of Totley and Dore could be outlined (roughly) as from Lady Cross and going N.E., across Totley Moss to the top of Brown Edge (1252 feet west of Totley Brickyard), where the Holmesfield boundary is met to the S.E. Then, across the foot of Blacka Moor estate and the post-Dore Enclosure-Act-made farms in Whitelow Lane and Sheephill Farm. We finish at Ringinglow.

STRAWBERRY LEE, THE FIRST FARM NEAR TOTLEY MOSS

The foregoing is sufficient to prove that Strawberry Lee Grange, a medieval and finally, a possibly early-nineteenth-century farmstead, was the original farm for Totley Moss. Today it is thrown down, and the land derelict and waste, but less than fifty years ago it was a good moorland holding, and one-hundred-and-twenty years ago, the only farmhouse near to Totley Moss. It is a monument to the neglect of 'sporting' landowners of the past and the gradual reduction, and/or, elimination of sheep and cattle-grazing on the moorlands. It is an expression of the neglect in not repairing, renovating and modernising farm houses and buildings, after the incremental gains of the Enclosure Acts and early land, and rent, improvements of the early-nineteenth century had been absorbed by the three succeeding generations of landowners, and more modern forms of taxation began to atone for the previous neglect of social services.

ABOUT BEAUCHIEF ABBEY

Totley Moss and Strawberry Lee were possessions of the dozen Premonstratensian Monks ('White Canons') of Beauchief Abbey and their abbot, who first settled on the estate surrounding the remnants of the present church in, or about, 1183. Their home estate, generally stated, included the line of today's, post-war widened Abbey Lane, Greenhill village, the old bridleway, and present road, between Greenhill, Bradway and Upper Bradway Farm, long known (if modernised and widened since the war) as Hemper Lane and Bradway Lane, to Upper Bradway Cross. This Beauchief Abbey boundary cross which stood beside the junction of the ancient bridle roads to Holmesfield and Totley, just inside the field wall corner, at the junction of the road to Bradway House, Bradway Bank, and Totley Rise, was fixed at the southern boundary and watershed of the original 'home' estate of the Abbey. The photograph in the 1930 issue of the *Sheffield Clarion Ramblers' Booklet* shows a square morticed base and delicately tapered shaft upon which the original Cross head was fixed. I understand, from a friend, that, during 1935,

it was removed into the yard of Bradway Grange Farm by the new resident, or owner, Mr T.T. Osborne, who succeeded Mr T.J. Tinker. From Upper Bradway Cross, the boundary continued down the hollow of The Lumb (deep woody hollow) and Bradway Brook – or the present course of the L.M.S. railway line from Bradway Tunnel to Dore and Totley Station. Then it pursued the River Sheaf to Beauchief.

These medieval monks grew fat upon the chunks of territory 'granted', chiefly between the twelfth and fourteenth centuries, by landowners who, impressed by the belief that they could compound for the sins of this life by conceding part of their wealth to the church, were sometimes rewarded by the title of

Beauchief cross base and shaft.

Fox Lanes crosses.

honorary canon of the order and the right of burial within the private burial ground of the monastery. By so doing they, presumably, obtained preference in selection for life in the next world – unlike the Polish priest, during 1936, who sold choice plots and places in the land of the hereafter to his credulous flock for 10/- to 40/- per plot and place, and, in a more enlightened age, was arrested, and not permitted to 'get away' with the profits in this world.

It is suggested the Upper Bradway Cross should be declared a national monument, and be refixed in the former position which, within a few yards, was probably the original site of the Cross.

THE MOORLAND GRANTS TO BEAUCHIEF ABBEY

Beauchief Abbey was well provided with grants of moorland and there were such 'grants' at Fulwood, Rivelin, Wigley, Beeley and Harewood Grange. These and many other 'grants' of land in lower and more agricultural districts can be examined in the Rev. Samuel Pegge's rare, but laborious and largely unexplained, collection of documentary information known as the *Historical Account of Beauchief Abbey*, published in 1801, and a shorter, if slightly extended, *Historical Memorials of Beauchief Abbey*, by the late S.O. Addy, issued in 1878. I have chiefly gathered, and explained, the items from Pegge's volume, but from the finding of bridle roadside and boundary crosses in Holmesfield, Barlow and Brampton parishes (one of which I re-discovered on the Moorhall side of Leash Fen, and another at Beeley and Harewood boundary), I suggest that among the charters of Beauchief burnt in the fire at Lichfield Cathedral during the early-eighteenth century were documents referring to other 'grants' of moorland in these parishes.

COMMON PASTURES OF PADLEY ARE MONASTIC IN 1285

Another charter and grant of 1285 proves that, long before the ducal owners and squires could use the dishonest Enclosure Acts of 1789–1839 in the North Derbyshire moorland area for the purpose of 'swapping' and bartering land, and linking up their present, or recent, 'sporting' estates, the monastic business organisers linked up their little grants of pasturage which, often, they leased out to the surrounding farmers and yeoman at an annual rental, or under a long lease. In 1285, Richard Bernak (Bernac) granted to the 'canons' of Beauchief Abbey, 'common of pasture' 'everywhere' in his manor of 'Paddeley' for their cattle of all kinds kept at the 'Grange of Streberiley' (Strawberry Lee) – Bernak's charter may have been the first grant, or the usual confirmation made by the heir to the estate of the manor, of the earlier grant made by his father, or predecessor.

Another grant (undated) made by William de Dron(e)field and his wife, Agnes, confirms to the 'canons' of Beauchief the 'common of pasture at Streibeisley', (Strawberry Lee), 'for goats and other animals', 'as set forth in the charter which they have from Lord Willielmo de Memil', (the Meynill or Meinel family of Balborough Manor).

Without investigation it would not be possible to say whether this presumably thirteenth or fourteenth-century document is a confirmation of the Hathersage, or the Padley grant. Matthew de Hathersage, as we know, married Anora Meynil of Barlborough. The fact deduced from the 1285 Padley grant, however, is that the monks of Beauchief would, at least, have the additional profit of free grazing of moorlands lying to the west of Burbage Brook.

MONASTIC LEASE OF STRAWBERRY LEE IN 1461
The first reference to the leasing of land at Strawberry Lee or parts of Blacka Moor and Totley Moss, is a lease of 1461 under the seal of the chapter, or 'in domo capitulari', granted to 'John Faunchall', of certain parcels (or pieces) of land and meadow in the place called 'Streaberry Lea', for a term of sixty years at an annual rental of 14/- – probably equal to about £20 today. The demise runs – 'Such, his assigns, as to the same abbot and monastery and their successors, have not been enemies nor hurtful' – meaning that if this son or grandson of the 'John Faunchall' (living in 1417 and, probably, of Fanshawgate Hall, Holmesfield, or his heirs), were not 'good boys' in the eyes of the Church, the lease could be revoked.

Another item in the foregoing document is that a small portion of land at Strawberry Lee upon which a small cottage was built, was reserved to the monastery – the next reference, after 1285, to the original Grange, or stone dwelling, at Strawberry Lee which I had thought stood beside the three (now two) decayed rowan trees called by the Totleyite 'The Three Ships'.

ANOTHER LEASE IN 1530
The last known lease of 'Streberyley' (Strawberry Lee) was granted to a Thomas North, on 1 October 1530, for seventy years, at a rental of 6s. 8d. – 'beyond 6s. 8d. to be paid by him (North) to the chief lords'.

After the Dissolution of the Monasteries and their great estates (1535), which followed the business, and marriage, quarrel of Henry VIII with Rome, the success of the Protestant Reformation was probably prepared by virtue of the fact that the monastic estates were divided among the cutest of the nobles and squirearchy in 1535–8, and they had no subsequent desire to change, and probably lose, some of their regained church territory and later power.

THE LATER OWNERS
After the 'Dissolution' the rent of the Abbey lands of Beauchief, however modestly, was valued at £150 a year, and for the usual 'good and faithful services', rendered by these gentry, the fortunate Sir Nicholas Strelley, on 10/4/1537, for a payment of £223 in cash, was rewarded with the cheap bargain, or prize, of the Beauchief Abbey lands. This prize also included 'all houses, buildings, land, meadows, pastures and commons belonging, which Thomas North holds to farme', and Strawberry Lee was in the possession of the Strelleys, the succeeding Pegges, and the Pegge-Burnell family until, probably in or about 1900, it was bought by the late Duke of Rutland to form part of his shooting estate, and became part of his great Longshaw Moors Estate and grouse preserves of 12,300 acres – the largest in Derbyshire.

A 1535 INVENTORY OF STRAWBERRY LEE
The record of the 'Household Stuff' at the Grange of Strawberry Lee is given in the inventory of the Abbey, dated 2/8/1535.

It consisted of 'on materas' (1 mattress), '2 shetts' (sheets), '2 blanketts', '2 covletts' (coverlets), 'an old covynge' (covering or carpet?), '3 grete pannys' (large earthenware pans or bowls?), and '2 small' (pans?), '2 potts' (stewing or water pots?), '2 almeris' (cupboards, pantries, or safes), '5 mylke kitts' (milk cans), 'on loome' (for wool weaving), '3 doblers' (doublers used for wool spinning), '2 count' setts' (countersetts), '00 borde' (board?), '2 trestilles' (trestles), 'a pair of combs' (woolcombs), and 'a branding iron' – for branding sheep or cattle.

The facts of the above record, whether correct, or minimised by previous abstractions, cannot be checked, but it is possible that the monks of Beauchief, at 'the Grange of Streberily (1285)', 'the small cottage' and small portion of land at Strawberry Lee (1461), reserved for themselves a portion of the good, and the rough, summer grazing of cattle and the all-year-round rearing of sheep or goats for the supply of milk and meat.

STRAWBERRY LEE FARM IN 1691
An inventory I took from the Derbyshire Archaeological Society's *Journal* for 1881 is highly interesting. It reads as follows:

'A true and perfect Inventory of all and singular the Goods, Chattels and Creditts of Strelley Pegg, late of Beauchieffe [Beauchief Hall], in the County of Derby, Esq., deceas(e)d, taken, vallued, and appraized the fourteenth day of

December, Anno Domini, One Thousand six hundred ninety one, by Thomas Burley, John Rotherham junr, Godfrey Webster, and Charles Dixon; as followeth:

At Strawberry Lee
Item seaven score weathers [castrated rams] and seaventy-five ewes – or £53 10 0.
Item hey [hay] there – or £3. 6. 8.
Item one cow in calv'd [in calf] – or £2. 10. 0.

Although the greater part of the walled-in land at Strawberry Lee (now about 90 acres) probably was cleared and, almost certainly, walled-in later than 1691, and the rudely shaped fields are earlier than the Totley Act of 1839 (the latest Enclosure Act in the North Derbyshire moorland area enclosing 1188 acres of common lands), it is apparent that cleared land and hay-making was common at Strawberry Lee before 1691, and the pasturage of Blacka Moor good pasturage for sheep. The super-abundance of bracken on Blacka Moor and similar places today is the sure sign of what should be, and some day must be, regarded as the criminal neglect of rough pasture land.

THE STRAWBERRY LEE FARM AND BUILDINGS DEMOLISHED IN 1936

The rambler and lover of old moorside farms were shocked, in February of last year, when they saw that the farms and buildings were being demolished, and that the only trace of this familiar landmark was the ruins in the little farm yard. The rambler, moreover, asked, and wondered why and found no answer!

We would fain hope that, some day, moorside farming will again be a feature at Strawberry Lee, and a house and farm buildings be rebuilt; with the right to 'turn' sheep and young cattle on the moor and Totley Moss – before the expected national necessity for extensive agricultural development demands the taking of drastic steps with owner and occupier which, mildly initiated and resorted to during the 1914–18 war period, were speedily, and conveniently, dropped in 1919. One of the fields might be used for school and Sunday school parties, but it would appear that the remainder of the enclosed land, after woeful neglect some years before the war and since, could, within a period of ten years, restore Strawberry Lee to its former position as a good moorside farm and 'tea-place'.

THE FAMED BULL AT STRAWBERRY LEE

(See also the section, *The Old Sideboard and Strawberry Lee Bull's Head* in the article, *The Story of 'Fox House Inn' and Callow Farm*. Ed.)

We well remember the 'stuffed' head of the fine bull which, after purchase by

Mr Thomas Rowarth, at the Longshaw sale, reposed in the top room of 'Fox House Inn' and, after he left the inn, was given to the Longshaw Estate Committee, and now reposes in the Warden's Room in the east rear of the Lodge.

I was informed that the Duke and Duchess of Rutland admired this animal and, after it was killed (about 1886?), the 'stuffed' head became one of the 'trophies' in the Longshaw Shooting Lodge. This bull was reared and 'kept' at Strawberry Lee farm during the stewardship of Tommy Mottram, who worked the farm and land for the late Mr George Sampson, of Beauchief. One of his sons, Mr Edward Sampson, the late surveyor for the Norton R.D.C., now in retirement at Heysham, and to whom I am indebted for a number of facts relating to Strawberry Lee, says that his father, George Sampson, bred West Highland cattle on this farm, and, 'one year, when the Royal Show was held at Newcastle, he exhibited at the show and beat the Scotsman in every class in which he showed.' This bull's head, from one of the exhibits, was the one presented to the grandfather of the present Duke, and Mr Edward possesses the Duke's autograph letter of thanks.

THE SITE OF STRAWBERRY LEE MONASTIC GRANGE
The lover of Strawberry Lee desires to know the exact site of the monastic 'Grange' (Old French for barn or granary, and usually a barn, and farm, attached to an English monastery) which preceded the early-nineteenth-century farm, and its two-gated yard and restricted outbuildings.

'The Three Ships' (now two dead rowan trees) which, Mr Partington assures me will be replanted by the Sheffield Estates Committee, are at, or beside, the site of an old building, and a little spade work would probably reveal the exact place or foundations. The two dead trees today stand a little beyond the end, and the top, of the second field west of the 'yard' of the recent Strawberry Lee Farm and its demolished buildings – at a distance of approximately 400 yards west of this recently demolished farm house. The six-inch-to-a-mile Ordnance Map, surveyed in, or shortly after 1876, shows the trees growing inside the 'V'-shaped corner of this field.

Although there may be doubts as to the site of the monastic Strawberry Lee Grange and whether the 1285 recorded house and buildings fixed in this high place fell into ruin or disrepair before, or after, 1691, it is possible that Peter Pegge-Burnell decided to build his new, but ill-fated (1820–30) Strawberry Lee Grange on, or about, the site of the original Grange.

Mr Edward Sampson supports my old thought and theory that, possibly, if excavations were made on this site, some interesting foundations might be revealed, and he also remembers the dressed stones fixed in the adjoining field walls.

THE MONASTIC GRANGE BECOMES BUILDING MATERIAL

The pre-war note I took from Jacques Green, the gamekeeper, and wrote on my six-inch map at the time was 'Mr Coates, of Dore, led many a load of dressed stone from the site of Strawberry Lee Grange', and I was told that the stone was taken for the building of some of the Dore New Road stone villadom, probably not later than the seventies. I was not able to obtain the exact date and trace the facts to their source, but they will stand. These loads of stone were probably bought from the agent and owner of the Pegge-Burnell Estate, at Beauchief.

A little rough-worked stone may be detected in the field walls here and there and, twenty-five years ago, I saw two or three smaller shaped stones. The chief feature today is a large well-worked and shaped roof-corner stone (corbel?) of several hundredweights, and too heavy to lift by hand. This would assist in assuming the nature and height of one building. The others have disappeared. The altitude above sea level of the old building is about 1200 feet, or about 100 feet higher than the ex-Strawberry Lee Farm and buildings.

THE ORIGIN OF THE HOUSE BY THE THREE SHIPS

Mr Edward Sampson, from his picture book of memory, indicates that my unproved theory of the site of the original 'Grange of Streberiley' (1285) and 'small cottage' (1461) being beside the Totleyite's landmark of 'The Three Ships' trees (now two) should be placed among the many lists of not proven and still to be found.

He declares that Mr Peter Pegge, of Beauchief Hall, in about 1820–30, decided to build a moorland residence at Strawberry Lee and to call it 'Strawberry Lee Grange'. The building was erected, and the roof timbers fixed when a terrific gale blew it down, and it was never rebuilt. The site was near 'The Three Ships'. There was, or is, in existence at the Estate Office at Beauchief, an old drawing of the front elevation of this 'S.L.G.' as it was built, and Mr Sampson well remembers the Georgian design of very plain dressed ashlar stone, with a doorway in the centre, a room on each side, and two upper rooms – with three windows – all with 'Y' shaped archings. There was a plain parapet wall-and-stone balustrade – similar to the one at Beauchief Hall. This Peter Pegge (d. 8/2/1836 aged eighty-five) who assumed the name of Pegge-Burnell, after becoming heir to part of the estate of Darcy Burnell, of Winkburn, spent some time at Strawberry Lee, for his nephew, Broughton Benjamin Steade (also a Pegge-Burnell) by sign-manual, d. 30/5/1850, aged seventy-five, married Peter's illegitimate child by Elizabeth Dalton, and Elizabeth lived at Strawberry Lee Farm.

WHEN STRAWBERRY LEE WAS A GOOD FARM

Mr Edward Sampson's grandfather and father, who were agents to Peter

Pegge and his successors, farmed the land on Beauchief Abbey Estate and at Strawberry Lee, and stocked it with Scotch sheep. The old shepherd (and, as I have heard, good stocking knitter) Thomas Mottram, of Strawberry Lee, in his earlier years, would go up into Scotland and drive the sheep home along the by-ways and bridle-ways and, occasionally, in spite of good shepherding, a few would travel back to the Scotch hill sides from whence they came. 'Droving', however, was generally superseded by rail trucking in the seventies and early-eighties of last century.

'Tommy's' proficiency in women's work is supported by a note from Mr Edward Sampson to the effect that his father (George) would send the old clothes to Strawberry Lee and 'Tommy' would cut them into tiny strips and knit them into the cloth hearthrugs which were so popular fifty years ago. At one time there were probably ten or 12 of these hearthrugs in Sampson's house at Beauchief.

'Old Tommy' died at 'S.L.', and he was one of the local shepherds who probably attended the first very local sheep dog trials which, about Christmas 1895, or shortly after, preceded the first official 'trial' in 1898. The last generation of Sampsons spent many happy days there, and their father (George) drove up in the dog cart or wagonette and left it at the sheep-wash. Edward well remembers the old footril near the bottom gate to the moor, which was worked with a pony, to draw the coal. There was a large horizontal wheel formed in wood, like a windlass, elevated from the ground, and the pony was harnessed underneath it.

'BOW-LEGGED TOMMY'
'Old Tommy', their shepherd, was bow-legged, and it was little use trying to stop a Scotch sheep in a door way, for the sheep made straight for the 'gap' between Tommy's legs, and 'through they went'.

He had a stentorian voice, and the Totleyite was wont to say that he could hear 'Owd Tommy' shouting at his sheep and dog on Strawberry Lee and Blacka Moor when the Totleyite was standing beside the 'Cricket Inn', at the foot of Totley Recreation Ground.

The young Sampsons collected birds eggs, and 'Tommy' made several rare additions to their collections – one being a night-jar's eggs, and another a batch of 'moor-peeps' eggs which contained a large green one. On examination it proved to be a cuckoo's egg.

SHEEP-SHEARING AT STRAWBERRY LEE
The sheep-clipping was a rare gathering at Strawberry Lee. The neighbouring farmers and shepherds attended, and other dipper-helpers, and Strawberry Lee clipping was the biggest in the district. Then came the big supper, and the

sing-song – 'and didn't they put some beef and ale out of sight'. These however, are the dead days, and machine, hustle and bustle, has succeeded.

CATCHING THE NAVVY FOWL THIEVES AT STRAWBERRY LEE

The older men will remember the row of Navvies' huts opposite the (today) Rifle Range headquarters house in 'Moss Road' and beside the Recreation ground etc., and the 'doings' of these rough men during the making of the Totley Tunnel. About this time (probably 1890) Strawberry Lee was troubled with the navvies' dogs roaming over the moor and worrying the sheep. The woodman was sent from Beauchief Estate to help 'Tommy' to keep a lookout, and he took an 'old pin-fire' gun and some cartridges.

'Old Tommy' got 'a small barrel in' for the occasion, as 'it was no use having company in the house and no beer'. But, on the second night, when they were in the house sampling Berry's 'Strike-me-Stiff' – or as we said, forty years ago 'Berry's Lion Ale and look at me for a tanner' – they heard a commotion in the hen-roost. They went to investigate and found two navvies busy with Tommy's fowls. One was in the roost handing them out, and the other was at the foot of the ladder, receiving them.

THE 'SHOOTING' AND THE SEQUEL

Then came the scuffle. The man at the foot of the ladder escaped, but the man at the top had to run the gauntlet. Tommy and the woodman, however, were 'well lined' with Berry's brew, and the second man got away.

The woodman then had a sudden brain-wave and, stepping in the house, he seized the old pin-fire gun, and, as Navvy No. 2 was getting over the yard gate, he was presented with a dose of buck-shot in his nether regions, and carried it away, yelling and bellowing as he went down the moor.

So the matter seemed to end, but, possibly a fortnight later, after Tommy had called at the 'Cricket Inn' and, as usual, stayed until 'turning-out time', and was wending his way towards Strawberry Lee, a burly navvy stepped-out of the darkness as he was going through the bottom gate to the moor. In the navvy's forcible language he told 'Old Tommy' he would 'do him in' for shooting him a few nights previously.

And, to quote 'Tommy's' own words:

"Well, ah mays na moor ta doo bur ah crack'd 'im one o'er t'eead wi mi ashplant, an' ah down'd 'im an' left 'im. Ah went dahn t'next mornin' ter see if 'e wer still theer. Oh 'e'd gone reight enuff, but ther' wer plenty o' blood abaht."

THE END OF POOR OLD KITTY, THE HOUSEKEEPER

There was a sad side to Tommy's reign at Strawberry Lee for, when the navvies were there, he contracted small pox during the epidemic which prevailed (about 1902) and, in another way, 'downed' a goodly number of the tunnel and line makers.

'Tommy' lay abed in the house, thoroughly 'isolated', and his old housekeeper (Kitty) went to Totley Bents for some groceries. On her return she encountered a heavy snowstorm and, overcome by the exposure, she laid down and was buried in the snow – less than 100 yards from the farm house door. She was not found until two days later when Dr John Aldred, in paying a visit to his patient, noticed a mound in the snow and, on closer inspection, he found it was poor old Kitty, frozen to death.

THE JUBILEE BONFIRE AT STRAWBERRY LEE

In the Victoria Jubilee year (1897), Strawberry Lee was marked out as one of the places in the official list, and a huge bonfire was made on the top of the hill, west of the farm house.

My warmest thanks are due to Mr Edward Sampson for his valuable contributions.

'THE MONKS' PATH' APPROACH TO STRAWBERRY LEE GRANGE FROM 'CROSS SCYTHES'

What I have christened 'The Monks' Path' and, until after the eighteenth century, the chief approach to Strawberry Lee, will eventually, become one of the well-used public entrances to this free territory from the motor bus terminus at 'Cross Scythes Inn', Totley. I, and our club, have used this path for many years, and only the cussedness of Chesterfield R.D.C., or the tenant of the moors, can excuse the placing of a trespass board (autumn of 1934) beside the horse gate in the field wall at the north foot of Wimble Hol(m)e Hill, about 220 yards S.E. of the (Feb. 1936) demolished Strawberry Lee Farm house and buildings. A publicly acknowledged path, for the 500 yards to, and along, the N. slope of Wimble Hol(m)e Hill would not frighten one grouse bird in one month.

Coming up the main road to Baslow, and arriving at the seven road-doomed (widening) cottages at Lane Head (the first four of stone, and the last three chiefly of brick), and turning right (the old bridle road is seen in the field on the right below the three houses), we descend and cross Monnybrook (lower down called 'Needham's Dike'), and then ascend to the once Brookhill Farm and now headquarters for the Territorial campers and rifle range firing parties. We are now in (Totley) 'Moss Road' proper and rise between the walls on the ancient bridle road where the sheep, goats and cattle of the several Totley yeoman farmers, and of the monks of Beauchief, were driven hundreds of years before stone walls were generally built. After passing Bole Hill Lodge (right) and reaching the junction of the alternate walled-in lane the summit of the enclosed lane is ahead. At the gate and wall corner we turn abruptly (right) and soon descend gently down the north slope of Wimble Hol(m)e Hill to the horse-gate and field wall.

THE CART ROAD TO STRAWBERRY LEE
The lower cart road to Strawberry Lee Farm, from Totley Bents and Recreation Ground along Strawberry Lee Lane and, from the farmyard, to the Stony Ridge to Fox House main road (which commenced at the now abandoned ganister workings of Pickford and Holland's, Totley Brick Works, and pre-war quarry and ganister working) probably was not made until after 1818. The latter was the date of the opening of the Sheffield–Fox House Road.

We will now deal with other approaches to and features of Blacka Moor Estate.

COW SICK AND STRAWBERRY LEE PLANTATION
As you pass along the cart road from Strawberry Lee towards Stony Ridge toll bar site and the main road (going N.W.), and pass through the field gate to the moor and cross a little hollow, you see the beginnings of the Cow Sick (or Cow Sike) feeder of Blacka Dike and then walk beside the westerly wall of the modern and narrow, Strawberry Lee half-grown plantation and its rhododendrons. The latter, at least, were planted by order of the late Duke of Rutland, after the purchase – about 1900 – and the then dilapidated wall of the plantation was rebuilt.

THE SHEFFIELD–DORE–FOX HOUSE BRIDLE ROAD
You may continue your leisurely sauntering in the narrow plantation for a long half-mile towards Meg and Jin Hollow and, if you look as you walk, you will eventually see, and trace, the course of the sunken old bridle road which led from Sheffield, via Dore, to Fox House and beyond. It was in daily use until the opening of the Sheffield–Fox House Road.

WIMBLE HOLME HILL, LEE SICK AND BLACKA HILL
I will not sing of the beauties of Blacka Moor, of the golden and brown and the gay and sober and the changing hues of bracken, ling and heather; or of its semi-wildness and remoteness from the road speeder and suburban villadom. A wise man will learn and appreciate his Blacka, and the greyer-green tones of Strawberry Lee, and its ancient, because haphazard-shaped, fields.

On the south, or Totley Moss side of Strawberry Lee, is the steep heathery bank of Wimble Hol(m)e Hill (1144 feet) and, beneath it, the little tricklet, rising in the once called Wimble Hole (wimple, or wimble, is to meander or wind).

Beyond the easterly field wall it becomes a stream and is dignified by the name of Lee Sick (sitch, sick, or sike – for small stream, or drain) as it runs down to join Blacka Brook at the foot of the hollow.

The Bole Hill (1020 feet) and Bole Hill (ex-shepherd's) Lodge are on the right and east of Lee Sike, and the old 'Bole', or lead smelting place, or places thereon, are on the windy ridge S.W. of the lodge and a trenchy track leads to, and beyond, it.

Blacka Hill proper is the rounded moor immediately north of the recently demolished Strawberry Lee farm and buildings, and is only a prosy shaped hill when seen from below. The newly-made path towards the Meg and Jin Hollow, main road entrance to Blacka Moor, goes across Blacka Hill.

STRAWBERRY LEE SHEEPFOLD AND LENNY HILL

Entering the Blacka Moor estate from Totley Bents and Recreation Ground, by the lower road called Strawberry Lee Lane at the ganister workings and old quarry (again abandoned several years ago), the fields of the old Hallfield Farm and small wood, and Lee Sick streamlet, are on the right, and a few yards after crossing the brooklet (left) and old disused Strawberry Lee Farm sheep fold and sheep wash, we have Lenny Hill.

LENNY HILL

The open rough ground at the end of the fields (right) is called Lenny Hill (about 850 feet). The word may be derived from 'lennucky', a term used for poor, or barren land. From this point, the cart road bends to the left and rises toward Strawberry Lee Farm site.

SHORT'S LANE AND BLACKA BOTTOM

Another approach to Blacka Bottom is from Dore Townhead, and, as we approach the bend and descend towards Redcar Brook and the bridge, with the new Children's Holiday Home on the left and short of it, we can see the sunken course of the ancient Dore-to-Fox-house, etc., bridleway going down the slope of the first field. After crossing the bridge and turning left, we enter Short's Lane and, in 600 yards, the prettiest portion of the Estate, at Blacka Bottom. The late Mr H.W. Hancock, of 'Rushley', Dore, informed me that Short's Lane is named after an old man named Short, whose cottage was removed 'years ago'. This occupation lane ended at the old quarry (right) as we enter into Blacka Bottom and the private cart road goes S.E. to Hallfield Farm which, I am told, once stood perhaps 500 yards to the west.

Forty years ago Short's Lane was an 'El Dorado' for local blackberry pickers, and there was only space for one cart, and not two, to pass. Today, however, we know that, to outvie the suburban dweller and the more active of the unemployed, the 'native' must get up early in the morning. The long stretch of the seven steep fields (right) of Swift's Hill Sides are on the right, and the village blackberry picker, formerly, had a remunerative time.

BLACKA DIKE
The pre-1867 one-inch-to-mile map gives the name of Blacka Dike to the main stream after it receives the tricklet which comes from the N.W., but the 1876–80 six-inch map awards the name to the main stream which comes from the S.W. – and the same inch map calls it Eaglescliffe Dike. The stream which rises in Meg and Jin Hollow is not baptised.

BLACKA PLANTATION – OLD AND NEW
A few more trees between these two latter streamlets would improve the landscape, and we may remember that, in the usual English tender way towards landowners, the Plantation was cut down about the end of war-time, and the late owner was not compelled to replant.

This plantation was previously felled about 1864 and provided timber used during the making of the present (Midland) railway line direct to Sheffield, via Dronfield and Dore. The replanting and after-care of the last plantation was not skilfully carried out.

SWIFTS' HILL SIDES
On the opposite (N.) side of the Blacka Bottom (valley) and, long ago, becoming part of the wild and uncultivated moorland, blackberry, bracken and gorse patch, etc., are remains of field walls, which prove that the hus-bandman was busy after the Dore Enclosure Act of 1809 and its Award of 10/4/1822. The late, learned, in local lore, and well-respected Mr H.W. Hancock, of Rushley, Dore, who died 22/2/35, aged eighty-three, informed me that this land was cleared by the Swift family, of Roundseats Farm (off Whitelow Lane). To this day the 'natives' give the name of 'Swifts' Hill Sides' to the northern side of the valley, from the brook side to the field walls along the top of the steep bank.

One of the Swifts, perhaps as long as seventy-five spring-times ago, was wont to lead his horse with the old-fashioned wooden-pegged harrow down the steep slope, and he would carry the harrow on his back on the return journey, because the horse could not pull it up the steep slope.

ROUNDSEATS SCHOOL LAND
The Dore Enclosure Act gave the names of several persons to act as Trustees of the village school, and also the acreage of land allotted to the school. Mr H.W. Hancock's grandfather, and the latter's brother were among the Trustees. He informed me that the beginning of the Trust was the fact that some years previous to 1809, the freeholders of Dore (his ancestors included) raised money by subscription among themselves to encroach upon the common at 'Rouset Moor' (later called Roundseats), to the extent of a few

acres (about six) – using the subscription to fence and rid (clear) the land. After letting the land to a tenant, the rent was used to pay a schoolmaster to teach 'a certain number of poor children' of the township of Dore. The school, built on the site of the old chapel, in 1821, was endowed with £30 a year for the instruction of 30 scholars. The Enclosure Act Commissioners, in the Award, allotted more land to the same object and, in all, about 60 acres of the 5000 acres enclosed under this Act.

Roundseats Farm is up a slope, on the right, as we enter Short's Lane – coming from Dore Townhead, and the much older High Greave Farm is behind us – to the north.

MEG AND JIN HOLLOW
(See also the section, *Meg and Jin Hollow* in the article, *History upon Sheffield Corporation's Moorlands*. Ed.)

Proceeding up the old plantation ride we eventually arrive near the Sheffield–Fox House Road and, turning to right of the drive, come to the boundary wall and a formerly pretty hollow, which presents the appearance of a nasty rubbish tip – after the straightening of the road bend (1930) lately christened (by a speeding motorist only) 'The Devil's Elbow'. We have chiefly to thank Councillor H. Kirk for acting on the hint and for the welcome planting (1935) of saplings on the sides of the road, but we wish the City Fathers would give the low side and slope of the road a 'decent dress' of shrubbery. The old bridle road to Dore and Sheffield, in two places, can be seen crossing the hollow.

I have not found any acceptable meaning for Meg and Jin or old renderings of the name. A local rendering, but apparently without printed record or date, is that two girls, or young women, named Meg and Jin perished near the ancient bridle road in this Hollow. Old renderings of the name are required.

Blacka, similarly, is difficult to explain beyond saying that Blacka connected with black, sombre, or dark, would equally fit the Dike on this Estate, or the similar named streamlet which forms the chief tributary of Haywood Brook – under White Edge.

PRIMITIVE MAN AT BLACKA AND STRAWBERRY LEE
Unfortunately the archaeologist who seeks for the evidence of the existence and contacts of the primitive early Britons with our moorland areas, often works alone and, occasionally, selfishly, and much rich evidence of working places, tools and instruments (flints, stone and other axes, daggers, hammers, etc.), is scattered, unpublished, or lost. Otherwise I could probably prove that primitive man not only used, but lived, or worked, beside a number of our Derbyshire moorland bridle roads.

My friend, A. Leslie Armstrong, F.S.A., told me, fourteen years ago, that he found a number of flint implements near 'The Monks' Path' to Strawberry Lee where it goes along the north slope of Wimble Hol(m)e Hill, and that most of the weathered (or bare) patches on the slope yielded a few flints.

This article, however, must give full credit to Mr W.M. Cole, 22 Nether Green Road, Sheffield, for his recent persistent and painstaking research work on this public moorland estate where, today, the archaeologist has much more liberty than on other local and, as they say, 'strictly preserved' moors.

BOLE HILL

A trenchy bridle road goes N.W. through the gate and a few yards west of the approach to Bole Hill Lodge, to a little above, and beyond, the Lodge. Then it swings sharply round to the left and S.S.W. and, afterwards, going a little to the right (W.) of the ridge it proceeds almost to the corner of the wall at the gate exit of the 'Moss (bridle) Road' to the open moor of Totley Moss.

There are several bare patches strewn with lead smelting debris on this windy ridge. The fuel used may have been obtained from the many primitive pudding-hole, thin coal workings seen chiefly below the ex-Duke's Drive under Brown Edge (coal was worked hereabouts as late as 1830 – Glover's *Gazetteer*) going S.S.W. towards Thickwoods Lodge and Owler Bar – or/and from, the burning of wood and charcoal in the hollow to the north.

A layer of charcoal under a covering of peaty soil is perceptible at various points. There is a little pond near the top of Bole Hill and a few made hollows from which thin flag stone may have been taken.

The trench track, slightly more 'cart roadish' nearer the top, is probably the alternative bridleway often found on a moor and hill slope. Beside, and W. of the wall of the enclosed lane on the east side of Bole Hill, is clear evidence of another alternative trenchy track – also a little below Bole Hill Lodge, both inside the moor.

Mr Cole found two large flint implements and a number of smaller worked flints on Bole Hill.

The view from Bole Hill is one of the best on the S.W. side of Sheffield, but until time has mellowed them, the suburban spread of post-war villadom is a feature – like pinky stains upon a crumpled green carpet.

NEAR STRAWBERRY LEE

On the left side of the rising cart road, and at a point approximately 200 yards east of the site of the demolished Strawberry Lee ex-farmhouse and buildings, there appears to be the remains of a small stone circle with one large raised stone in position. The others lying in formation are entirely or partly covered with bilberry or heather bushes. Adjoining this, and approximately 20 yards to the south, is a small artificial mound, possibly in relation to the circle. More flint flakes have been located near this point between the cart road and Lee Sick. Bateman, in *Vestiges of the Antiquities of Derbyshire*, refers to the opening of a large tumulus on Strawberry Lee – but where? It is probable that this tumulus was situate on Blacka Hill, approximately 370 yards N.N.E. of Strawberry Lee Farm site and nearer Cow Sick, as Mr Cole located the remains of at least two tumuli on this hill. In the vicinity of one he found the remnants of a Bronze Age flint dagger, charred by fire, in addition to other worked flint implements and flakes.

Sunken places adjoining the two destroyed tumuli indicate primitive hut sites, as worked flint was found just outside the indentations in the ground.

LENNY HILL
Probably has unwritten history and association with early man, and one pointer to this conclusion is that a search on the crown of this ridge of Lenny Hill, between Blacka Dike and Lee Sick, revealed flint flakes.

GIANT'S CHAIR NEAR BLACKA PLANTATION
The late S.O. Addy's *Glossary of Words used in the neighbourhood of Sheffield* (July 1888), in the introduction, says:

'Before we reach the Han Kirk Hill [now called Houndkirk – G.H.B.W.], the road makes a sharp bend, and we cross a weird valley which lies at the foot of the hill, and is called Meggon Jin Hollow. Below, and on the other side of the road is the Giant's Chair. The Giant's Chair is not marked on the maps, but it is remembered by the old inhabitants, several of whom have mentioned it to me. The proximity of Giant's Chair to Han Kirk Hill (Giant's Church Hill) is not without significance'.

Again, confirmation, and old renderings of the name are required. 'Han Kirk' is perilously near to 'Ahn Kirk' – good dialect for Houndkirk.

The plan in the glossary shows 'Giant's Chair' in the N.E. boundary of Blacka Plantation, and about 150 yards from the Sheffield–Fox House Road – near the boundary wall at the foot of the Meg and Jin Hollow, below and a little south eastwardly of, today's 1930-made roadside tip. The site, shape, and size of 'Giant's Chair' is lost, and it may have been broken up for wall-stone, etc. Possibly, like Caer's Chair, or Pym Chair (on Carl Wark and near Edale Head), it was a large isolated gritstone, and the result of the water-wearing, etc., of two 'rock basins', one overflowing into the other and wearing away the lower basin into the form of a 'Chair'.

Hallam and Ughill Moors

The Forest of Rivelin

From S.C.R. Handbook, 1950/51. *This was almost the last* big *moor article Ward wrote, for he did write a few articles of length about Kinder Scout just before the plateau finally gained public access in the late 1950s. This article was written, as he says, to lay down fact and story ready 'for the day of liberty to all', however qualified it be, the beginning of the new era. Ward expected the new era to begin after the 1949 National Parks Act, something perhaps to be borne in mind by anyone expecting the new era to begin after the Countryside and Rights of Way Act 2000.*

A **1270 Grant**. Mr John B. Wheat, M.A., in *Garret Gleanings* (*Hunter Archaeological Society Transactions 1930*), unearthed a valuable thirteenth-century document from his lawyer's rooms at 8 Paradise Square, Sheffield.

This Thomas, Lord Furnival charter of Sheffield Manor, is a copy, upon which Mr Wheat's great-grandfather wrote, probably one-hundred-and-twenty-nine years before 1930, 'no date, about 1270', and further endorsed it with 'Remarks on Furnival's Grant and Mr Gibson's letter, 15th May 1791', is worth reproducing for ramblers. I have inserted all explanatory words in brackets and added notes. This 1270 charter, not punctuated, is:

'Know all men present and to come that I, Thomas ffurnival, the son of Lord Thomas ffurnival, have given, Granted, and, by this my present writing, have confirmed to Ellys [Ellis] of Ugghill, and all men of Ugghill, Nether Bradfield, Thornsett, and Hawkesworth, the Herbage as it lies in length and breadth between Ugghill Brook, Eventrevick, and the way leading from Hope to Sheffield, Bradrake, Seven Stones in Horderon, Weanston, to the Water of Agden, for the depasturing [or out-pasturing] and agisting of their own proper Cattle, to be taken Yearly, without any hindrance of me or my Heirs, as they have held the same to ffarm at the Will of my Ancestors. To have and to hold the same of me and my Heirs to the aforesaid Ellys [Ellis] of Ugghill and his Heirs, and all ye men of Ugghill, Nether Bradfeld, Thornsett, and Hawkesworth, and their Heirs, with free ingress and regress, and with all the Appurtenances [other rights belonging to farm properties, or holdings] the aforesaid Herbage freely, quietly, and in peace: All the Men [tenants – yeoman or copyright] of Ugghill, Netherbradfeld, Thornsett, and Hawkesworth, and their Heirs; rendering therefore yearly to me and my Heirs, four marks in

Silver [then worth 1³/₄, each and now fully 40 times more] at two terms of the Year, viz; one half at the ffeast of penticost [Whitsuntide], and the other half at the ffeast of Saint Martin [Martinmass – or 11 Nov.], for all secular [civil – not clerical] services and demands, and moreover, I, the said Thomas and my Heirs, the af(or)s(ai)d Herbage to Ellys [Ellis] of Ugghill and his Heirs, and to all the Men of Ugghill, Nether Bradfeld, Thornsett, and Hawkesworth and their Heirs, will Warrant [guarantee] and against all men for ever defend by these presents. In Witness whereof to this my present writing I have put my Seal, these being Witnesses: Elia de Medhope [Midhope], Thomas de Mountne [Mounteney], Thomas de Sheffeld, Robert de Eckylsale [Ecclesall], and others. Dated at Sheffeld, on Sunday next before the ffeast of Saint George the Marter'.

Some Explanations

Thornseat – from upper Bradfield Dale, to Strines, Pears House – once medieval farm – and back to Back Tor end of Derwent Edge.

Hawksworth – that part of Bradfield which ends at the flat moor summit – still called 'Howden Edge' (Howden estate boundary line) and sources of Agden Brook. It is denoted by stones from Back Tor (N.N.E.) and, from about 350 yards E. of Howshaw Tor, a mile-long (Saxon?) trench boundary along Cartledge Stones Ridge, goes almost to the summit of 'The Duke of Norfolk's Road' – Bradfield Enclosure Act awarded public way – on 9/3/1826; which must soon be liberated.

The way leading from Hope to Sheffield – this is Stannington–Moscar Cross, etc.. 'High Riggs' Road, then a bridleway which, from Beacon (now Beeton) Farm, crossed Rod Moor top, and through Crawshaw Head buildings.

Bradrake – now Broad Rake – even then (1270) a crudely defined tract of land – is the 11-mile trench boundary of Rivelin Forest.

Seven Stones Circle – 1 mile N.W. of the Crow Chin summit edge end of Broad Rake, is on Hordron Edge, 600 yards S.S.E. of Cutthroat Bridge, beside the Sheffield and Bradfield–Moscar Cross–Hope ancient bridleway in this 1270 charter, and gives ancient support for our claim under the 1949-passed National Parks, Access to the Countryside Act. A Hallamshire boundary (1637) says 'Beaven Stones' and 'a place where certaine Stones are sett upon the ends, haveinge markes in them'. Where are they now? See T. Winder's *T Heft an' Blades o' Sheffield*.

The Wainstones (Wagon), or Wheel Stones, are on Derwent Edge.

The Water of Agden – means to the sources of Agden Brook and Cartledge Stones Ridge watershed.

The Medieval Forest of Rivelin Boundary

The previously thought first charters which mention the 'common way which leads from Sheffield towards Darwent', and 'the road leading from Hope towards Sheffield' (identical as far as Moscar Cross), are the third Lord Thomas Furnival's charters, of 10/8/1297. Lord Furnival gave to the tenantry (yeoman freeholders) of Stannington, Morewood, Hallam and Fullwood, herbage and foliage throughout the whole of his forest of Rivelin 'as it lies in length and breadth between Malen [Malin] Bridge, Belhag ['Bell Hagg Inn', and thereabouts] and Whiteley Wood on the one part, and a place called Stanedge and the common way which leads from Sheffield towards Darwent on the other'. (This common way, which, S.W. of Moscar House Farm, going W., in 1½ miles, crosses Derwent Edge, 500 yards S. of Wheel Stones, is, since 1933, a freed track – due to our writings, S.C.R. work, and the Peak District F.P.S. victory.)

The yeoman freeholders had liberty to turn in their cattle and to gather green and dry wood and, in return, had to pay Lord Furnival and his heirs, four pounds of silver yearly, in half-yearly payments, at Pentecost, and at the feast of St Martin.

The inhabitants of Ughill, Nether Bradfield, Thornset, and Hawkesworth, within Bradfield Chapelry, and Sheffield Manor, were also granted 'common of pasture on the moors between Ughill Brook, Gwentree Sicke, the way which leadeth from Hope towards Sheffield, Broadake [Broad Rake is meant], Sevenstones in Holderon [Hordron] and Wainstones on the water of Agden – with a reserved rent of four marks'. Wigtwistle inhabitants were granted 'the like privileges on their own moors', and similar rights were granted to the inhabitants in, or by, Loxley Chase.

No one can, from the foregoing rough boundaries – with ancient mark stones broken up and lost, etc. – give exact descriptions, but, leaving the filling-in to future investigation, or comparisons with other unknown charters or medieval documents, etc., I essay it as follows:

Hallam Moor and White Path Moss Boundary
The Firth, or Forest, or, generally, uncultivated moorland, of Riveling (Rivelin) would go from today's Malen (Malin) Bridge, up Rivelin Brook for 11 miles, to about the Stepping Stones and Mill Dam, and then rise to opposite the foot of the straight, and long Hagg Lane – S. of Mill Dam. Then, up to Bell Hagg and/or to Lydgate, and down to Whiteley Wood, up Porter Brook to Carr Bridge, and rise up to the ancient (1574 recorded boundary) 'heap of stones', and then county boundary mark at Ringinglow. Thence it followed the Deep Sick source of Limb Brook, and along the county boundary and watershed-line of Friars Ridge (Beauchief Abbey lands), to Stanage Pole, and Edge, to the Crow Chin point and bend of Stanage Edge. Here it – to me – undoubtedly turned from N.W. to N.E., down the 1½ miles of ancient Broad Rake trench (to its eastward bend), until it merges into Oaking Clough, a little above (S.W.) the present Redmires Reservoir conduit and at, or by, the con-fluence of the two head feeders of Oaking Clough which, in another three-quarters of a mile, joins Hollowmeadows Brook and becomes the Rivelin.

Thence it follows the Rivelin to Malin Bridge. Intelligent Sheffield ramblers and lovers of ancient moorland and boundary records should, with the passing of the National Parks Bill, in 1949, before 1953, be able to see this Rivelin Forest 'Broad Rake' trench boundary line, as of right and manhood. All I can say is that, at last, I have published these facts and lines of location and as was possible, they will not be lost. This trench way track must be claimed under the 1949 Act.

A Rivelin Forest Boundary is also in Ronkesley MS. 1153 – in Sheffield Reference Library, as:

'1559, Oct 3. At the General Court of Francis, Earl of Shrewsbury, an order was taken betwixt the tenants of the Firth [a section of the Forest, or rough lands] of Riveling and the Firth of Hawkesworth for variance [a dispute] among the respective limits and boundaries, which was pronounced on the said ground by the Earl's Officers, with assent of the inhabitants, 12 June, 1 Eliz. 1559'.

'To begin at Lady Seat, and so descending down the hill to a place called the Stony Ditch [a Dike, or Sitch?], and so from thence following up after the ditch [Broad Rake] that parteth Sheffield and Bradfield parish unto the north end of Stanage [which corresponds with Crow Chin]. If beastes or cattle stray beyond the limits they shall be neighbourly and quietly driven unto the said mears [mears, or boundaries] without any sleating [or dog-driving], chasing, or impounding. It is ordered that this decision shall be entered into the Court Book at Sheffield'.

Evidently the tenants of Rivelin and Hawkesworth walked the boundaries with the Earl's stewards, and agreed, or accepted, the decision, on the spot. But, so roughly described, where are the mark-stones today?

Lady Seat, like Lord's Seat on Rushup Edge, may be the summit of today's Kay Flat, the highest part (1330 feet) of the still well-kept Ughill Moor, a little E. of the top (1321 feet) of the long, walled off, now heathery, Stake Hill Road, which, joining old High Riggs Road, comes up from Sugworth Road and, as Mr George Goodinson tells me, in his early years, it had a wooden pole at its summit – like the Edale to Chapel-en-le-Frith bridleway usually native-called 'T'Stake'. Kay Flat summit is a good half-mile slightly N. of W. from Crawshaw Head House – where, today, and when Mr Ernest Wilson was the gamekeeper (until 1948) we had, and have, a refreshment house for ramblers. I have not observed any cairn upon this flattish moor top. Ughill Moor may be well-kept, but most Peak and S. Yorks. moors, for fifty years and more, have been noted for bad draining and for old heather not fit for sheep, or even grouse. Heather over ten years old, except for grouse shelter, is practically rubbish.

Loftshaw, once the 'loft', or upper wood, is the rough slope a good half-mile N. lower down, and between (left of) Stake Hill and Sugworth Roads.

Rivelin Forest boundary on Hallam Moor, from Kay Flat summit, or the lost name of Lady Seat, may well have been more or less S.E., down to the confluence of Hollowmeadows Brook with the Trout Sike, and Oaking Clough streams (not 20 yards apart), by the mossy 'Slippery Stones', and where the united streams become the Rivelin, at about 150 yards S. of Weather Cote Farm. The course of the spring at 1175 feet level, rising at 400 yards S.W. of Crawshaw Head house (long covered-in down the fields and flowing towards Weather Cote Farm) may, I suggest, have been followed by the boundary.

'Stony Ditch'. Mr George Goodinson, the last of four generations who served the Dukes of Norfolk as gamekeepers and or water-bailiffs on Hallam Moors, or the upper Rivelin stream, and lives at Fox Holes Lodge, built for him and his wife (*née* Fox), on the side (S.) of the lower Rivelin Reservoir, in 1891, gives me the clue to 'Stony Ditch' – Dike, or Sitch – in the 1559 record.

He confirms that the spring, rising, and still seen, 400 yards S.W. of Crawshaw Head House – a few yards above (N. of) the present footpath from opposite Fold Farm, on the Sheffield–Glossop Road, leading to Upper Hollow Meadows Farm and Crawshaw Head House – was, when he was a lad, an open stream. Then, probably about seventy years ago, it was covered-in down the three fields, in a S.E. direction and, from beside the footpath which now leads straight N.N.W. from beside Hollow Meadows school house (W. of it), to ensure a pure water supply for Weathercote Farm, on the S. side of the main road. Goodinson distinctly remembers that this lower part of it was then called Stony Sike. Until definite refutation appears, this explains Stony Ditch in the rough boundary document of 12/6/1559, which, ignoring Oaking Clough, confirms the Broad Rake trench boundary.

The Rivelin Forest boundary then followed up the attractive, steep-sloped Oaking Clough, almost due S., for three-quarters of a mile, to Sheffield Water Works conduit line leading from the Black Clough most northerly source of Rivelin to Upper Redmires Reservoir – made in two sections. The earliest section, of 2587 yards, appears to have been made in, or about, 1855–60, as far as Oaking Clough – by the Sheffield Water Company – and the little pond, and sluice, to turn excess water into Rivelin Reservoirs. The second length, from Oaking Clough to Black Clough, of 2640 yards, was made by Sheffield Corporation, in or about 1888, shortly after acquisition of the Water Works Company. This Redmires 'Catchwater' is sometimes called Oaking (or Oaken) Clough Conduit. The Upper Redmires Reservoir, 1150 feet, 98 feet higher than Barbrook Reservoir, was finished in 1853–4, the Middle Reservoir (1100 feet) in about 1835, and the Lower Reservoir (1050 feet) in 1847. From this conduit crossing where the flat flood-silted bottom could be made a little pond, odd feet deep, the present boundary line follows the westerly bend of Oaking Clough 800 yards, but from 20 to 80 yards north of Oaking Clough stream, which may have been the original boundary line. At this point (800 yards) is the S.W. bend of Oaking Clough's chief feeder, which, in another short half-mile, practically begins at the 'Foul Hole' moss and bog in which I once 'rantied' during a heavy winter snow. Gamekeepers keep away from it!

From this 800 yards point, looking, and going W., on the soppy ground (in wet weather), in less than 150 yards, one sees, and could pursue an almost straight line of trench way boundary (Saxon?) which, if here and there half filled with storm deposits of sand and gravel, is easily followed 1900 yards, to within 100 yards of the surviving dozen low 'daystone' (outlier) rocks at Crow Chin, (about 1470 feet) on Stanage Edge. The general direction is W. half S.W.

The Reverse Way, from the gritstone blocks at Crow Chin edge, and about 400 yards S. of the surveyor's tower-like structure erected for Derwent-Rivelin Reservoir conduit tunnel (1910) four miles, 612 yards long (12 yards less than Severn railway tunnel), is N.E., half E. The cliff face of Stanage Edge here, about 600 yards N. (un-named), is the 1477 feet level.

The boundary trench, or Broad Rake 'ditch that parteth Sheffield and Bradfield parish unto the North end of Stanage' (1559 record), begins about 150 yards from Crow Chin edge, and varies from 2 to 8ft deep, and 8 to 15ft wide – or even wider where this ancient civil engineering did not provide an easy flow for flood water. At the first 600 yards or so, it is almost filled in and heather-hidden for some 60 yards, but quickly seen ahead. In a similar distance is a slight bend, either way, and, in the heathery trench, a left bend for 40 yards, then a right bend, and a deepening narrow trench – down the first perceptible slope. Next, in about 60 yards, is a Cutgate-like flood-washing width of 25ft, followed by a bank-burst, made by old flood washings, which formed a new flood-tricklet. The way, however, is ahead, on the flat, filled-in, green strip, and, in 80 yards, the heathery trench resumes a little to the right. In another 400 yards one arrives at Oaking Clough stream. The last 150 yards are confusing. Old floods have made two apparent channels – the right one probably the original. Both 'peter out' in soppy, flattish, brookside ground, where the trench ends. Mr Ernest Wilson tells me that, after the great fire on Hallam Moor, in and about July 1868, navvies engaged on the construction of Bradfield reservoirs (Agden in 1869 and Strines in 1871)) made a trench across this moor. Mr George Goodinson, however, emphasises that this trench was made from the Black Clough most northerly source of the Rivelin – in a southerly direction – towards Foul Hole. It should be mapped, and named. 'Fire Trench, 1868'.

The Sheffield and County Boundary, now N. and N.E., along Stanage Edge and End, to Moscar Top, Heathy Lane and Moscar Cross, was made by the legal settlement, in 1724, of a Sheffield–Hathersage Manor boundary dispute in which, recorded in 1637, it is claimed that Crow Chin to Seven Stones circle, Hurkling and Wheelstones and Strines Edge, was their land. In a Sheffield boundary, even in 1574, Bradfield had it!

The origin of Kay Flat is not known to Mr Ernest Wilson, the 1920–48 game-keeper for Ughill Moors. Like 'Lodge Moor' and the 'Otter Piece' on N.W. side of Kay Flat and the heathery, walled-in Stake Hill Road – Otter Piece being right of (E.) the path from High Riggs Road to Sugworth Hall, – it may refer to two men who were 'awarded', or bought, moorland after the Bradfield Enclosure Act (1811) Award of 9/3/1826. (George Goodinson says that until sold, round about fifty years ago, 'Otter Piece' was owned by a Mr Otter, who had Moor Lodge, a little S.E. of Sugworth Hall for his shooting box – and shot over Otter Piece and also Lodge Moor – or 'Piece'.)

Another fact is that, when I walked due N., from beside the field and moorside wall, at a point on High Riggs Road, 400 yards due W. of Crawshaw Head house, for almost 600 yards, to the N.E. bend of the plantation wall, I refixed a rude stone, not 150 yards S.W. of the plantation wall – inside the moor. It is 2ft 3in high, 15in to 18in wide, and 6in to 8in. On the S. side of it is a deeply chiselled 'H', about 6in long by 3in wide. A second upright stone, about 300 yards S.W. of this plantation corner wall is about the same height – about 14in wide and 6in to 8in – but unmarked. The 1896-revised six-inch-to-mile map shows seven stones across Kay Flat and I found odd stones, heather-covered, which, as Mr Ernest Wilson confirms, are survivors of those which formerly extended beyond the seven, across all Kay Flat, to almost the junction of Stake Hill and High Riggs Roads. It represents, he says, the boundary of a 50 acres piece of moor which a deceased owner of Ughill Moors, Mr W.S. Laycock – the head of W.S. Laycock's railway carriage fur-nishing works in Portobello, and, later, at Millhouses (who incurred tremen-dous underwriting losses against the sinking of the *Titanic*) – bought from the late Mr Henry Vickers (solicitor) and Mr W. Trickett, the Load Brook firebrick works and ganister-pit owner. He thinks that the 'H' may be for Mr Hammerton, of Sugworth Hall, a previous owner? It may possibly have been owned by a J. Haywood, a Hardy, or B. Hounsfield, who were three of the founders of Bradfield Game Association, in 1819. But see Bradfield Enclosure Act Award.

Lodge Moor – or 'Piece' is Bamford Lodge Moor. Bamford was first game-keeper on these, or neighbouring Bradfield parish moors whose tower-like house, now a tumbling ruin, not inhabited for more than eighty years, was called Bamford Lodge. Bamford Lodge would be built for him by the Duke of Norfolk – in, or about, 1810. But, whether Bamford was underpaid, or sold game he 'preserved', he so neglected his duty that grouse became scarce and 'he got the sack'. The Bradfield Game Association commenced at 'three guineas a year per gun', and the owner, the Duke of Norfolk, appointed new gamekeepers. See Hunter's *Hallamshire*. These Norfolk ducal grouse shooters, like the Rutlands, did not wait for the Enclosure Act (1811) Award of 10/3/1826 before they raked-in grouse-moor rents.

Broad Rake. Old English 'brad' for broad, is generally accepted, and this Saxon, or hill, trench-boundary line was written 'brad' in 1270, and, even then, was ancient. However used, as it was, in later document and case-evidence, in a generally wider sense – of under (W.), behind (E.), or to either side of Crow Chin and Stanage Edge hereabouts – 'rake' is emphatic in its meaning. 'Rake' is well known, and Wright's *English Dialect Dictionary* confirms much of what we know. It is 'a track, path, or course (especially a steep, narrow one), a range or walk for cattle, sheep, etc'. In addition to a sheep walk or area where certain sheep graze, it means, in Derbyshire limestone areas and in old lead mining districts of N. Yorkshire, a vein of lead, chiefly near the surface, which, in Derbyshire, usually runs E. to W. along high ground. In plain terms, it is, in this case, a broad line – or boundary.

Three things are dear to me and older ramblers who participated in our research and joint twenty-five years' fight for 'Derwent Road', a road now (since 1933) won, which goes from the gamekeeper's house we all knew in Strines Lane End – the home of our late consummately aggressive ramblers' enemy, 'Jack' Twigg – over Derwent Edge to Derwent. It is not yet won from behind Moscar Cross (pulled down, during war-time, 1941, and buried, though I hear it was re-erected in 1949), down the walled-in Parson's Piece Moor trench way to the (Strines Lane) gamekeeper's house itself.

The first is the mention of 'the way leading from Hope to Sheffield' and 'from Sheffield towards Darwent', in the two documents of 1270 and 1297. The two direct ways divided at Moscar Cross, the Hope Road going down Parson's Piece Moor, then along Hordron Edge, past Seven Stones Circle (recorded in 1270 and 1297) and coming under scenic Bamford Edge in a trench way to almost opposite 'Yorkshire Bridge Inn', and then to Lidgate Farm, a little south of it.

The second is the mention in the early, and later, document, of 'Bradrake' and 'Broadrake', which indicates what I previously propounded, i.e. my find that this lost, or latterly confused, place name is not that part of Stanage Edge on either side of, or just below, Crow Chin – that bend and nose of this long edge (here about 1470 feet) situate at 1½ miles S.S.W. of the 1185 feet (Moscar) summit of Sheffield–Glossop Road.

Then, thirdly, and probably pre-Norman, it is the 11 miles of wide trench boundary line (like Cutgate, or Sewards Lode trenches, on Wilfrey and

Howden Edges, and on Cartledge Stones Ridge), and easily traceable, which leads, straight and direct, a little N. of the upper S.W. sources of Oaking Clough, to Crow Chin.

Gwentreesicke, or Eventrevick – Ughill Brook Boundary. I cannot certainly define 'Gwentree Sicke', or 'Eventrevick', in the 1297 and 1270 boundary documents. Wherever it ended in 1270, the name of Ughill Brook, in the nineteenth century, begins at the junction of Royds (cleared land in a wood – plenty of it here, on E. and W. sides) Clough – which flows down the steep-sided woody hollow on the S.W. – and the stream from the W. under the road bridge at Tinker Bottom, that, in its infancy, S.W. of Turner Walls Barn, is now called Wet Shaw Dike. Ughill Brook, from this point – 300 yards S.E. of Ughill hamlet, flows E. to Damflask Reservoir, under steep Rickett's Bank, N. of Rickett Field Farm. Dealing first with 'vick' and 'Sicke' (1270 and 1297), it is evident that the Wet Shaw Dike source of Ughill Brook most resembles the sick, sitch, or 'syke', which, common on High Peak or S. Yorkshire moorsides, means a drain, a shallow-sided streamlet, or upper moorland brook-feeder, or the several fork-like sources of a river. At present I suggest that Wet Shaw Dike was the stream boundary line hereabouts – and not the deeper, clough-like Royds Clough Brook. But 'Eventre' and 'Gwentree' are greater name-problems, and 'Gwen', for fair or beautiful, or 'even-ash', the leaf of an ash tree having little leaflets – a lucky find or charm – is guesswork. I leave it with my supposition that Wet Shaw Dike is the upper part of 'Gwentreesicke', and that the lost name of Lady Seat, near or at the summit of Ughill Moor, may be another clue. When will I see the documentary proof?

Enclosure Act Justice. Mr J.B. Wheat's article (referred to in paragraph one of this article) shows that these late-thirteenth-century Furnival grants, or charters, were used in deciding claims during local administration of the 1791 Sheffield Enclosure Act. A Mr Gibson took up the case 'on behalf of the poor', and a Mr Wood (another solicitor?) advised the Enclosure Act Commissioners 'as to the rights, or otherwise, of so unusual a claim', wrote Mr Wheat. Mr Wood advised that the poor had no right to common grazing or other right, the burning of bracken ashes ('fearne' – manure?) for keeping geese there, or for Galloway ponies which carried their cutlery or files, to or from Sheffield from Stannington parish – where the claim was made. Excellent law, for, in entailed estate, no living owner could bind his successor and, though the yeoman farmer, for a hundred years, had always allowed his labourer, etc., to put odd geese and fowls on the moor, to take dead wood or bracken for bedding or manure, and get peat for home fires, it was only a moral right! On Totley Moss Moor, in 1816, the custom was that the poor cut their own peat, and the farmer-commoner took half the peat – for the cost of leading it. Excellent law it was, for, in these Enclosure Acts, all, except the Lord of the Manor and big local landowner, and the odd-man among the farmer common-right owners, got little more than 'paupers' pennies' of award land

– and then paid rent for the enclosed commons their stock grazed on! The poor were sent empty away! These tricks could not be done today.

Rivelin Commoners' Rights. A Ronksley MS. No. 4165 (copy) quotes an interesting verdict of Sheffield Manor Court of 4/10/1733 as follows: (apparently an abbreviation) 'Confirms former paines [i.e. fines or penalties] To keeping fence brushed [filled with brushwood, of thorns, etc.] and ditches scoured [free-running] adjoining the highways – pain 6/8d.'

To keep swine well ringed 6/8d. pain [to prevent rooting-up]. 'For gathering dung off the Common, pain 6/8d. [to prevent deterioration of pasturage]. For graving turf [cutting peat] £1. 19s. 11d. [only freeholder farmers-yeomen, etc. would have the right to cut, or grave, peat]'.

'For putting cattle upon the commons called Riveling Wood, having no common right to do so, a fine of £1. 19s. 11d.' 'For any persons putting cattle on said common of Riveling Wood who is not an inhabitant of the Liberty of Stannington, Moorwood, Hallam and Fullwood, a fine of £1. 19s. 11d.'

'For burning bracking on the above Common, not having right to do so, a fine of 6/8d.' [whether bracken was reserved for bedding, or for burning only in certain places or circumstances is not known, to me]. My additions in brackets. This document gives a good idea of the Commoner rights in Rivelin Forest, or Firth – then called a 'Wood'.

Moorland Coal Pits. The following (inverted) extracts are from *Memoirs of the Geological Survey of England and Wales*, by A.H. Green, C. le Neve Foster, and J.R. Daykins, dealing with this area, publisher Longmans Green & Co., London, 1869.

'**Ringinglowe Colliery**. In a section of this colliery are the following details: shale 81ft; closely grained sandstone 17ft; shale 98ft and coal – fair quality 1ft; black coaly shale 9in, and inferior coal 2ft 9in. Then underclay 1ft, and Third Grit.'

Presumably, it was a shaft 196ft to the first good seam. This colliery shaft was in the old wire mill yard.

The account of the upper boundary of the Third Gritstone layers was carried (in the description of the Rivelin valley) to as far as a conduit above the Redmires Reservoir, and, in regard to Oaking Clough and Coal Pit House – 'The coal lying on the top of the rock has been worked in the upper part of Oaking Clough, and again about Coal Pit House, but the pits have been long abandoned, and, except at these two points, the line of the crop is very uncertain, but there seems to be little doubt that Hallam Moors [now, often wrongly called Stanage Moors – G.H.B.W.] are covered by a broad spread of the grit-stone. A fault in the upper boundary was seen in the brook, the coal and its underlying clay being bent up into a vertical position on the north side against a mass of coarse grit on the south side'.

'Though we can make nothing out of them ourselves, we give the three following sections which were found among the papers of the late Mr W.B. Mitchell Withers, of Sheffield' – a prominent Sheffield surveyor and architect.

'(1) **Bore Hole in Oaking Clough**. Soil and clay 7ft, Bind 10ft; (1) Coal 2ft; Bind 21ft; Coal (Third Grit Coal) 2ft 6in; Fireclay 2ft; Hard Rock (Third Grit) bored into 17ft. [In Gin Piece, or Gin Piece Plantation – G.H.B.W.?]

'(2) **Bore Hole on Stanage Moor**. Peat and Soil 5ft; Rock 32ft; Coal 1ft 6in; Fireclay 2ft; Gritstone rock 29ft; Rattler, or Cannel Coal (Third Grit Coal) 5ft 6in.'

'(3) **Open Pit on Stanage Moor** – 'Coal Pit House'? Peat, and (query loose blocks of) gritstone 12ft; Coal 0ft 1in; Grey rock 18ft; Shale 4ft; Rattler, or Cannel Coal (Third Grit Coal) 5ft 6in.'

One could sit secluded from the world beside Redmires Reservoir conduit where steep, narrow, Oaking Clough suddenly becomes a saucer-like hollow, and the stream could be dammed-up into a pond several feet deep. The late Mr Thomas Winder, A.M.I.C.E., told me, in a letter of 9/5/23, that 'there was a small dam at the top of Oaking Clough when I was a lad' – i.e. 1865–70.

It could have been a pond for the early pit-workers below Oaking Clough Plantation, but George Goodinson says it existed before his day, and avers that it was made to arrest the flood siltings of upper Oaking Clough after the construction of the two Rivelin Reservoirs in 1855–60.

Moorland Place Names. Looking ahead, S.W. of the conduit, where it crosses Oaking Clough, and the southern feeder from Broadshaw Plantation joins it, we see to the right of the latter, 'Stanedge Lodge'. Some 500 yards S.W., at the top of the bank ahead, is the small, square Oaking Clough Plantation – 1260 feet. Behind, unseen, is the (20 acre?) walled-off field called Rape Piece. The easy smooth slope on the S.W. side of upper Oaking Clough – towards High Neb, is High Lad Ridge, but Mr Geo. Goodinson never saw remains of any ancient 'pile' or heap of stones which denoted an ancient British cairn – like the 'Lad Stones' on Wetherlam. If any cairn, or pile, was here, it would probably be used for field walls after 1791. There is, however, a half-mile line of soppy moor between it and Rape Piece, and Gin Piece Plantation. George Goodinson says there was a horse-gin worked for a coal pit or trial-hole within this latter (game) Plantation and filled-in before 1870. In all, this one?

mile of Oaking Clough is a modest imitation of the change from shapely to solemn seen in the lower and upper Abbey Clough.

Coal Workings. Several undefined Oaking Clough coal workings are soon seen on the near S. side of the main stream S.W. of the Culvert crossing, and between the stream of Oaking Clough Plantation. The plain stone building a few yards W. of the culvert-crossing of Oaking Clough, is the post-1897 grouse-shooter's cabin built by the late Mr W. Wilson.

Another 1869 extract says: 'The coal lying about at Coal Pit House was some of it bright and clean and some of it very earthy cannel or carbonaceous shale', and the joint authors say that, 'if the foregoing three sections are trustworthy about this part, almost close upon the Third Grit, is a bed of sandstone, 20–30ft thick (29ft and18ft in two or three), on which rests another coal bed, marked (1) in the three sections, but very variable in thickness'. They say that, 'the rock 32ft thick in (2), may not be sandstone as the hard stony shales are often called by colliers'.

Waterloo Pit at High Neb. The thoroughly ruined 'Coal Pit House', about 18ft square, now 2ft to 4ft 6in high, with a south doorway, and a rubble heap between it and the open Wilson-made grouse-shooter's pony shed close beside the rubble heap (made after 1897, out of the Coal Pit House), is not 150 yards S.E. from the summit of High Neb (1502 feet) – the highest altitude within Sheffield – and three-quarters of a mile N.W. of the point where the Roman-used, eighteenth-century paved Stanage Pole to Brough Road crosses Stanage Edge. The natives call it 'T' Coal 'Oil'. It was named 'Waterloo Pit', and according to *Derbyshire Archaeological Society Journal, Vol. 17*, this was one source from which John Bagshaw, of Abbey Grange, obtained coal in the reign of George I. The line of Waterloo Shooting Butts, which ended near it, are a later continuation of this name. The 1845–50 one-inch Ordnance Map shows 'Coal Pit House' here, and the old pit shaft (long filled-in?) about 100 yards directly E. of 'Coal Pit House'. I also hear of a partly filled-in bore hole on the easterly side of the latter.

Stephen Glover's 1829 *Gazetteer of Derbyshire* states: 'Stanage Pole, S.W. of the pole, 1½ miles N.N.E. of Hathersage, 1st coal (formerly)'. N.N.E. of Hathersage is approximate, but Glover erred. It is 1½ miles N.W. of Stanage Pole, and, evidently, this pit was closed before 1829. But, ye colliers of 1950, what a place to walk to and work at!

(Broad Shaw, on the first Ordnance Survey Map, and since excluded, goes eastwardly from Crow Chin, between the upper stream sources of Oaking Clough and the field walls on the N.E. It may have been partly wooded.)

'Along the escarpment of Broad Rake, to Crow Chin, towards the N. of

Stanage Edge, millstones have been made out of the grit. They were described as fit for grinding oats, but too 'nesh' (weak) for beans or barley.'

Bore Edge is mentioned in this 1869 book, but not located. On the first Ordnance Survey Map (1840–50) it is the edge behind Cattis Side Farm to Kimber Court, on the E. side of Brookfield Manor parkland (Hathersage), and since forgotten by our map-makers.

'A thin coal and fireclay have been worked on the top of the sandstone at Moscar Plantation, but the clay is said to have been of bad quality' – p. 62, 1869 book.

This working should, if correctly stated, be traceable in Moscar Plantation, on the S. (left) side of Sheffield–Glossop Road, the W. end of which ends at the highest Moscar Flat level of this road – 1185 feet. The last 1869 extract is:

'The crop of the clay [fireclay? – G.H.B.W.] may be clearly traced by the aid of old workings to the northeast of Bamford Lodge' – p. 66, of 1869 book.

The still public path, on High Riggs Road, (N.), from about 500 yards short (N.E.) of the top, and junction, of Heathy Lane, goes N.N.W. down by the moor-side wall, to Sugworth Road. Bamford Lodge ruin is about 350 yards to the right (E.), and the old workings, N.E. of it, are near the north boundary wall of the little 'Lodge Moor' – or 'Lodge Piece'.

Lord's Seat Farm (1260–1310 feet) is post-Sheffield Enclosure Act – 1791. The plough-furrow lines of 'Rape Piece' tell us that, in early Victorian years, this high land grew rape, a plant allied to the turnip, for its herbage, oil-producing seeds and rape-cake, and useful for fattening lambs. Mr Geo. Goodinson assures me that his father, Fred (1841–1927) said that, before G.G. was born, not only was rape grown here, but oats (black), turnips and potatoes. The Highland 'longhorns, alone allowed on the moorland from 1897 to 1914, were, as 'natives' said, partly there to frighten-off trespassers. Successful, stout, 'lawyer', B.P. Broomhead (Broomhead, Wightman & Moore, Bank Street), who leased Hallam and Moscar Moors for a goodly number of years, and 15/12/93, was killed (aged fifty-nine) at the then level-crossing at Sheffield Victoria Station, farmed Lord's Seat tolerably well and was a grouse-shooter well respected by his farmer and cottager tenants. He lived at Wales Lodge, Kiveton Park – formerly in Broomhall Park – and, 1890, added 'Colton Fox' to his name – to inherit another fortune from Miss Mary Benson Fox, a relative of his first wife.

After 1897, the farm was gradually neglected and land-use decayed. I understand that the last farmer was Mr John Marsden (who went to Cow Close farm), and the last occupant, Mr W. Wingfield. Fifty years ago, 30–40 young cattle were summer-grazed on this farm and an old friend of mine took some of them, yearly.

The house was emptied (1939) and demolished in 1944 'Fairthorne Lodge' is now the one inhabited house on either side of Redmires Upper Reservoir.

The 'Lord's Seat'. The reputed medieval thirteenth-to-fourteenth-century Lord Furnival's Lord's Seat, was at or near this farm house. The late loved J.R. Wigfull, A.R.I.B.A., wrote that the Sheffield Enclosure Act Award Map (1805) shows that: 'in the centre of a large area containing 215a. 2r. 19p., and occupying about the same position, there is a circle described as the Lord's Seat Plantation'; and I agree with him (*Hunter Archaeological Society Transactions, Vol. II*), that 'this name probably perpetuates the Lord's 'set', or 'seat' – a hunting lodge'.

An item in a post-mortem enquiry into certain Lord Furnival properties, etc., held at Sheffield, in 1383, is: 'Two pieces of pasture, together with wood and deer, and hunting for the same, at the Mores [mor is Saxon for moor. G.H.B.W.], and Ryvelynden £4-0-0' (*Hunter Archaeological Society Transactions, Vol. I*).

The Lord's Seat 'Chapel'. Presumed history says that here, or near here, Dissenters came and worshipped during the period of the vile 'Five Mile Limit' Act, 1665, that prohibited all Nonconformist ministers from holding a service within five miles of any town, or place, where they had previously ministered. Catholics 'got it' similarly and worse, in the previous one hundred years. Before 1559 Protestants were 'roasted', etc., and equal 'martyrs' to those now 'saintified' by the train-pilgrimages to Padley Manor Chapel, etc. – two murdered priests in 1588. Protestants however, are, not yet, 'martyrs' in Franco's 1936–50 Spain!

In one of the (late) small outbuildings at Lord's Seat, like a small dairy, which the natives called 'The Chapel', there was a flat stone bench, roughly about 4ft x 3ft, and two vertical holes in it – one at each end. My living informant well remembers the two rusty iron chains, each about 18in long, fastened in the stone. He remembers it being authoritatively stated – and his authority was a relative who could 'go back' to about one hundred years ago – that a Bible was once chained to the stone table, and used here, by Dissenters who after – or even before? – came to testify to their faith and creed during the post-1665 period. This stone, and these chains, disappeared between the 1914–18 and 1939–45 wars; and he does not suspect the house tenants. These later Dissenter pilgrims came here perhaps too frequently – so it is suggested. But where is it, the table, and chains, now, and who will say, and remove these doubts? Possibly 'Fulwoodites', and their earliest Unitarians, came here, more or less secretly – with 'lookouts' fixed – to worship here.

Stanedge Lodge, very seldom visited by strangers, but seen by every road-walker, is 700 yards N.N.W. of Stanage Pole. This shooting house and game-keeper's house, 1386 feet, was named 'Lumley Lodge' on my first Ordnance Map (pre-1850) which does not show the Ambergate–Rowsley railway line section – commenced in 1848. The name could be for 'the meadow by the wood' and as being near the original medieval 'Lord's Seat' – or the Lord's Seat Farm house site, 600 yards to the E. This house was rebuilt by the late B.P. Broomhead (d. 1893, aged fifty-nine), in the early years of his lease of Hallam Moor – in or about 1869. He used it for his shooting box and summer-house – and for the friends he regularly invited.

Agriculture around Redmires. The even shape of fields shows that all modern farming on the N., W. and E. sides of upper Redmires Reservoir is post-1791 Sheffield Enclosure Act. Today, in the last stage, due to Sheffield's Water Purifiers, only one house remains (the Doncaster-built Fairthorn Lodge), and, 1947, the first, monastic-medieval Fulwood Booth Farm, on the E. side, was demolished after emptying in 1937 and, in 1949, earth taken away to put over a disused, filled-in, Crookes (town supply) Reservoir. The twin cottages below ex-'Ocean View' pub (until 1885) just E. of it, called Marsh Cottages – and the land, where Mr Fred Marsden was born, were 'downed' in 1936. Fairthorn Green House, at the foot and corner of the road-rise towards Stanage Pole, became a shell in 1934, and the 'Grouse and Trout', an unwanted, but welcome roadside inn, and its land bought by the late Mr Wm Wilson for £3000, in 1897, lost (?) its licence in 1915 because it was too near to his moors. The water purifiers made it an empty shell, in 1934 – and, at present, it remains so.

Stanage–Moscar–Bamford Moor Railings. In our 1925 *Sheffield Clarion Ramblers' Booklet* we asked whether the 1924 fixed mile of iron railings, from N.E. side of Stanage Pole to Stanage Edge top – by the late owner, Mr Wm Wilson, of Beauchief Hall – did not encroach upon the presumed 30ft width of this public road. The reply is still awaited. These 1924 fixed railings, in 1934, were extended on the same (right) side of this road to the 'New Road' (1771 Act branch road), under Bamford Edge to about half a mile S.E. of 'Yorkshire Bridge Inn' – roughly another two miles – by the then presumed owner, the late Mr T.K. Wilson. The railings (1934) on 'the New Road' and Yorkshire Bridge side rusted rapidly and since 1945 have been replaced prin-cipally with wooden stakes and wide-mesh wire.

The 1939–45 war brought a frantic rush for iron railings and gates etc. – for melting down from house-garden, estate, park, and other walls – even tombs in cemeteries – and their wholesale removal. Much was used, and some wasted, and much cost up to ten times its value in removing! Some removals were unnecessary, or silly, and we stopped one home-side bit of folly! But here were possibly 30 tons of railings and supports which insulted the scenery, and beside a lorry-traversable moorside road! The C.P.R.E. – all of us – tried, from city to county authority, district planning officer, even to the Ministry H.Q., but in vain, and we grimly congratulated the moor-owner upon his exemption. Two ex-late owners' old gamekeepers told me that the 1924-mile of railings was deliberately fixed to keep out sheep as well as Ramblers, from these moors, and we concluded that in 1939–45, they had been, anticipatedly – and equally – fixed – in 1924 – to keep in sheep (and Ramblers out) that, during national necessity, had to return to the moors! I add another trifle.

Mr Valentine Heywood, then chief reporter of *Sheffield Independent*, who lived at Fairthorn Green House, in a letter to me of 2/1/1926, referred to the (1924) line of these iron railings as follows: 'Under some old deed Mr Wilson can compel the Sheffield Corporation to erect a wall round certain property – I do not know where it is – which would cost some thousands of pounds. On one occasion, when the Corporation bought some land from a charity, they found Wilson had shooting rights for which he paid £5 a year, but he refused to continue this payment to the Corporation, and, I believe, only pays 10/-. He threatened to force them to build the wall if they did not agree'.

Mr Heywood, confirming the general view that these railings, in part, encroach on the public highway, said that Sheffield Highways Committee then had all the admitted facts, but were reluctant to act because the owner would retort in making them build this wall, and they were waiting for a new owner who, to them, would be more accommodating (Mr W. Wilson, at Beauchief Hall, died on 2/8/1927, aged seventy-seven).

The Hallam Moors, then including odd adjacent farms, and approximately 2500 acres, were auctioned by Eadon and Lockwood's, on 5/7/1927, and, then, had a rental of £365.15.0d. p.a., with shooting rights over these farm lands. A bid of £15,000 was not obtainable, and, apparently, the reserve was £20,000 (Mr Wilson, in 1897, paid £43,000 for the moor, and the rentals for land and houses were £446 a year. Included was £3000 for 'Grouse and Trout' inn).

They were shortly afterwards said to be privately sold to the late Mr T.K. Wilson, of Fulwood House, Sheffield, and his nephew, Mr G.R. Wilson, is understood to be the present owner.

Stanage Edge Quarrying and a Curiosity. Passing Stanage Pole, going N. and N.W. along the Roman-used road from Sheffield–Long Causeway to Brough, and (left) the Golden Car bridleway to Stanage Cottage war-ruin and Hathersage, in about 900 yards one arrives at Stanage Edge. Here the sharp-eyed innocent trespasser promptly observes, when going along the Edge (N.W.), a green and heathery (long disused) old road, about 10ft wide, and, sees that, in the first 50 yards, part of it has been quarried away for the easily-got top blocks of gritstone and, along the first 300 yards of it, 20–30ft of the summit layers have disappeared. Beside this eighteenth-century quarry road, made after the 1771 Mortimer Road Act, and the branch road from 'Yorkshire Bridge Inn', and before arriving (in about 200 yards) at a nameless streamlet, one may easily miss a low surface rock on which a deeply chiselled letter 'G', about a foot long, was chipped, by a quarryman, 150–180 years ago? Another low rock is carved with 'F M'.

Where the road crosses the streamlet is a rough, slab-topped culvert, about 3ft 6in x 2ft 6in. (See the similar culvert – E. – beside Froggatt Edge, eighteenth-century 'Millstone Road', miscalled a 'Drive', and never a public road.) For some 50 yards the road is built-up and has a dry-walled edge – for the use of lorries. N.W. of the culvert this road is slab-paved and, in about 150 yards, it turns left, downhill, between the cut-away rocks and, bending, descends to the older quarry road, which, under the Edge for a good two miles, goes from the road leading to Stanage Pole, to a little W. of High Neb, 1502 feet. A second quarry road descends from the Edge to the older quarry road at about 200 yards short of High Neb (S.E. of) which, at close quarters, derives its name from a pointed 'nosey' rock.

Millstone – and Rivelin – Edge Quarries

A record refers to millstones taken over Baslow's ancient (wooden?) bridge contrary to order and, in 1500, of a Thomas Harrison fined 6/8d., by Baslow Manor Court, for his sin. We also know that Dronfield's village squire, Mr Rotherham, in 1737, had Hathersage's Millstone Edge Quarry, and that Rivelin Edge Quarries were 'discontinued because Rotherham would not let them be worked for fear of injuring the other, and had taken Millstone Edge Quarry with this object'. (In an Enquiry into certain Lord Furnival lands, etc., at Rotherham, in 1332, we read: 'Also they say, there is a certain stone quarry in Ryvelvngden worth, yearly, forty shillings, but, this year, it is worth nothing, for want of tenants'. *Hunter A.S.T., Vol I.* It must have been a big quarry – situated E. of 'Norfolk Arms'.) Mr Rotherham, or another, may have quarried along Stanage Edge before 1700, for Mr S.O. Addy, in his fine *Hall of Waltheof*, (1893) said: 'I have an old document relating to the making of mill-stones on Millstone Edge more than two centuries ago'. Faulty millstones are seen under Stanage Edge – also under Carl Wark, etc., and the probably, 1600–1700, paved 'Long Causeway' and Roman-used road from Stanage Edge to Redmires, and Sandygate, Lydgate, Sheffield, and beyond, provided an easy downhill way, for drugs or lurries.

Prof. G.R. Potter and Miss Mary Walton, in *A Fragment of a Compotus Roll of the Manor of Sheffield, 1479–80 – Sheffield Hunter Archaeological Society Transactions, 194*, revealed this: 'To a man of Hathersage for a pair of millstones and carting them to Whiston Mill [three miles S.E. of Rotherham – about 15 miles – G.H.B.W.], altogether 14s.' Possibly these millstones came from Stanage – and who knows?

Totley Moss Bridleway

Godfrey Dalton (seventy-four), in my evidence – copy of a Holmesfield-Totley moorland commons grazing dispute (1816) said: 'He knew the late Mr Rotherham's father (d. 1794) getting millstones in the Millstone Edge, in the Liberty of Hathersage, and carrying them on the road near Totley Moss [Totley Moss bridle road is meant], and Mr Rotherham repairs [repaired] the road, which Totley never did'. But Rotherham had to get his drugs or lurries across Longshaw Park, via Hollowgate, behind Longshaw Lodge, and across Totley Moss, and, perforce, repaired it. Apparently the Rotherhams had Millstone Edge quarry for fully forty years, until about 1794 or 1797, when John and Samuel died – and then a Cecil married a Miss Rotherham, and the 'Rotherham-Cecil' line eventuated.

Old Quarrying Method. Dr Erasmus Darwin's (1731–1802) long poem: *Botanic Garden, Economy of Vegetation*, 1795 – in a footnote, gives an item for students: 'It is usual, in separating large millstones from the silicious sand rocks [underlying softer, thinner strata. G.H.B.W.] in some parts of Derbyshire, to bore horizontal holes under them in a circle, and fill these with pegs made of dry wood which gradually swell by the moisture of the earth, and, in a day or two, lift up the millstone without breaking it'.

Darwin, a physician at Nottingham, Lichfield, and Derby, was grandfather of Charles R. Darwin (1809–82), the great naturalist.

Sheep Grazing – 1332 and 1906

An old Hallam Moor gamekeeper told me that sheep-grazing on this moor – much later than on many I have recorded – ended in 1906. A preliminary was in, or about, 1905, after two gamekeepers drove a flock of sheep from Hathersage to Sugworth Hall land, and, doing the usual, they strayed towards their old pastures, and, observed by the Moscar Moor gamekeeper (R. Dolman), reported, or confessed it to the late Mr Wilson Mappin who, also buying White Path Moss Moor (1897) from the Duke of Norfolk, instantly banished all sheep, and then half ruined Fulwood Booth Farm – emptied 1937, and destroyed 1947. However, Mr W. Wilson 'had a fancy' for some 30 to 40 Highland longhorn cattle, which, ages-long a feature of Peak and S. Yorks. Moors, were allowed to remain until about 1914. But they also, as natives said, frightened trespassers away!

History reveals that Sheffield's Lord of the Manor, Thomas, Lord Furnival (d. 1332) granted to the prior of Beauchief Abbey (Sheffield) his grange of Fulwood, all lands belonging to the grange, and common of pasture 'throughout all Fullwood and Riveling for all their cattle except goats'. Now, the nation must return to the position in pre-1332 before the grouse-shooting 'preserver' and beast-banisher was invented, and the taxpayer pays the hill-farmers subsidy! An assessment of hill-farm present production and potentiality is now proceeding, and, in the near years, an idle farmer, assured of his reasonable price for graded animals, a decent living, and freed from the middleman market-manipulation, will be summarily 'outed' or punished – after a fair period for amendment. Farmer and keeper have told me of odd moors, not far away, where old tricks are now tried in a nicer way, but, as usual, fear to allow use of their names. Equally, a moor-owner restricter of full Access to the shepherd will, before long, receive 'short shrift' when saying a grouse moor must be kept quiet if it is to be any good; and trying so to act – as also the hill-farmer who, in this farmers-revolution-period, deliberately over-stocks the moor with sheep or beast, gambles on a good year, and – financially – endangers his neighbour-farmer too. Another equal task is to train a new regiment of hill-shepherds worth their wages, and to revive the days when the shepherd was the finest man upon our hillsides.

The Duke gets a 'Tip'

The late Duke of Norfolk, Sheffield's Mayor in 1895–7, the last who lived at The Farm in Granville Road, before it became Midland Railway Co. offices after the line-widening, and extension of Sheffield station in 1903–4, was well known for his 'Norfolk' jacket and habit of 'mixing' and losing his identity – which we liked.

Mrs Gertrude Goodinson, wife of George Goodinson, and née Fox, daughter of a late vicar of Stannington, told me this story. On one occasion the Duke, on a crowded platform at Sheffield Midland station, and seeing an elderly lady with several parcels, asked if he could help. She said, "I'd be grateful if you would. The porters seem too busy to notice the likes of me."

The Duke found a seat, and, putting the parcels on the rack, said, "Now I think you will be quite comfortable." Then replied the old lady, "Yes. Thank you my man, and here's a threepenny bit. You've earned it. I don't suppose you get paid like this every day," and the Duke responded, "No, indeed, I don't."

The Duke, speaking humorously of this incident said, "It was the only money he had ever earned," and he wore that threepenny bit on one of his watchchains.

I forget the year when I recorded that the late Duke was turned off his land by a tenant on his Derwent estate who failed to recognise the Duke in dishabille! Ducal rents and power are one thing, and Communist cruelty another, but the Duke could throw off his trappings, if my father, and many others, could say that the hierarchy of the R.C. Church probably secured odd million pounds from the Norfolk estate during his lifetime.

Another celebrated titled personality I know of who, equally, could sometimes be 'fed-up' with these ceremonial say-nothing-well functions, went to do his show-work and, on returning to quietude and to his guide and prompter, asked: "What's the next **** job I have to do?"

Many stories could have been written about the navvies who worked on the water tunnel (1910) from Priddock Clough, under Bamford Edge to the upper Rivelin Reservoir, and which was followed by the late owners' 1911 claim (Mr W. Wilson) for easement, or compensation – because his grouse had less water to drink due to the abstraction of water from the moor. The round value of the claim was £5000, and £3650 for the loss of water.

Mr Hanson, a Huddersfield surveyor, estimated the loss at £4000, but Mr Edward Holmes (Sheffield), engineer to Derwent Valley Water Board, referred to 'no surface disturbance', the draining away of water suggestion 'ludicrous', and said £100 'nominal damages' was sufficient. The case was heard before Col. Welland, at The Surveyors Institution, Westminster, and the award was £1350. The average yield of grouse on this moor, from 1906, was then stated to be '2619 per head a year'.

Here is a wee one: A well-respected foreman navvy – a burly six-footer – one week-end night, walked up stony, steep Fox Hagg from the navvy's huts on the S. side of Rivelin Reservoir, to the 'Three Merry Lads', on Redmires Road. Verily, he drank more than 'one above his nine' but, somehow, he had to return and, unable to walk arm-in-arm all the way, one of his nearest relatives, and another man I know, brought him down – walk or stagger, creep or crawl, or slide. Eventually they left him snug and snoring. When he came to, he discovered the 'backside' of his new 'blue Melton'-cloth trousers were in a truly sorry, torn condition. Then, there was a little more than 'you did it' said to the two who brought him home! The two then explained, as best they could, that he could not come down all the way 'straight-end up', but that, here and here, he had, literally, to be pulled, or slided-down.

And did you hear that very old gamekeeper-beater's story of the grouse-shooter who, when a fox came within nice range of his gun, instead of shooting it – as the gamekeeper would have done – took off his hat!

Vale. This may be the last big moor article I'll write and add to my list. It will be, like others, free to every good rambler in due time. It has been the least-trespassed, best-keepered moor I've known – with Kinderscout, on 'Snake Inn' and Downfall side. Trespassers go today, and, if they do, take their own risk. This article is only to lay down fact and story ready 'for the day of liberty to all', however qualified it be, the beginning of the new era.

There is much we have not said of this one footpath moor possibly saved to us, first, by the Redmires-Rivelin Reservoir navvies in 1830–60. Cowper

Stones–Stanage–Derwent and Howden Edges to Crowstone Edge walk is probably the finest, longest moorland edge walk in England – with the edge-walk around Kinderscout. The truth resides in no man, and if any write and prove error, or add useful data, I hope it is printed!

Ringinglow – Fun and Fact

From S.C.R. Handbook, 1950/51. In the section on The Ringinglow 'Deep Sick Coal Pits', the Biblical reference for 'Ichabod' is 1 Samuel 4, verse 21 – 'The glory is departed'. Ward devotes a sizeable chunk of this article to the Irishman, Henry Kelly, the ruins of whose household and outbuildings are still plain to see between Brown Edge quarries and the road from Ringinglow to Upper Burbage. 'Who can add to this Kelly biography?', Ward asks. With the benefit of Census returns to which Ward did not have access, the biography can be filled out a little. Henry and his wife Bridget Kelly were born in Ireland around 1817 and 1825 respectively. They probably came to England at the height of the Great Famine of the latter 1840s. Around 1850, they were in Manchester, but they must have subsequently crossed the Pennines and settled in the house at Ringinglow in the early 1850s. They had two sons, Paddy and Barney, and two daughters, Mary Ann and Catherine. The story about Barney Kelly running away is recorded in a local 'gossip song' called 'Fulwood Farmers and Neighbours', supposedly written around the year 1900 by Josh White, who lived at Hollins View Farm on Crimicar Lane, Fulwood. [Thanks to Dr Ian Russell for that last bit of information.]

These pages, largely, were the result of conversations (1921) with the late Mr Herbert Trotter, some pleasant rambles through snow-slush, and some research – and they are, now, 'touched-up' and added to.

Though born at Fernfield Farm – half a mile W. of 'Dore Moor Inn', S. side of the (1816) Sheffield–Fox House Road – he spent youth, and early manhood too, at Ringinglow. Herbert was the now very rare stonemason who could quarry, 'hew', 'dress', and 'fix', his own work, and wore the nigh-forgotten trade sign of white woollen cord trousers, cleaned with bath brick. I cannot forget his vivid memory and gift of location, for I visited every place he described and wondered at his correct directions. Then sixty-two years old (1921) and living, and dying (1928–9) in Bigod St., in the Park district of Sheffield, away from heatherland, he then wore his years lightly, and was a truly 'breezy' Upper Hallamite. He was uncle to Mrs Edith Walker (*née* Dagenham), wife of Frank Walker, both Clarion Ramblers in 1913–18, and after.

Roads and Boundaries. This roadside hamlet began after the 1757 Road Act – from Sharrow, Psalter and High Lanes (now sillily labelled 'Ringinglow Road') to Ringinglow, and there dividing. One section went along Houndkirk ('Ankirk') Road, to Fox House, across Longshaw Park to Yarncliff Lodge,

Grindleford Bridge, Sir William, Great Hucklow, Tideswell, Hargatewall, Wormhill, and Buxton. The other went to Upper Burbage Bridges, Overstones Farm, Hathersage Dale and village, up the hill and down, to Hillfoot Cottage (from beyond 'George Hotel'), Mytham Bridge, Hope, Castleton, and up The Winnats, to Sparrow Pit and Chapel-en-le-Frith. Later (1811 Act), the direct road was made, under Mam Tor and Rushup Edge.

Ringinglow is in Upper Hallam (Fulwood), within Sheffield, but the ancient Manor of Ecclesall, and, until 1/4/1934, the Sheffield–Dore boundaries (in the Norton R.D.C. area), followed up the Limb Brook, which, at Ringinglow, should be called 'Fenny Brook'. But, above the old Barber Fields copperas works and coal workings, it meets, at Houndkirk Road, the Fulwood boundary. Here old Ecclesall ends, and the ex-Dore and Sheffield (Fulwood) boundaries continue along the brook, S. of the wee 'chapel', to Ringinglow–Upper Burbage Bridges Road – at 200 yards W. of the 'Norfolk Arms' Hotel, and a little short of the (W.) end of the first field W. of Fulwood Lane junction with the above road. The boundary line crosses to the N. side of Ringinglow–Upper Burbage Bridges Road at the commencement of the wee road bend (one mile beyond 'Norfolk Arms') and goes to the summit – at Burbage Head, 1361 feet. Here, at the roadside, is the old Hathersage–Dore boundary stone – now 'Sheffield' – the old Dore boundary going S., and Hathersage-Hallam (Sheffield) boundary W.W. by N., along 'Friars Ridge', once Beauchief Abbey lands boundary, to Stanage Pole and Edge.

The late Mr Priest's stone house (1911), 'Moorcot', on Houndkirk Road, a little S. of Fenny Brook, built after he left 'Norfolk Arms' – about 200 yards to the N. – is in old Dore parish.

'Ringinglawe' 1574 and 1637, is in 'A boundary or breefe note of all the meres and bounds of Hallamshire, betwene Whiteley Wood and a place called the Waynstones [i.e. – Wainstones]; namely between the lordes landes of Hallamshire and the lordes landes of Ecclesshall and Hathersedge. Gone over and viewed and scene the sixt day of August Anno dni one thousand fyve hundredth seaventy and fower, by these men whose names are here, underwritten', etc. Ringinglow is described as 'Also from the said stone called Stowperstocke to a great heap of stones called Ringinglawe, from wh(ic)h one Thomas Lee had taken and led away a great sorte [i.e. a great number of] of stones being by one sicke or brook which

Badger Houses on Houndkirk Moor.

parts Derbyshire and Hallamshire' – Hunter's *Hallamshire*, p.18.

Think of a pre-historic mound of stones, before 1574, between 'Norfolk Arms' and 'Moorcot', beside the brook and Houndkirk Road, perhaps 60ft diameter and 15ft high. Dore, Ecclesall and Hallamshire boundaries met here, and another cairn should be built. The late Mr Thomas Winder, in his fine *'T' Hefts an' Blades o' Sheffield'*, prints Harrison's 1637 Survey document, and I note 'Ringin Lawe', and 'Stowperstorke'. Ringinglow is 1080 feet altitude.

A local explanation. 'Ringing' – as in 'Ringing Roger' (rock), on Kinderscout, 'beats me'. Rhian, rinnen, rin, etc.,means to flow, run, or a stream, and could refer to infant Whirlow (Fenny) Brook, or to the ring-in-the-low. But these won't do!

Modern Ringinglow, not unlike my own Moorwoods Lane, complains that certain common suburban facilities are slow in arriving, but probably the first house there is the present octagon 'Round House', old catch toll-bar house probably built about 1758–60 – after the 1757 Road Act. The old 'Weigh House', opposite the 'Round House', was pulled down before 1922. Herbert Trotter told me the story that the tolls were let by annual contract and it was usual for the displaced toll-bar keeper to go into the Weigh House until the next toll-keeper 'lost his job'. In Herbert Trotter's boyhood, Weigh House was a 'dame's school' kept by a Miss Lawson, and 'Billy' Winterbottom, after-wards an Oxspring wire mill owner, was the 'big lad' – and 'chucker out'.

The Chapel, about 80 yards, nearly due S. of 'Norfolk Arms' (right side of road), first 'Methodist', is said to have been built chiefly by the efforts of a Mr Rhodes who, an old man in the 1860s, was the preacher. He occasionally preached to a congregation of one, and Herbert Trotter said his father acted during his absence. The lads mocked him, and once he left the pulpit and broke a stick over the head of a boy named Latch, but Herbert was the real culprit. The land was let at £1 a year ground rent, and, when Charles Marsden ('Norfolk Arms') obtained the land from William Roebuck ('Round House'), there were 'twenty years owing'. Marsden put in the bailiffs, the money was collected and paid, and Marsden at once released it. Our friend, Mr J.B. Himsworth, in *Hunter Archaeological Society's Journal* (1946), gave a drawing of a plan on the back of a lease of two acres of land and buildings (then a shed?) opposite (N.) Round House – then 'Toll Bar House'. The land corresponds to the length and shape of the walling on the 1914-revised six-inch-to-mile Ordnance Map, as far as Fulwood Lane (W.), and E. of 'Norfolk Arms'. The space occupied by the later wire mill and row of six cottages (and two next to them), was then a plantation. 'Ring o' Firs' farmhouse is not shown. This two acres was then leased for ninety-nine years at £1 p.a., and, today, is it worth £200? The document (1946) was possessed by Mr E. Goddard Stokes. The Hathersage toll bar was on the W. side of Houndkirk Road junction, and

Houndkirk Road toll bar on S. side of the Hathersage Road – both beside Round House. The 1802 leaseholder's name is not stated. Ringinglow – post 1757 – like Ashopton hamlet – post 1818 – grew after the modern highway, and whether there be proof or not of the earlier 'Ring o' Firs' (first?) farm being a 'pub' before the 'Norfolk Arms' (1820–30?), the book, *Walks in the Neighbourhood of Sheffield* 1844 (in Sheffield Reference Library) says: 'All that the stranger includes as appertaining to Ringinglow is a good house of entertainment on one side of the road and an unseemly tower on the other which, until these few years past, served as a toll house, and lodged the keeper and his family'. The explanation is that the Sheffield to Fox House Road (1816 on Whirlow Bridge parapet) had made this toll bar useless and diverted the bulk of road traffic.

Low, law, lowe, or lawe, is generally accepted and common to Derbyshire hill country, and in the Lowlands; is a rounded hill, heap of earth or stones, barrow, or tumulus and sepulchres of ancient British, often found upon the summits. We can connect 'low' and 'lawe' with the 'great heap of stones', and leave it there.

T' Ring o' Firs. The following legend was often believed by past generations and older natives of recent years. About 400 yards W. of 'Norfolk Arms' along the road to Upper Burbage Bridges, on right (N.) side of the road, was a small walled-in ring of trees, known as 'T' Ring o' Firs'. The roadside wall is still in the form of a crescent moon, and the circle wall, inside the field, about 12 yards diameter, was pulled down a little over thirty-eight years ago, by Mr Henry Broomhead, the farmer at 'Ring o' Firs Farm', the last two houses at the west end of Ringinglow (N. side of road). Mr Herbert Trotter said that, sixty-eight years ago, the 'ring' was then planted with Scotch firs, and a few large trees were decaying there when he was a boy – ninety years ago. The 'Ring' was re-planted and now (1949) there are but two anaemic birches (three in 1922), and one sycamore there. They should be replanted, the circle-wall rebuilt, and the site of the legend preserved.

The legend is that, long ago, a man, coming over the moors, in winter time, was lost – on the first Tuesday evening in the month – and, hearing the Sheffield parish church bells, he walked on, and was saved. It is added that this ring of trees denotes the spot where he heard the bells, and that he gave a piece of land, in bequest, to secure that, for all time, Sheffield parish church bells should be rung on the first Tuesday evening in every month. The story has appeared before but, alas, there is no record of it in the Charity Commissioners' report of bequests, or charities, to Sheffield parish church – and its bells did not ring on the first Tuesday of the month. The old Sick and Dividing Society, at the 'Norfolk Arms', during Mr Priest's tenancy – before 1911 – was called 'The Ring o' Firs' S. and D. Society. There could be truth in the story – but where is it? The late Mr R.E. Leader, in *Sheffield in the Eighteenth*

Century, suggests that the story arose around 'one immemorial custom, now fallen into disuse – the practice of ringing on Tuesday evenings during the winter months, from the Tuesday after Doncaster Races to Shrove Tuesday'. Mr Leader could not find any 'foundation for this pretty romance, and Town Trustees and ringers have never heard of the legacy. Another theory associates the Tuesday evening peal with market day, and a further explanation is that Tuesday was the ringers' chosen practice night'. Historians agree that old charities were not always devoted to their original objects, but, in this case, the difficulty is to find the date, or the name!

Old 'Pubs' and 'Ring o' Firs' Farm is now two cottages, and the archway over the westerly cottage door suggests that it was a barn, or shed. The land W. and N.W. of it was cleared after the 1791 Sheffield Enclosure Act, and the house may date from about 1800. I understand that, not improbably, it was, like the 1936 Corporation-murdered Oxdale Lodge twin houses on Houndkirk Road, a roadside beer-house, before the 'Norfolk Arms' was built – like unto Mount Pleasant Farm, at the top of Andrew Lane and its junction with Fulwood Lane – known as 'T' Bog Trap'. Other Fulwood beer-houses, open during the construction of Redmires Reservoirs (1831–54), were David Lane Farm, near Fulwood Hall, and Jeffrey Green Farm, by Bennett Grange. The latter was 'kept' by 'Sally' Earnshaw, and the former was called 'T' Oil i' t' Wall'.

The Club Feast. The late Mrs Crawshaw referred to the old club feast – of the 'Ring o' Firs' Sick and Dividing Society held at the 'Norfolk Arms'. Whit Monday was Club Feast at Ringinglow and she said that during Charles Marsden's occupancy, there was a band, and the members walked in two-and-two fashion, behind the banner. The band played before 'the big houses', and others, at Fulwood, and listeners were expected to pay whether or not they enjoyed the music. The procession went down Angram Lane, Woodcliff, Carr Bridge, Chapel Lane, Brook House Hill, Fulwood church and vicarage, and returned by Stumperlow Hall, Whiteley Wood Hall and the 'Hammer and Pincers'. The dinner, usually beef or mutton, vegetables, pies (and plenty of beer), was cooked in one of the 'softening ovens' of Ringinglow Wire Mill, and some members had 'thick 'eeads' next morning. I was told there were some outside 'attractions'.

Workmen's Sprees. Mrs Crawshaw remembered a few incidents. On one occasion, Charles Marsden refused to allow the feast-makers more beer. So they sent a man with a donkey and loosely tied the empty bottles on its back. One bottle slipped, 'all t' others soon did t' same, an' mooast on 'em wer' lost'.

In those mid-century days, workmen, when 'on the spree', 'made a good job of it', and then, 'like jolly, jolly sailors', worked for more. The men at Ringinglow Wire Mill 'balanced-up' every three months, and, meantime, could obtain 'strap' for food and general supplies at Broomhead's shop, at Hathersage! Broomhead, by the way, was son-in-law to Robert Cooke of Hathersage, who, apparently, was the first owner of Ringinglow Wire Mill.

'Oxstone Dale Road'. About 1200 yards W. of 'Norfolk Arms', along Upper Burbage Bridges Road (left), we reach the junction of 'Oxstone Dale Road' moor path, which leads to Houndkirk Road and its junction with 'Jumble Road'. Older inhabitants call it 'T' Sod Walk', or 'Sod Fence', from the sod and turf bank on the east side of this Dore 'awarded' Road, 30ft wide. Herbert Trotter said the bank was made by the Duke of Rutland's gamekeepers, for grouse shooters, before the 'invention', and adoption, of shooting-butts – in 1860–70. During Herbert's boyhood, they used to pull down bits of the bank and vex the keepers. A gamekeeper, about thirty years ago, began to play usual tricks with this path, and I 'looked up the fact' and the 'Hallamshire' F.P.S. erected public notice boards. Long Lane, called 'Long Line', from Dore, was made to connect with Ringinglow – when Sheffield to Fox House Road was made – about 1816 or after 1757?

'Kelly's' At the junction of 'Oxstone Dale Road', looking N., towards Brown Edge, and, 20 yards E., there is (or should be) a short line of old wall, and, some 40 yards N. of the short wall; and about 60 yards inside the moor (N. of the Upper Burbage Bridges Road), are two small remnants of walls and foundations of a cottage and outbuildings – in 1921 and after, very plain to see.

The remnants were then insignificant and, from time to time, stone had been taken for walling, etc., but, sixty years ago, when I was a youth, the ruins were more substantially intact. It is 'Kelly's', a house until 1876–7, and, *vide* the late Herbert Trotter, and others, in its latest years, it had four rooms – two up and two down – and was inhabited by Mr Henry Kelly, an Irishman, and his wife, Bridget. Henry, at first, worked for Mr Preston, who built the house. Peat was dug nearby, and Preston installed a small engine and boiler, and a small press and shed – for the pressing of peat for, as I was informed, the making of a potash manure – or the pressing, or drying, of peat, before sale. The business did not pay, and Preston went abroad, leaving Kelly in the house – at a rental. But Kelly, remaining there, never heard of his landlord, and never 'paid the rint'. (Trotter told me that Preston eventually made an inglorious return and took his sister's watch – Mrs Flint, Bower Hill Farm, Fulwood – 'and several others, to repair, and never returned them'.)

Peat, it is added, provided part, or all of the boiler fuel. Kelly kept goats and fowls, and sold bony chickens, and often gave odd ones to friends. He cleared a small patch of moorland and grew oats, 'about six inches high' – as Trotter jocularly said – and potatoes. And, he added, 'when yo' were bad, and a pal of Kelly's, yo' could send for a drop of good watter fro' Kelly's' – and the excise men never discovered that illicit still.

Kelly also worked at Brown Edge Quarry and carried stone slates – on his back, in a saddle padded with straw – to the spot where they were left to have frost, and 'weather', before 'scabbing' and 'striking' (scaling and splitting) into required sizes. The Sheffield (Hallam) commons 'went in', in 1791, and possibly, any previous lease had 'run out'. 'The Duke' began to press for payments, and Kelly began to remove some of the brass and scrap from the engine and boiler, etc., with his donkey and a sort of 'cart'. The police once watched Kelly down to the 'Hammer and Pincers', detained him, and 'told the Duke', but 'they couldn't prosecute him' – possibly because no owner (Preston) could be found. Finally, Kelly was 'turned out', the remaining scrap and materials were sold by auction to 'Jack' Young (Pond St.), the only bidder (who gave the furniture to Kelly), and the house was deserted – about 1876–7.

'When t' first Bumble Bee cum'. Perhaps it was an old custom, and, in these uplands, represented the coming of summer, or the bringing of hives to the moors (revived, after 1918, by Sheffield Bee Keepers' Association) for, fully sixty years ago, it was customary to bring as many as 100 hives, at 1/- per hive, to 'Moorcock Hall', while Joseph and Hiram Trotter lived there. He informed the curious that he put flour on some bees as they left the hive, and, slipping away to Norton, often found they had arrived at their 'home' before him. But, whatever the origin, Herbert Trotter told me that, when the first 'Bumble Bee' was reported, Mr Henry Hancock, the owner of Brown Edge Quarry, 'put five bob on t' men's two bobs, an' sommerdy went off wi' a barra (barrow) fer some gallons o'beer fro' t' 'Norfolk Arms'.' There were many sprees and 'beanoes' at Kelly's, or at the quarry. Kelly's son, Barney, played his concertina, and the band was 'made up' with a fife, tin-whistle, and a jew's harp – and there was plenty of singing, shouting, and clapping by the 40 or 50 quarry employees. 'Owd Kelly' wouldn't be put out , so they played 'Battle o' Boyne Water', and 'drew his Irish blood'. 'Then 'e'd shoot at 'em wi' 'is owd carbine', after the rollickers hoisted a black flag over his chimney; and the men would hide in the heather, out of his way. There were usually several 'fetchings' of beer and, one year, they were at Kelly's house, dancing and larking with his two buxom daughters, Catherine, Mary Ann – and two sons, Pat and Barney – when Kelly came in, and, objecting, tried to turn them out with a steel bar. Two men were at the foot of the stairs – in danger – when Henry Hancock, coming to the rescue, put Kelly's head up the chimney, over the peat fire, until he cried for mercy. But, finally, Kelly came in again 'an' cleared 'em aht wi' 'is steel bar an' owd carbine'. Once Kelly tried to back his old donkey into an old Moss Coal Pit shaft; 'bur it wouldn't commit sewicide that rooad'.

Poaching. The late Mr William Fox, of 'Norfolk Arms', Rivelin, was, before marriage, a gamekeeper, and lived at Bassett Farm, Andrew (now Andwell, and why?) Lane. He suspected 'Barney', and, lying in the heather, saw him shoot, and pick up his bird. 'Barney' then fled and, doing twelve years in the

Army, his sin was not purged. Herbert Trotter said, in 1921, that, if alive, Barney was, possibly, a wire cleaner in Sheffield. Who can add to this 'Kelly' biography?

The Ringinglow 'Deep Sick Coal Pits'. About 250 yards W. of 'Moorcot' cottage, was the first of the two Deep Sick Coal Pits – Deep Sick being the moorland source of the Limb (Fenny) Brook. Other surface evidence of shale and 'pudding hole' bellpits are almost opposite the 'Ring o' Firs', with a deeper hole, into which peat drainings fell. Higher up Upper Burbage Bridges Road are later workings where a shaft was sunk, and further pudding holes are seen – also on the S. side of the road (fully 600 yards W. of the 'Norfolk Arms'), near where it makes a slight bend. Coal was wound by a hand windlass, and the tubs were pushed along the pit bottom, over stone flags. Both workings lie inside what is called 'Lady Canning's Plantation' (called 'Kenyon's Plantation' in an 1852 Geological Survey Map), which, felled about 1870, contained good larches but, during the last fifty years has been another Ichabod of grouse-moor forestry, ruined by neglect and preserved rabbits, etc. Herbert Trotter's great-grandfather, Robert, was a Scot. His parents came to Durham to work a corn mill, and it was said that some colliers kidnapped him when he was a youth, and brought him to Barnsley. At length, he deserted them, sought work, and, arriving at Marsh House Farm – on S. side of the road to Ringinglow, a few yards W. of its junction with High Storrs Road – asked Mr Lowkes, the farmer, for a job. There was no work, but, pressing for a job, 'bread for work', the farmer 'set him on'. Robert helped to sink the first coal pit, or working, beside the three roadside cottages (N.) at the top of 'High Lane', Ecclesall – about 600 yards W. of Ecclesall church – now 'Ringinglow Road'.

Robert married, lived at Carr Houses, Fulwood, and started Deep Sick Coal Pits (so called on the first – 1850 – Ordnance Map). He built a small tool-sharpener's cabin beside the first (easterly) working, a few yards on the S. side of the bridge, about 150 yards S.S.W. of 'Norfolk Arms' (the pit was about 200 yards S.W. of 'Norfolk Arms'). Farmers brought lime from the then famous Stoney Middleton lime quarry kiln to Fulwood, Ecclesall, Sandygate and Rivelin valley farmers, and returned with a load of coal – apart from local 'fetchings' to Stony Middleton, etc. But carters, and others, 'pinched' the coal, and Robert, deciding to live 'on the job', built a parlour to the cabin – now the 'Moorcock Hall' two storey lengthways. Robert was assisted by his only son George. Robert was asked to pay rent, as Dore commons were 'awarded' on 10/4/1822 – Act of 1809 – but he didn't see why, like many others. Nevertheless, owing to his wife and 'to save trouble', he paid the 5/- a year demanded and thus, inconveniently, gave away any squatters' claim he had. Every half-year he went to the Rutland rent audit at 'Peacock Hotel', Owler Bar, and ate the free dinner. But, after Robert's death, his widow and son George had to pay three guineas a year! The mining right, however, would be rented.

George Trotter's four sons – Joseph, John, George and Hiram – more or less, assisted him, and one daughter – Ann. George Trotter died a little before 1859, at a goodly age, and to make life more tolerable added another 'storey lengthways to Moorcock Hall' which disappeared in and about 1911. Part of its rubble went, I'm told, into wall material, etc., for 'Moorcot'. I was told that Hiram Trotter's widow left it about 1887, but Hiram Trotter, 'of Ringinglow', who died 2/6/1903, aged seventy-seven, at 21, Ringinglow, and his wife Helen, on 18/12/05, aged seventy, is on a Fulwood churchyard grave stone. The house was abandoned in 1887–92, suggests his grandson, Hiram. Hiram Trotter's father, Joseph, worked the pits before they were abandoned – about 1862.

This pit is recorded by Glover's *Derbyshire Gazetteer*, 1829, very accurately as: 'Ringinglow Bar, S.W. of the inn ['Norfolk Arms'?], 21 miles N.N.W. of Dore, 2nd coal, crowstone'. I conclude that this working may have commenced during the operating of the Dore Enclosure Act, 1809 – Award of 10/4/1822.

Other Pits. I am reminded of a drift, near Carsick Grange – about 200 yards E. of Carsick Hall and Carsick Hill Road, perhaps some 500 yards S.E. of Sandygate Golf Club House, and that, about ninety years ago, a pit, from which coal was drawn by a donkey, drum, and rope, was worked below Dobbin Hill, on the slope above Ecclesall church, on the right (E.) side.

Herbert Trotter's Anecdotes. Herbert told about the quality of Ringinglow coal, and we can compare our experiences with the muck, and shale, and quick-burning coal we have had to buy since 1940 (and 1946 nationalisation), at six times the 1912 price for better coal; and say that it is time the now decently-paid young collier should begin to display the spirit of nationalisation, and respond to the call for the higher man. "One looad o' coil made two looads o' ass (ashes), an' one o' soot. It 'ud boil owt an' rooast nowt. When we wert makkin' t' foire up fer t'neet, mi muther 'ud pur a bucketful on, a' slam t'uvven dooar across it. If t'uvven dooar worn't slammed across it yer didn't need tellin', fer yer 'eeard a click, an' turned yer 'eead away – ter miss gerrin' yer eyes knocked aht. It wer' loike t'battle o'Balaclava" – his explanation being that a certain amount of copperas (sulphate of iron) was in the coal. Herbert was "one of nine", and didn't love "the good old days". "It wer offen porridge an' milk fer brekfast, an' tea an all, an' yer' ad ter gobble it – if yer spoon stuck up i' t' middle on it. Offen enough ther' worn't even bread an' fat wi' it! We'd basins wi' blue marks on 'em, an' we'd run fer t' first dooas on it, an' t' biggest 'ud get t' biggest sarvin' (serving). We got meight abaht once a month, an' it wer offen sheep's 'eead an' pluck (entrails) at that! Mi first job wer' wi' Charles Marsden, at 'Norfolk Arms', (1868) an' Ah'd a shillin' a week, wi' bread an' fat chucked in. Ah worn't a dud, bur Ah wer' sixteen yeear owd afoor Ah'd larned ter tell t' toime bi t' clock."

Herbert recalled the great frost and snow of 1880–1, when "it wer nineteen weeks wiart onny brass. Snowdrifts wer' up ter t' top o' t' Ringinglow 'aases, an' yer cudn't see aht o' t' winders; an' up bi t' Sod Walk, t' rabbits ud etten t' bark off o' t' branches an' t' trees. Deead uns wer' all ower t' graand and all – 'undreds on 'em."

Trotter's reference to the pest of rabbit-preservation on the Duke of Rutland's Longshaw Moors – for his shooting parties – when, as native, or poacher said, and told me, "parts o' t' moors wer' snided wi' 'em" – and, today – 't' pre-sarved foxes as etten t' rabbits an t' graase an all." Progress! "An' one owd keeper's killed aboon a' 'undred foxes on is moor" – Burbage.

The great snowstorm of January 1814 is noted in Hallam. All the roads, Ringinglow, etc., were blocked, and some 80 carters and carriers' coaches and wagons were held up. "They'd etten up all t' 'ay i' Fulwood afoor t' rooads wer' oppened ageean." Robert Trotter lost a son about that time, "an' they carried 'im all t' way ter Ecclesall church wiart crossin' a fence all t'way, fer ther' worn't many fences ter cross abart theear at that toime."

WALKERS come out TROTTERS. Herbert's great-grandfather (Robert), and his only son, George, both "went a cooartin' ter Tidzer (Tideswell), 28 moile theer an' back! T'lasses went inter t' church as WALKERS, an' they cum aht TROTTERS! An' one o' George's sons did t' same thing. She wer' as pratty as paint, but she wudn't Trot – she jilted 'im instead."

Moorland Grazing. Herbert remembered that, in his early youth, far more sheep were kept on Burbage Moors (than before the 1914 war), "thaasands 'on 'em", – and Peter Priestley, of Mitchell Fields, and 'Kester' Green, of White Edge Lodge, were the Duke's shepherds. Highland bullocks, or stirks, were fattened on the now corporation-destroyed (1936) Strawberry Lee monastic farm (although grazing has revived a little since 1943), and a number 'wintered' on Longshaw Park pastures. William Feasey, and, later, William Fox, of Far Bassett House, and John Siddall – at the 1936-Corporation-destroyed twin 'Badger Houses' ('Oxdale Lodge', on the first O.S. Map – one an ex-pub), were gamekeepers.

Brown Edge Quarry and 'Moss Coal Pits'

These, *vide* the first O.S. Map, were N. of the junction of 'Oxstone Dale Road' (Sod Walk) and Ringinglow–Upper Burbage Bridges Road, and were, quite probably, worked about one-hundred-and-twenty years ago – by, amongst others (before 1860), Philip Andrew, of Green House Farm, in Andrew Lane, half a mile N.W. of Ringinglow – probably named after him, or another member of the family. *White's Directory*, 1841, gives Joseph Andrews, Fulwood, as quarry-owner, Redmires (Brown Edge quarry?), and Philip Andrews, Fulwood, a farmer. In 1845, Philip Andrews is a coal owner and farmer. There are primitive 'pudding holes', or bell-pits, beyond and below the rubble-remnants of Kelly's House – of the kind best seen on, and by, Bucca Hill. It is possible that some crow-coal was got from Brown Edge Quarry, and there were, at least, two shallow shafts between Kelly's House and the field walls of 'Ring o' Firs Farm'.

The Brown Edge Quarry (a quarter of a mile long – to Brown Edge Farm) was a stone-slate quarry before 1836, and noted for roofing slate, flags, and building stone. Herbert Trotter said it was worked about 1860, by a Mr Chaddock, then by 'Sam' Hancock (an older relative of Fulwood's monumental mason), and, later, by his brother Henry. Philip Andrew had the quarry for a period, and prior to Mr Chaddock. Brown Edge Quarry was closed about forty-eight years ago. Seventy years ago, 40–50 men were employed; and wages were about 18/- a week, with 22/- or 24/- for stone-getters and dressers.

Ringinglow Wire Mill and Coal Pit

The one-inch-to-mile Geological Survey Map of 1852 – slightly revised, 1866 – shows 'Moss Coal Pits', 'Deep Sick Coal Pits', and 'Coal', at Barber Fields, but not the Ringinglow Wire Mill Coal Pit. The wire mill was built in 1844, and there was a date-mark on the chimney. The mill was on the right (E. side), as you turn N. W., along Fulwood Lane, and immediately behind the row of six stone-built cottages, built for the wire mill workers – two more between them and the 'Norfolk Arms'. It is understood that the Mill was started by Robert Cooke, of Hathersage (in *White's Directory* for 1837), and his son Robert, and came into the possession of a Mr Broomhead, of Hathersage, odd years after 1855 – when the mill closed down for a time. It was last worked by a Mr George Winterbottom, of Barnsley, who, manager for Cooke, took it over, and a Mr Fieldsend became his partner.

Probably about seventy-eight years ago there was a strike. The employers and apprentices were working "but t' gaffers wouldn't pay t' price, an' t' ware'us gor afire. Men thowt it worn't insured, but t' gaffers 'ad insured it a month afoor, an' cleared a thaasan' quid aht o' t' job" – so it was said. The firm had obtained coal from Barber Fields drift-workings, several hundred yards to the S.E., and with this or, probably, other earlier, capital (in the 1860s?) they found coal and sunk a 196ft shaft, in the wire mill yard. 'Joe' Trotter (Herbert's uncle) and Sam Millward were colliers and Hiram Trotter (Herbert's father) engine-man, and John Mills, the banksman.

Water troubles soon stopped the pit (when?), but Hiram Trotter's great grandson (also Hiram Trotter) tells me that an attempt to drive an under-ground road, and join up with the Barber Fields drift and seam – and so increase production and make a two-way carting trade with lime and coal – did not succeed. But had the coal been worked? The shaft at the N. end of the wire mill yard was ordered to be filled-in by the authorities in 1901 – after the late Alderman J.R. Wheatley bought the Ringinglow property. The chimney, the local landmark, fifty years ago, gradually declined and, latterly, was assisted by a desire for scrap-stone.

A little before 1912, a dangerous portion was pulled down to a few feet above ground level; but none remains now. Many years ago, Herbert Trotter took down the lightning-conductor, "an' made tooastin' forks fer nearly ivvrey-body i' Fulwood!" Mr G. Winterbottom, the last owner, afterwards started at Barnsley, and ended life at Oxspring Wire Mill. After Winterbottom left, the men, and others (unemployed?), took available brass and other scraps, and sold it. Needle wire was drawn here, and some 30 wiredrawers' blocks were in use. Herbert Trotter added that, in the mid-nineteenth century, Fulwood and Ringinglow were 'little gold mines – for wiredrawers?' Men walked to Ringinglow and Hathersage, and paragon-wire mills, from Fulwood (one? and six miles), Dronfield (six and nine miles), and Mickley (four? and seven miles), and good wiredrawers could earn 20/- a day. The late Mrs Hugh Thorpe, of Stanage Cottage, in 1912, told me of three wiredrawers who, at weekends, walked home to Thurgoland (14 miles) along the Hathersage–Moscar bridleway, beside the phallic Moscar Old Woman Stone and Stanage End – now alleged to be private, but when was it closed by order? (Those who ordered, and/or destroyed, the Old Woman Stone, have never, to our knowledge, admitted the fact; but it was drilled and broken up in December–January 1931–2 – the finest phallic stone in The Peak – and lost National Monument.) This 14-mile walk was about 1870 and, eventually, the three wiredrawers married and settled in Hathersage. For a while, after the mill closed, there were 'hard times' at Ringinglow. The late Mrs Crawshaw told me that, one day, the wire-drawers wanted a holiday, and a good 'sub'. So one man 'made it up' to ask for 'a fiver' to buy a good suit of clothes, and the 'boss', probably scenting trouble – but knowing it was no use denying – gave the required cash. The men had their spree, and, when they returned, the 'boss', asked: "As ta got thi suit lad?" The man duly replied: "No, but we've getten plenty o' good linin(g) insoide, mester."

'Gerrin inter bed'

Here's one of my stories, which I heard in the 'Norfolk Arms'. "It's sum toime nah, bur Ah remember, one day, when Ah'd bin knockin' abaht t' moors' abaht noine yeear sin', takkin nooats fer mi article on Ringinglow, Ah dropped inter t' 'Norfolk Arms', theear, fer a drink. They wer' all natives i' t' taproom, an Ah went in, an' joined 'em. T' conversashun swung rahnd ter what silly things sum chaps does when they've getten a looad on, an one on 'em telled this tale:

'It wer' afooar t' war (1914–18) an' one neet, gerrin' on i' t' yeear, Ah went ter t' 'Norfolk Arms', an gor' as drunk fer less nor aif a craan as it ud tak' thirty bob for nahadays. Ah waddled dahn Angram Lane, an' t' next thing Ah remembered wer' bein' wakken'd up bi t' bobby. T' owd lad didn't want a job just then, an' 'e 'appened ter know who Ah wor. So off Ah popped, an' after Ah gor alf way up t' 'ill, Ah cum dahn ageean ter find aht wheear Ah'd started froo'. After a bit, Ah gor 'ooam all reigh – sumwheear up at t' top o' Crimicar Lane, an' afooar so many o' t' nobs 'ad cum ter live theear.

'Then Ah offed wi' me clooas an' get's inter bed straight away. An when Ah wakken'd up, sum 'aars later, Ah fon aht as Ah'd stripp'd misen, an' bin liggin under t' kitchen table, mooast o' t' neet. Ah wor nearly frozzen wi' cowd, but nowt 'appen'd after it'."

'Norfolk Arms' – Green House Paper Mill

In 1836, Mary Green was licensee, and *White's Directory*, 1845, gives Charles Marsden, paper manufacturer, Rivelin, as landlord of 'Norfolk Arms', Ringinglow. In 1864 he is also a quarry owner (at Bennett Grange Quarry, one mile W. of Fulwood church?) and, in 1871–2, living at Bennett Grange, a Mr Garrett having succeeded to the licence. Herbert Trotter's first job (1868) was at 'Norfolk Arms', under Mr Marsden. His Rivelin ex-paper mill and its excellent paper, is well known, but Marsden made paper at a two-storey mill (roofless in 1921), 44ft x 22ft, beside Hood Brook, in Warren Wood, under Sheepwash Bank, 300 yards E. of Green's House – a pretty sequestered spot. The elongated pond is there, and a zig-zag road was made to join the road a little E. of the bridleway, near (the ruins of) Stanage Cottage.

The paper was carted to Sheffield, and sold at about 9d. per lb. The largest weekly output was about seven tons, and paper "was made in long sheets and hung over rails, or rafters, to dry". The mill was abandoned about 1881, and appears to have been started by an uncle of Mr Marsden – both Hathersage men.

A Ringinglow Song

Charles Andre[w]'s the man, on the bank he did stand,
An' aloud to Joe Trot[ter] he did call.
He says to Joe Trot[ter], "now get a good stock,
For Ringinglow's waitin' o' coal".
Sim Mellor made answer; an' says: "I'm the man;
I'll get you some toppers as soon as I can".

Chorus: Hero, gallant and brave,
For the honour of Ringinglow town.

Up comes owd Crawsha'[w] wi' 'is pony so clever;
An' says to Charles Andre, "ah've got some coals to deliver",

So 'e stood on the top till 'e 'eeard the men shout,
Then 'e whipped up 'is pony, an' drew the coal out.
Joe Trot mended 'is fire an' went to 'The Feast' –
'E went, an' 'e left it a week at the least;
An' when 'e cum' back 'is fire worn't dun,
For the smook in the elements darkened the sun.

Sim Mellor an' Albert in t' gardin did go.
Albert says to Sim Mellor: 'Tha 'as a fine show'
Then up jumped a bee, an' stung Albert i' t' 'ee;
An' bunged booath 'is eyes up till 'e cudn't see.

Robin an' Grannock they went dahn to t' tahn:
They called in a gin shop, an' spent 'aif a craan.
As Robin drank one glass, an' Grannock drank two,
They booath gor as drunk as mi daddy's owd shoe.

These lines refer to the coal pit in Ringinglow Wire Mill yard.

Charles Andrews lived near the 'Bog Trap' old pub, while Crawshaw, a Ringinglow resident, was born at Dungworth. Sim Mellor lived at Fulwood and Joe Trotter at 'Moorcock Hall'. 'The Feast' is Fulwood Feast.

The late Mrs Crawshaw, mother-in-law of Mr H.A. Stone, J.P., gave me the five verses of this local ditty, and, possibly, some Ringinglow lover will supply the remainder, and the writer's name. Mrs Crawshaw was an Elliott, born at the fine old Stumperlow Hall (1839) when, temporarily, it was divided, and several families lived therein.

Mr Dixon left Stumperlow Hall, and Sheffield, in 1925–6, and, we think, it is due to him that the 'developer' in the roads did tasteful work in trees, grass verges and gardens, which gave relief to some most pleasingly designed villas, and screened-off some that no town-planner should have allowed.

Hiram Trotter Stories
In addition to the care of the 100 bee hives in summer time – at 1/- the hive – Hiram grew hardy roses which, in the advertiser's manner of ten names for one variety, must have a name. The Rev. J.T.F. Aldred, M.A., the vicar of Dore (1849–94), had four sons, Philip, Shirley, John and Christian and, one day, before 1892, they went to Hiram's 'Moorcock Hall' to buy a score of roses. Hiram duly named and labelled them – 'Queen Alexandra', 'Duke of York', etc., and, 'threw one in for luck', and off they went, down 'Long Line' towards home. Then one young Aldred discovered that the 'one for a coddler', was nameless, and 'that would never do for father'. So Christian returned and asked Hiram to baptise it. Then said Hiram: "Well, it's a bit of a devil – Ah've

crissened twenty on 'em for yer missen, an' tha reckons ter be a parson, an' can't crissen one on 'em thissen. It's a bit off, isn't it!" Christian had recently been ordained!

Hiram was working for Sam – or Henry – Hancock, at Brown Edge Quarry, and building a stone fowl house, near to it, when Hancock told Hiram to pull down part of it; because "tha 'asn't put dooar oil in, an' t' fowls can't get insoide it". Hiram then reminded his 'boss' that, only a short time previously, he was doing another job, and then "tha worn't perticler to a yard or two, an' nah thart grumblin' abart a bit of a fowl oil!"

Saluting 'the Cloth'. Hiram Trotter's son (also Hiram) tells me about his father, when attending Dore Church School, in the seventies. The schoolmaster, from inside the school, could see the vicar, the Rev. J.T.F. Aldred, when approaching it, and, straightway, the boys and girls, separately, were conducted into the school yard, and lined up, on either side. The girls curtsied, and the boys bowed as the vicar passed by into school. Hiram, on one occasion, refused to bow to 'the presence', and the schoolmaster gave him 'a tanning' and informed his father of the serious offence. Father added another thrashing, and Hiram decided that further 'indiscipline' was not worth the reward it received.

When I attended St John's Boys' School, Park, Sheffield, in the eighties, we were only obliged to stand, and bow to the vicar as he entered the boys' school, on the upper floor of the building. But, on our way, when playing in Bernard St., we had to shout "Heyup, t' parson's comin", and beware of the Rev. James Gilmore's umbrella, and, probably, his somewhat playful physical admonition if we were caught.

Here endeth the chapter, and if any one can add to it, or correct it, let him write forthwith, for the whole truth, however loved, resides in no man, of whatever creed or politics. History has many mistakes.